the Dream Girl

OTHER BOOKS BY ANTHONY PIETROPINTO, M.D.

Beyond the Male Myth
with Jacqueline Simenauer

Husbands and Wives
with Jacqueline Simenauer

The Clinic (novel)
with Elaine Piller Congress

Not Tonight, Dear:
How to Reawaken Your Sexual Desire
with Jacqueline Simenauer

the Dream Girl

THE IMAGINARY PERFECT WOMAN
ALL MEN HIDE

Anthony Pietropinto, M.D.

ADAMS PUBLISHING
Holbrook, Massachusetts

Published by Adams Media Corporation
260 Center Street, Holbrook, MA 02343

ISBN: 1-55850-533-4

Printed in the United States of America.

J   I   H   G   F   E   D   C   B   A

Library of Congress Cataloging-in-Publication Data
Pietropinto, Anthony
     The dream girl / the imaginary perfect woman all men hide /
Anthony Pietropinto
         p.   cm.
     ISBN 1-55850-533-4 (hc)
     1. Men—Sexual behavior. 2. Men—Psychology. 3. Sexual fantasies.
     4. Man-woman relationships. I. Title.
     HQ28.P56   1995
     306.7'081—dc20   95-19450
                                                              CIP

This publication is designed to provide accurate and authoritative information with
regard to the subject matter covered. It is sold with the understanding that the
publisher is not engaged in rendering legal, accounting, or other professional
advice. If legal advice or other expert assistance is required, the services of a competent professional person should be sought.
         — From a *Declaration of Principles* jointly adopted by a Committee of the
American Bar Association and a Committee of Publishers and Associations

Cover design by Janet M. Clesse

This book is available at quantity discounts for bulk purchases.
For information, call 1-800-872-5627.

To my wife, Joy Ann, and my daughters, Rita Diana and Laura Joy, with deep appreciation for their assistance and support in the creation of this book, and for making so many previous wonderful dreams come true.

Table of Contents

An Apology

ANA:
I daresay you all want to marry lovely incarnations of music and painting and poetry. Well, you can't have them, because they don't exist. If flesh and blood is not good enough for you, you must go without: that's all. Women have to put up with flesh-and-blood husbands—and little enough of that, too, sometimes; and you will have to put up with flesh-and-blood wives.
—GEORGE BERNARD SHAW, MAN AND SUPERMAN

*I*t is customary for an author to begin a book with an explanation of why it was written. In this case, I also have to include an explanation of why *The Dream Girl* was almost *not* written.

The Dream Girl is about men's secrets, especially the best-kept ones, and why men have so much difficulty establishing and maintaining committed, monogamous relationships with women. It is a book written primarily for women, but I hope men will read it, too, because the best-kept secrets are those that men somehow manage to keep even from themselves.

The skeptical reader, although she might be willing to kill for such a book, will, understandably, ask, "If these secrets are so universal and so influential in men's behavior, why hasn't anyone written about them before? Is it possible that something that has been going on for centuries would be almost entirely neglected by the psychological experts?"

In 1907, Sigmund Freud wrote a paper that made the then-startling revelation that people have daydreams and fantasies. People didn't start having daydreams or fantasies when the twentieth century began, they simply did not talk about them. While the storytellers, poets, and novelists provide ample proof that fantasy has always been with us, it took Freud, with his new technique of probing uncensored personal thoughts, to confirm that *everyone* has daydreams. Freud explained that people were ashamed of daydreams because they considered them childish. Children fantasized about what they would do as adults, which was a praiseworthy part of the maturational process. Adult daydreams were regressive and unproductive, shameful pastimes best left concealed.

For these same reasons, men do not speak of the dream girl. The fantasy begins in adolescence or even earlier, when men are immature, sexually inexperienced, and vulnerable. The dream girl is the boy's first attempt to deal with his unmet needs for adult love and validation as a man. She is different and far more complex than the women in magazines and videos who provide a focus and release for his growing and unfulfilled sexual drives. The dream girl is individual and personal, not shared by magazine readers and video viewers in the manner of the current sex goddesses and porno queens.

Men do not speak of their masturbatory fantasies and experiences, however natural and prevalent they may be. They are not adverse to revealing and embellishing their sexual adventures with real women, for these are the exploits of mature, competent men, while anything else is the province of boys driven to puerile, inferior methods of gratification.

Similarly, they do not speak of their dream girls, who are supposed to be inadequate stand-ins for the real women who will someday share their lives. When a real woman comes along, the dream girls will be discarded with the other worn-out playthings of childhood. Any admission of her past or present existence is a painful reminder of vulnerability. Vulnerability may be powerfully attractive in women, but it is an overwhelming liability for men, whether revealed to the women they desire or to the men whose friendship and respect they value.

But men do not always discard their *Playboy* collections once they acquire regular access to real sexual partners. And the dream girl does not always vanish with the appearance of a human lover. As the pile of provocative magazines lies hidden on a high shelf or under a bed, the dream girl lurks in dark recesses of the mind, wielding her potent influence and creating problems for her unsuspecting rival.

I do not think many people of either sex would deny that the relationship between the sexes needs some improving. About half of all marriages end in divorce and many of the remaining ones are intact only because the partners lack the support systems, finances, or initiative to go their separate ways. A substantial number of spouses, both husbands and wives, are unfaithful at some time, probably at least half the men and a third of women. An untabulated statistic is the number of romances that begin so promisingly and end short of the altar.

There have been books in abundance that have aimed to help couples establish, maintain, and advance a loving, healthy relationship. These usually stress communication and interaction. They emphasize trust and the sharing of confidences. Their premise is that a shared appreciation of a problem and mutual efforts will lead to a solution.

This approach is useless when the problem is undetected from the start. If a man does not know what is bothering him, he cannot enlist the help of a woman in combating the problem. He cannot find the problem if he does not know where to look. He cannot find answers if he does not have the questions.

I am a psychiatrist who has been practicing for thirty years. Prior to that, I had a few years' experience as a boy and an adolescent male, which contributed substantially to my understanding of men's development. I have co-authored four books, some of which have led many to regard me as a "sex expert," although I prefer to concentrate on sexuality, with all of its psychological ramifications, and I abhor the one-treatment-fits-all behavioral model, developed by Masters and Johnson, that is employed by most "sex therapists."

I have read a lot, in my capacity as a doctor, author, and literate human being over the last thirty years. In all those years, with one exception, I have encountered no mention of the dream girl. The exception was the final chapter of my own book, *Beyond the Male Myth,* written in 1977.

One might question whether, if no one else has thought the dream-girl phenomenon important enough to investigate, the subject is worthy of attention. I think the problem has been that therapists and writers have been exploring the infinite ramifications and byways of one major artery of human behavior, the interpersonal, and neglecting the intrapsychic. Whenever I see a couple with a problem, I encourage them to say, "Is it me? Is it us? Is it them?" Are we having difficulties because of one of my own hang-ups, because of a problem in our communication and interaction, or because of the extreme demands placed on us by our families, our jobs, or society in general? The dream girl, a very personal fantasy conceived in solitude, belongs to the "Is-it-me?" realm, but the difficulties she generates are manifested in a later relationship; therefore, everyone, including involved therapists, incorrectly tries to fix a basically good, unbroken partnership.

Therapists do not always ignore intrapsychic factors. When a women engages in a series of relationships that involve abuse or a man professes feelings of inadequacy, the therapist may explore conflicts that began in childhood or adolescence. But nobody asks about the dream girl, because she has never been included in any of the standard texts used by psychiatrists and psychologists in training. Nobody did screening tests for the Epstein-Barr virus in 1960, either.

I am often reminded of an old joke about a drunken man, frantically searching up and down a street one night. He told an inquiring passerby that he had lost his wallet and the man offered to help him look. After many fruitless minutes, the Samaritan said, "Are you sure this is where you lost it?" The drunk replied that, as a matter of fact, he missed the wallet on a street several blocks away. "Then why are we looking here?" his helper exploded. "The light's a lot better here," the drunk replied.

Therapists tend to cover territory that is advantageous to them because it is familiar or has yielded good results in the past;

however, digging in one area for relevant data buried elsewhere leaves nothing but empty holes.

Dream girls are not that difficult to track down, once you learn to follow their traces and to recognize them when you find them. Elusive, polymorphic, treacherous, of course—but far from rare and not invincible.

So, this is the first legitimate book about dream girls. I say "legitimate" because dream girls have appeared in fictional works. There have been many movies inspired by the dream girl. Comics and an occasional song have drawn on and perpetuated the dream-girl theme. Perhaps psychiatrists have shied away from investigating the dream girl because of her heritage as a childish fantasy figure— although if fantasy and regression are anyone's province, they are that of the psychotherapist. I have written this book to help women (and men) understand the dream girl and appreciate the seriousness of the emotional problems she causes, and to help them solve those problems.

That's why this book has been written. Now I would like to explain why it was almost *not* written.

I begin with an apology. I use this term not in the sense of admitting to something wrong and asking forgiveness, but in the classical sense of offering a justification for presenting material of a controversial and potentially offensive nature.

Publishing is a profit-making enterprise, albeit a risky one. I have read that two-thirds of the books published do not recoup the advances paid to the authors. While an author's main concern *should* be that of creating an original, well-written, and meaningful book that contributes to the world's store of knowledge and under-standing, with financial reward a distant second concern, publishers want lots of satisfied customers.

As a psychiatrist, I work in a business where the customer is *not* always right; in fact, the customer is frequently psychotic. While all patients must be treated with kindness and respect, the psychiatrist does not have to support their beliefs that Hillary Clinton is whispering obscene suggestions to them or that Michael Bolton is stealing song ideas from them through a microchip implanted in their brains. My patients sometimes cry and sometimes get angry. This is called *catharsis* and is part of the therapeutic work.

In most other fields, however, crying, angry customers are not considered the sign of a successful business. An angry customer is considered a dissatisfied customer. A product that makes you angry is one that either does not work at all or fails to deliver what you expected. No businessman wants to produce such a product.

Well, if you are a woman, this book will probably make you angry. I expect that it will, which is why I opened the book with Dona Ana's obviously angry statement, a perfect encapsulation of women's response to the dream girl. My twenty-three-year-old daughter, Rita, who helped with the research for this book and knew what to expect, got angry, nevertheless, at men's confessions. And some editors (female) passed on the opportunity to adopt this book, because they feared it would evoke negative feelings in women (themselves included).

Now, certain products that you buy are entitled, by their very nature, to rock your emotional equilibrium. If you watch television, Susan Lucci's soapy travails may move you to tears, Rush Limbaugh's commentaries may infuriate you, and Kathie Lee's 935th Cody anecdote may induce nausea, but, as long as the reception is good, you won't blame the Sony Corporation. Telephone calls from in-laws, creditors, and solicitors don't prompt crank calls to AT&T.

Similarly, authors should be entitled to bring disturbing information to readers, provided that the information is accurate and especially if the book promises to remedy, to some extent, the problem it exposes. George Bernard Shaw grouped three of his plays, including *Mrs. Warren's Profession* (referring to the oldest one), under the heading "Three Unpleasant Plays." The plays themselves are witty and delightful, but they do deal with disquieting topics.

So, I believe that books are allowed to be a bit upsetting. Too many pop psychology books fall into the *I'm-O.K.-You're-O.K., So-Who-Needs-This-Book?* genre. Others benumb the reader because she has already read the same book under three different titles. If this book makes you angry about something for the first time, at least it will have proven its originality. Placid people don't seek change—and, in certain areas, change would be welcome.

I won't say, "Please don't get angry." I will ask you to think about what makes you angry, since in your past relationships with men you have undoubtedly felt angry and some of that feeling was probably related to the dream-girl problem.

You will be angry at the dream girl herself. She sets an impossible standard against which all women are unfavorably measured. Nobody likes to be judged a failure, no matter how unfair that judgment. The dream girl is a bitch—although even bitches have their likable aspects, once you get to know them.

You will be angry (or should I say, angrier) at men. When they are in the grip of the dream girl, they are at their worst: demanding, selfish, irrational, juvenile, and foolish.

And you will be angry at me. (That's okay—as a psychiatrist, I'm used to it.) I'm going to ask you to be part of the solution. It's something I'd have to do, even if I didn't want to. You see, editors are never content with you describing a problem, even if you're the first to discover it. If I were to write a book with convincing evidence that aliens from outer space were inhabiting most people's homes disguised as items of furniture, would I be praised for warning the nation of this immense danger? No, the danger would not be published unless I could tell the reader how to rout the aliens in ten easy steps or less.

I'll admit that I am ambivalent about self-help books. As a psychiatrist, I am competing with myself. I practice psychotherapy, which is a wonderful alliance between an experienced, impartial facilitator and an introspective, active patient seeking self-understanding and self-fulfillment. A book cannot be a therapist: it offers information, but cannot add to it later; it advises, but cannot modify its counsel; it can address the masses, but cannot make allowances for individuality.

Still, a book has value. It sets its reader to thinking. I believe that only a fraction of the work done in psychotherapy occurs within the time-constrained session in the office. The patient's mind continues the process that was initiated in the session, following the direction, but progressing unaccompanied by the therapist until the next appointed rendezvous. Reading emulates the psychotherapeutic process in this regard. A TV viewer is an observer; a reader is a participant.

So, since they say if you're not part of the solution, you're part of the problem, you and I will have to work at the solution. I'm going to ask you to get to know the dream girl, even though you'd rather invite Sidney, Kimberly, and Amanda of *"Melrose Place"* to meet your boyfriend or husband.

I'm going to ask you to help men overcome the noxious influences of the dream girl, even though you may get so angry that you'd rather give up men entirely. But you won't, thank heaven, so you might as well make them more tolerable. Since you're going to be involved in relationships anyway, there is no harm in making them as enjoyable and mutually supportive as possible.

And, in case you're a man, I'd like to enlist your cooperation, too. Men *do* read books, despite what 90 percent of the publishers seem to believe. I read them myself and not just to see what my colleagues and competitors are up to; I actually enjoy them and don't consider myself an exceptional male because of it. A man may be reading this on his own or because his female partner had the good sense to throw it at him or leave it for him to stumble over.

If you're male, you're probably going to get angry, too. The book talks about foibles and vulnerabilities, to which no man wants to admit. It makes women somewhat vexed, and they are hard enough to live with even at their most amiable. It tells men's secrets. Shaw's Ann Whitestone says that men's secrets are "the things they tell everybody," but there are untold ones, and they are the ones the men themselves have forgotten. So, I am telling men their own secrets, the ones they learned as boys and lost track of, the way they forgot the combination to that old padlock or where they stashed that picture of the 1985 *Penthouse* Pet.

Finally, I am going to talk about other sensitive issues, including the stuff that cost a surgeon general her job. This book is not just about dream girls, it is about men's sexuality and all the things that contributed to its development and its essence. I won't claim that these are subjects nobody ever mentions, because, in these enlightened and sensationalistic times, there is virtually nothing that has not been exposed in print, photographed, or confessed to Geraldo Rivera's audience. Instead I will try to present these old taboos not as aberrations, perversions and abominations, but as part of the complex spectrum of male sexuality, crooked byways that feed troublesome impulses and actions into the straightest mainstreams of adult love and sexual expression.

The First Amendment guarantees freedom of the press. It does not compel an editor or publisher to print something that might offend a substantial portion of the readership and adversely affect profits. Pornography offends many people, but it seems to be profitable in the final analysis, so there is no dearth of pornography in print.

Sociobiology is less profitable. The word seems innocuous enough, as does its meaning. It is a discipline that attempts to explain the effects on social behavior by an organism's genetic makeup. While it is sincerely hoped that the popularity of *Jurassic Park* and the O. J. Simpson trial have brought to the American public an unprecedented appreciation of the importance and potential of DNA, sociobiology has been very threatening to women, in general, and female editors, in particular.

Since my premedical education required training in the sciences (the literature and writing courses were electives), I cannot reject scientific theories on the basis of someone finding them offensive. The idea of a bacterium invading my personal cells profoundly offends me, but I do not condemn antibiotic treatment because it was based on a distasteful discovery. I don't relish being influenced by a slew of genes that I was dealt by my ancestors without consulting me, or being run by a passel of aging organs subject to all manner of disease and malfunction—not the least of which is the gelid mass of brain tissue that does a barely passable job of coordinating my biological life processes while maintaining perception of my environment, communicating with my species, and trying to figure out what I'm doing on earth to begin with. I would prefer to be a disembodied angel, but my knowledge of my physical vulnerabilities compels me to conduct myself according to my body's limitations. Contempt for the physical may lead to mortification of the flesh and spiritual enhancement, but rarely to suicide. We learn to live with, if not love, our bodies.

When biology is invoked as an influence on behavior, especially that associated with one sex more than the other, people are less accepting. I can compare my circulatory system to a pig's, or my digestive system to a dog's, which medical research has done to great advantage, but I dare not compare sexual or social behavior even to that of those creatures most like man. "People are not animals!" one indignant female editor once said. (They are, actually: phylum Chordata, order Primate, genus Homo, species sapiens.) Like Dr. Doolittle, I never understood why people object to being compared to animals, since the animals usually come off better (or is that the reason?). In this book, I'm going to do it occasionally.

Sociobiology tends to support the theory that male and female brains are, like pelvises and reproductive organs, biologically different. This notion outrages feminists, who insist that men and women have identical brains and any manifestations that suggest otherwise were caused by differences in parental upbringing or social conditioning. Equality is not synonymous with identity. No two *men* are identical, including homozygous twins, so why should we expect males to be identical to females, even if deemed equals. In this book, we admit to the *possibility* of differences in male and female brains.

Freud said, "Anatomy is destiny." That was nonsense, even before the days of sex-change operations. Your sex certainly influences the course of your life, but it does not control it. Today, women drive 18-wheel rigs and RuPaul models gold mini-dresses on the runways. There are still far more male truckers and female (thank you, God) supermodels, and the exceptions understood that when they dared to buck the majority.

Any attempt to explain differences in male and female behavior on biological or genetic grounds, even unfavorable to the males (as is usually the case), is militantly opposed by female editors. They equate explanation with justification. If you say that males are polygamous or violent by nature, these women charge you with using such statements to accept such behavior and even encourage it.

The idea that naturally determined, even instinctive, behavior cannot be modified is absurd. What is civilization, if not the result of convincing individuals to conform their behavior away from natural inclinations and toward the common welfare? If we all followed our natural urges without inhibition, we wouldn't have indoor plumbing; maybe, not even indoors. So, this book accepts the premise that Nature may have programmed males and females differently and that, once we understand the cybernetics, we can update the software.

So, against the odds, this book has reached print. It helped to have a male editor, one who was still in touch with the dream girl nearly all men have encountered but few recall and appreciate.

Now, let me introduce my female readers to the dream girl. To my male readers, let me reintroduce her. The devil that you know is better than the one you do not know.

CHAPTER 1

Fair Warning

DON JUAN:

The visions of my romantic reveries, in which I had trod the plains of heaven with a deathless, ageless creature of coral and ivory, deserted me in that supreme hour. I remembered them and desperately strove to recover their illusions: but they now seemed the emptiest of inventions ...

— GEORGE BERNARD SHAW, MAN AND SUPERMAN

*D*on Juan is describing his feelings when confronting a real woman in a potentially sexual situation. He is frantically trying to resist his natural impulses and "spare her and save myself." He views her with all her imperfections. His ear, practiced on a thousand songs and symphonies, and his eye, exercised on a thousand paintings, tear her voice and appearance to shreds. He observes the telltale likenesses to her parents and envisions her thirty years hence.

Finally, he tries to summon up the dream girl, the perfect fantasy creature who had been his companion in lonely hours and provided the ideal to which he could aspire. The dream girl fades into a hollow illusion. Don Juan is powerless against the appeal of a living woman and falls helplessly into her arms, a victim of the Life Force.

Is the dream girl, then, vanquished? Does mature love triumph over boyish fantasy? Of course not. What Don Juan calls the Life Force might be more simply termed the sex drive. It is Nature's very efficient mechanism for keeping the world populated without unnecessary concern for humankind's higher sensibilities.

Don Juan had an infamous track record for his hit-and-run tactics. No sooner had he consummated his professed love than he was seized with misgivings and rode off to his next sexual adventure with never a backward glance. Perhaps his dream girl of coral and ivory was waiting for him in the next hamlet, maybe just over the next hill.

Not all men are Don Juans, but nearly all men start out like him. They have a potent sex drive that is practically indiscriminate in its targets, in constant conflict with the dream of one near-perfect woman who will meet all their emotional needs.

Eighteen years ago, I co-authored a book called *Beyond The Male Myth*. One of the major themes was the conflict men experienced between women perceived as loving, asexual mother figures and as seductive, passionate sex objects. The responses received in a survey of four thousand American men elicited evidence of this dichotomy again and again.

"You know, this prostitute/madonna complex of yours ... " my editor would sometimes start to say.

"Well, thanks," I would interrupt, "but I think Sigmund Freud should get the credit for that. However, Freud discussed the prostitute/madonna complex as a symptom that plagued neurotic men. What I'm trying to show here—and the survey supports me—is that the prostitute/madonna split occurs in *all* men, not just neurotic ones. Part of growing up involves being able to overcome the complex; Freud's neurotics weren't able to do it."

Neither Freud nor any of his descendants mentioned the dream girl, but I am convinced that she is as prevalent an inhabitant of the male psyche as the prostitute and the madonna—and even more problematic. She is a more potent archetypal figure because she is a more complete entity. The madonna meets the Oedipal need for unconditional love and nurturance, but she is not allowed a trace of sexuality. The prostitute accepts the burning desire for sexual release, but her uninhibited readiness threatens the male's adequacy.

The dream girl, the third member of this unholy trio, encompasses a full spectrum of attributes. She is a fuller figure than the all-good caricature of the madonna or the all-evil prostitute. She is easy to justify, difficult to attack.

Men yearn for the madonna, and this is immature. They lust after the prostitute and this is immoral. Toward the dream girl, they feel unwavering love and commitment—and what's wrong with that?

What's wrong is that men are supposed to love real women and have real marriages and live a real life—and the dream girl interferes with that course of events. If all went well, the dream girl would be a transient fantasy invented to help men prepare psychologically for an actual, mature love relationship. When a real, appropriate, and desirable woman came into a man's life, he would quickly discard the dream girl as an inanimate stand-in and replace her with the infinitely superior living woman.

But instead of a facile transfer of affection occurring, the dream girl often does not budge. Her would-be replacement either never gains access to the man's love or finds herself in stifling, crowded quarters.

Does this sound a little preposterous? Well, few women would deny that men seem to have a problem with commitment. They like women, they pursue women, they have sex with women. They profess love and the desire for marriage and the plan to raise a family. Yet, when the time seems appropriate or even overdue for them to make the unequivocal, nonreversible choice of the one woman who will be their lifetime partner, reactions range from hesitation to doubt to flight.

How do frustrated women explain (critically) such behavior? They may say the man does not want responsibility. Or he is immature and unready to assume the role of head of a family. Or that he is financially insecure. Or that he wants to play the field and dally with a number of women.

They may say that he is narcissistic and blind to the needs of others; that he is emotionally walled off and incapable of love; that he is tied to his mother's apron strings (if mothers still wore aprons). They may even bitterly say, "Well, what do you expect? *All* men are like that!"

What you *never* hear a woman say is, "He must be hung up on some unattainable fantasy woman that no real woman, myself included, can measure up to." Actually, when you put it in words that way, it *does* sound pretty farfetched.

Would a man really ever prefer the love of a fantasy to that of a woman? First, ask whether men ever prefer imaginary sex partners over real ones. That one's easy. Men who are anxious or dissatisfied with their sexual relationships often turn to fantasy. They may avoid intercourse, but still seek sexual release through masturbation. They may flirt with or actually proposition other women, even with very little chance of actually getting them into bed. If they do have intercourse with their wives, they may fantasize during the act that they are with someone else.

An uncommon situation? Hardly. Sexual desire disorder is the most common problem treated by sex therapists today, and *selective* loss of desire, in which sexual interest in a spouse is lost while interest in other outlets is maintained, is more prevalent than *pervasive*, where libido is nil.

"Nature seems above all to avoid the painful and aim at the pleasant," Aristotle stated two thousand years ago. People are part of Nature's province, so Freud, in explaining human behavior, proposed the rather obvious maxim: "People like to do what is pleasant and try to avoid the unpleasant." So, it is not surprising that when even something as generally pleasurable as sex becomes fraught with unpleasant sensations, such as anxiety or hostility, people will avoid it and substitute a form of satisfaction that, if somewhat deficient in the degree of gratification it gives, will, at least, be free from sources of displeasure and distress.

If people have such difficulty obtaining sexual satisfaction, consider how much more difficult it is to succeed in the complex area of love. Virtually any willing, or even reluctant, partner can provide physical gratification in a sexual act, but love is not as abundantly available.

One might argue that people can satisfy themselves sexually without benefit of a partner, but love, by definition, has to involve a second person. Real love is concern for another person's welfare. We hold the beloved in high esteem and value them above just about everything else. They reciprocate and feel the same way about us.

The need for love usually refers to the recipient aspect of the relationship. While it is praiseworthy to care for and cherish a partner, generally this is not a psychological *need*. The desire to be valued and validated is essential for most people. It is important to feel good about ourselves, to regard ourselves as competent, desirable, and, to some degree, exceptional. Ultimately, these feelings must come from ourselves. If someone feels inferior, the most loving and supportive partner will not be able to change that viewpoint.

Suppose a partner, rather than boosting self-esteem, undermines it? Or, more commonly, a partner is perceived as not supportive enough by someone who has neurotic feelings of insecurity. First, the injured party will withdraw from the partner, emotionally if not spatially. Then, the needy one will try to find someone more appreciative of him. Finally, if no real person is available, the seeker will supply through fantasy the validator he cannot find in reality.

The average man does not have to invent a fantasy companion when he experiences an ego crisis; he merely has to resurrect one. He returns to the dream girl who supported him before he was able to engage real women.

For every man, the dream girl once was there; for many men, she never leaves; and for even more, she makes periodic returns. She breaks up or befouls relationships in ways that are difficult to combat because participants and even therapists have no idea about what the problem is. Her presence goes undetected, not only because she is invisible but especially because her existence is unknown. Radiation and carbon monoxide are invisible, too, but we can detect them if we suspect them.

I once heard a lecture given by a medical expert in systemic lupus erythematosis, a pervasive disorder of the immune system where the afflicted form antibodies against their own tissues. The disease is often subtle and can masquerade as arthritis, mental illness, or various infections. The lecturer said, "We had a group of doctors who came here to study lupus, because they had not been finding cases in their own country. We taught them what to look for. They're finding the cases now."

So it is with the dream girl. Most therapists have never encountered her, but once you start looking for her, you will meet her again and again.

She Had a Name

Jeff was the patient who launched me on my career-long pursuit of the dream girl, culminating in this book. Finding his dream girl was for me like a detective solving his first crime or a paleontologist unearthing his first fossil. I suppose it was even more exciting than that, since there are many detectives and paleontologists, but I was probably the first tracer of missing dream girls.

Jeff was the type of patient that therapists used to call jokingly a YAVIS: young, attractive, verbal, intelligent, successful. In a field where so many patients are underachieving, limited in insight, and burned out from years of underproductive treatment, it is understandable that therapists would particularly welcome someone like Jeff into their offices.

Ironically, Jeff was sloughed off to me by a colleague who had been treating both Jeff and his wife, Theresa, before their divorce. My colleague, who also happened to be my boss at a clinic where we were both employed, apparently found Theresa far more interesting than Jeff and was soon conducting psychoanalytic sessions, even though his training had been in community mental health, not psychoanalysis. The doctor decided, especially after the couple decided to divorce, that his continuing to treat Jeff might have an adverse effect on his therapeutic relationship with Theresa, so he referred Jeff to me. Losing your therapist at the same time you lose your wife, no matter how partially happy you might be to get rid of either, is bound to be traumatic, and Jeff, despite his strengths, was wounded and vulnerable.

Jeff was a college English professor, tall, handsome and intelligent. He was good at what he did, but he would have preferred being a cop. Since he was a boy, he had wanted to be a law enforcement agent, preferably FBI, but at least a cop on the beat, admired and loved by those whose persons and property he protected. He never realized his dream, because he was color-blind. ("Officer, I did not go through a red light! How can you say I did?")

He never completely gave up the dream and the prof often packed heat. He was a member of a social club with a target range in the basement and he had a license to use a pistol therein. When you transport such a gun to and from the range, it is supposed to be unloaded, disassembled, and in a case. Jeff's was usually loaded and on his person, even when he was not planning to shoot at targets. He usually wore it to therapy sessions.

You don't have to go to psychoanalytic school to appreciate the symbolic significance of a loaded gun. Men who carry them tend to feel threatened, defensive, and usually a bit hostile.

Jeff never shot anyone, but he came close once and the event left him shaken. He was driving his car in a sullen mood one afternoon and stopped for a traffic light. Three teenage boys crossed the street and one, in the provocative manner of certain inner-city adolescents, pounded Jeff's front fender with his fist as he walked by.

Jeff leaped from the car, drew his pistol, and aimed it at the offensive boy. The kid stared down the barrel in momentary disbelief, then, maintaining his bravado, yelled, "Shoot me! Go ahead, what are you waiting for?"

Jeff felt very foolish. Obviously, he could not shoot the boy, despite his initial impulse. He was as helpless as his target, who now had the psychological advantage. The professor put the gun back in its holster and his body back in the car, as his adversaries ambled calmly off.

The incident helped Jeff get in touch with his own aggression. One day he confided, "All the stuff about my wanting to be a cop so people will respect me and love me while I protect their neighborhood is a lot of crap. I wanted to carry a gun so I could kill people!"

Mostly, Jeff and I talked not about guns, but women. Jeff met a lot of women and he was quite a charmer. He was bright and sensitive, as well as good-looking. He had a respectable, secure job. He was suave and attentive. He even played the guitar. He was "a catch."

The problem was that nobody ever caught him. Although he

professed to want a monogamous, committed relationship, months and months passed without his establishing a long-term bond with a woman.

There was a recurrent pattern. Jeff would meet a woman and they would begin to date. They would have sex, which Jeff found exciting and highly satisfactory. Since these women, who were all very attractive and personable, had other admirers, it was not long before the women would sever ties with Jeff's rivals and give him their undivided attention. Some of the women he dated had children, and Jeff would begin to bond with them, inviting them on outings and buying them gifts. It seemed as if the relationship was on an unwavering course down a church aisle.

Then, things would begin to go wrong. Flaws in the woman, previously unperceived, became progressively evident. The woman was irritable, demanding, selfish, inconsiderate or vulgar. She might have some virtues, but she was definitely not someone you would want to spend the rest of your life with. Fortunately, Jeff would have just met another attractive woman, who showed much more promise than the one he would be leaving.

By now it was apparent to me that Jeff would *never* find a woman to meet his standards for a permanent partner. I could no longer share his enthusiasm over the latest terrific woman he had just met; I had watched the scenario unfold too many times with the unvarying denouement.

He obviously had some woman in mind, one whom no real woman could ever match: a woman who could exist only in fantasy. Bingo, the dream girl!

"Jeff, what do you want in a woman?" I asked.

"Well, a strong woman."

I assumed he meant an independent woman, capable of self-fulfillment, secure in her own identity, and able to provide emotional support and help to her man. But I asked, anyway, "What do you mean by 'strong'?"

"Well, blond, tall, with a really good figure," he replied. This from a college professor who specialized in communicating through the English language! Okay, the dream girl often starts with a physical shell into which her personality gets gradually encased.

"Jeff, did you ever have a dream girl?" I bluntly asked.

"What do you mean by a 'dream girl'?" he asked.

"Did you ever fantasize when you were younger about the girl you would want to meet someday and marry? Someone who was the ideal woman for you?"

"No, I can't say that I did."

Despite such an unequivocal denial, I did not give up. Fantasy usually accompanies masturbation, so I decided to try that avenue.

"Jeff, do you have any fantasies when you masturbate?" Note that I did not ask *if* he masturbated, which would have tempted him to blurt out another nonproductive no.

"I rarely masturbate," he said (which is what all men say), "but when I do, the fantasy is always the same." The fantasy was a shocker, and not just because the dream girl wasn't a part of it: "I'm having intercourse with an attractive girl whom I barely know. When I'm finished, I look down at her with a feeling of contempt and say, 'That's all you're good for!'"

I knew that Jeff had some hostility toward and ambivalence about women, but this was rather extreme.

Could this barely known attractive sex partner of Jeff's be the dream girl? I didn't think so. The dream girl may be perceived as having negative elements, but she is thoroughly familiar to the man and not routinely a part of masturbatory fantasies.

And so the therapy continued and, unwilling to give up my theory that the dream girl was at the root of Jeff's problem with women, I would periodically ask again whether he had ever had one. The answer was always no.

Then, one day, the answer was not no. Instead, Jeff replied, "Well, I'm not sure you'd call her a dream girl. Her name was Susan."

"She had a name?" I gasped. "You're not sure whether you had a dream girl and she had a *name*?"

"Yes," Jeff admitted. He had concocted Susan when he was quite young, probably about eight. She was an adult woman, blond and beautiful. She was his secret companion who shared his imaginary adventures. These usually involved heroic exploits as an FBI agent or policeman.

What was the inspiration for Susan and where did her name come from? Jeff said he probably adopted her face from a wholesome-type wall calendar. One of his friends had an attractive mother named Susan. Jeff's imagination filled in the rest.

There she was, the classic dream girl, exactly as I expected to find her, even though any other therapist would have abandoned the hunt months ago in the face of Jeff's repeated denials. She was beautiful, but not lust-provoking; maternal, but not parentally prohibitive. She had been part of the secret daydreams and never considered them silly or impractical. Sometimes the helpful accomplice, sometimes the grateful victim to be rescued, sometimes the witness to an otherwise uncredited daring accomplishment, Susan was whatever Jeff needed her to be. In all her roles, she was his validator.

While Jeff's recent girlfriends appreciated him, they could never support his sagging ego the way Susan did. Any expressed wish to do something other than what Jeff wanted, any suggestion that he do something a little differently was taken by him as a scathing put-down and as evidence that the woman was a pushy bitch really interested in her own agenda.

But even the most passive and supportive of women could not have matched Susan's validation, for they knew only Jeff the professor. Susan knew Jeff the hero, intrepid and invincible. If there was a million-to-one chance that Susan existed in the flesh somewhere, Jeff the supercop never would. He was pure mythology.

Jeff knew that Susan was make-believe. She was not the product of a delusion, a psychotic false belief. That much insight had made Jeff banish her from his conscious mind many years ago. Yet, she had persisted as the impossible woman he intended to find. He had put aside his dreams to marry a real woman once and it resulted in misery and divorce. He was determined not to let the same disaster happen again.

Once Susan had been flushed out into the light, we could more easily explain in therapy the self-destructive pattern Jeff followed in his relationships with women. With hope we would no longer be continuously replaying "Desperately Seeking Susan."

There are millions of Jeffs in the world, each with his personal dream girl. They are victims of these phantoms, although they will get little sympathy from the women they have courted or married and then abandoned, physically and emotionally. They bail out of relationships that are salvageable and even sound because of a vague conviction that something is seriously lacking. They find fault with women who are actually exemplary. A therapist cannot fix the relationship because it isn't broken.

Dealing with the dream girl in therapy usually does not entail a positive identification. In working with Jeff, I doggedly persisted in getting him to recall and confront Susan; it took an inordinate amount of time. Not every dream girl has a name. Some are too shadowy to be classified as blondes or brunettes. Some stay constant while the man ages, but others undergo modifications to meet the man's changing needs.

So I don't probe relentlessly with the hope of eliciting a fully formed creature with a name and a biography. The dream girl is a secret, and premature or overaggressive intrusion on the therapist's part may cause the patient not only to bury her even more deeply but also to escape the therapeutic alliance. I took the risk with Jeff because back then I wasn't all that confident about my intuition and inferences. Today, I probably would have confronted him with the impossible standards he was setting for partners long before I had made a positive identification of Susan.

Have you ever been in a relationship with a man that suddenly went off course, taking an unexpected turn for the worse—with no idea why? Has your partner ever become moody and withdrawn, and when you asked him what was wrong, he said, "Nothing"? Has a relationship that seemed so ideal at the start dragged on interminably without proceeding to marriage because he "just wasn't ready yet"? Has he gone from being loving and supportive to aloof and critical, even though you're the same woman you've always been? Have you ever said to yourself, "He's involved with another woman," and then added, perplexed, "But he's always with me, so he *can't* be!"?

And in the midst of this rancor and discontent, the man is always protesting, "There's *nothing* wrong!" or "I don't know why I feel this way, I just *do*."

Hopefully, you've never been involved in any of the above situations. As a therapist, I see them all the time, so, fair warning! If you've escaped them thus far, there still may be pitfalls ahead.

When he says there's nothing wrong and there obviously is,

when he says there's something wrong with your relationship and there obviously isn't, when he acts like he's smitten with another woman but there is none—you're up against the little woman who wasn't there, the dream girl.

She may be invisible, but she's not invincible. She can be beaten. She *must* be.

~ CHAPTER 2 ~

A Dream Is Born

Then the Lord God said, "It is not good that the man is alone."

—GENESIS 2:18

*W*hy are there dream girls and why are there so many of them? Psychological entities generate and thrive in appropriate psychological environments.

Mold grows in dank crevices. Botulism organisms flourish in atmospheres of reduced oxygen. Algae proliferate in stagnant water.

Dream girls grow in isolation. They are not compatible with real women. They don't relate to more than one human and tend to disappear when friends are on the scene. But the young men who create them do not have to live in total isolation. If they did, they would possibly come to have hallucinatory experiences, as people do who suffer sensory deprivation, in which they could visualize the dream girl and hear her voice clearly.

The dream girl's requirements are simple: some time alone with one's thoughts and a void to fill. There is always a void in the beginning, for no one is born with a lover, unless you count those rare cases where members of royalty are betrothed from birth. And one can be alone with one's thoughts even in a crowd, so, like raising a plant from an avocado pit, just about any man can cultivate a dream girl.

At this point, perhaps we should address for the first time an issue that women are likely to raise, that young women also have fantasies regarding boyfriends and the men they will someday marry. Are there not dream men, as well as dream girls, and are they not just as problematic?

Yes to the first question, no to the second. We will return to the dream man and discuss him in more detail later, but for now we will make the following generalizations: the dream man's role is simpler, he does not have to be kept secret, and girls have more sources than boys of validation from real people as they grow up.

The dream girl emerges during those years that psychoanalysts call the latency period, the preadolescent span from ages six to twelve. People think that boys have little interest in, and even a contempt, for girls during those years, but much of the disinterest and repugnance is a reaction formation (expressing the opposite of your natural feelings and impulses) against a strong interest. Charlie Brown's unrequited crush on the little red-haired girl is a true-to-life depiction of the emotional agonies commonly experienced by little boys in the throes of playground passions.

What does Charlie want from the little red-haired girl? His drive is obviously presexual. At his age, even a date at the movies would be premature. All Charlie wants is to be recognized, appreciated, validated. The little red-haired girl is so remote that for years she was not seen in the comic strip and had no name. (She was finally depicted and named for the first time in a TV special, which considerably deemphasized her unapproachability.) The little red-haired girl does not dislike Charlie Brown; what is perhaps worse, she is unaware of his existence, much less his ardor. Charlie's pervasive inferiority feelings could be immensely helped by a friendly smile or a kind word from his classmate, but his inability to solicit a response dooms him to continued insignificance.

The girls in the *Peanuts* strip have similar but not equal problems with unrequited desire. Lucy tries to charm Schroeder away from his piano, but while she is as unsuccessful as Charlie, she does not have his ego problems. What she wants from Schroeder is tribute from him to feed her vanity, to be given gifts and adoration.

Her response to his indifference is not sorrow, but anger, and she remains as egocentric as ever.

Sally pursues the older Linus, who protests that he is *not* her "Sweet Babboo." Sally, unlike her big brother, Charlie Brown, is not deterred in the slightest. Sally has an innate understanding that boys are slower to mature than girls and that it is only a matter of time before Linus will succumb to her charms.

Peppermint Patty is the most poignant of the frustrated girls, having a crush on the least likely object, Charlie Brown. But while we ache for Charlie, it is difficult to empathize with Patty. Charlie is precociously introspective, Patty is oblivious to much of her environment. She is the only child who calls Charlie "Chuck" and who hasn't discerned that "the funny-looking kid with the big nose" is a beagle. She eschews dresses, curls, and feminine wiles; she is the archetypal tomboy, whom her sidekick, Marcy, calls "Sir." But unlike girls who adopt masculine ways as children in order to compete more effectively with male peers for recognition, Patty sleeps her way through the school day and adopts such dubious stratagems as blurting out, "Sixteen," because sooner or later sixteen will be the correct answer to a question the teacher asks. As a stereotype, she is the female equivalent of the jock, who excels in sports and fails at everything else, except the pursuit of the opposite sex. Female athletes, however, especially at the preteen level, score few points with boys, but Patty is as clueless in this area as in other matters.

Before developing fantasized love objects, children invent imaginary characters that meet more immature needs. It is curious that arguably the most popular comic strip today is *Calvin and Hobbes*, the subject of which is a six-year-old boy and his imaginary playmate, a large tiger, who originates as a stuffed toy. It is interesting that one of the first scientific books on the subject of imaginary playmates, written by child psychoanalyst Selma Fraiberg in 1959, opened with a description of "Laughing Tiger," the creation of her two-year-old niece. The friendly animal, who did not roar, bite, or scare children, was concocted by the little girl at a time when she was terrified by dogs. "Laughing Tiger" provided her with an ally; she could play with or scold this potentially ferocious animal and her control over him helped her to master her fear of dogs. When, at age three, she no longer had the fear, she lost her imaginary playmate as well.

There may seem to be little kinship between large tigers and attractive dream girls, but they share other common attributes besides being imaginary. To understand dream girls, we must understand their more primitive forebears, what their purpose was, and what they evolved into.

About 60 percent of children, both male and female, between the ages of three and four, have imaginary playmates. (If you count having dolls or figures, which the child animates in play, talks to, or carries around to share experiences, this figure would approximate 100 percent, but psychologists seem to count only creations that do not "channel" through a tangible prop.) The playmates may be human, animals, or indeterminate spirits. Boys almost always have male companions at this early age; girls may choose either. Sometimes there are small bands of companions, constituting a small family of their own. The playmates tend to develop around age two and are usually gone by age five.

A generation ago, imaginary playmates were thought to be symptomatic of some emotional disturbance or, at best, a defense against anxiety and loneliness. When careful studies were made, it was learned that, contrary to expectations, the children with imaginary companions were more intelligent, less aggressive, more cooperative, seldom bored, better able to use language effectively, and watched less television.

Children who were without siblings or firstborn did more frequently turn to imaginary companions, lending some support to the contention of Bruno Bettelheim that maybe such children were lonely. While he conceded that imaginary companions were a healthy reaction to loneliness, he asked, "But is it healthy to be lonely?"

Jean Piaget, a psychologist more interested in cognitive development than its emotional aspects, saw this type of imaginary play as a natural attempt for a child to incorporate symbolic concepts into his limited cognitive resources for classifying and dealing with new information. As the child grows older, he prefers structured games with definite rules to the more amorphous symbolic play.

Children always know that their playmates are make-believe. Even though they may frustrate their parents by insisting that a place be set at the table or a chair reserved for their "friend," children can easily distinguish between the imaginary and the real. Piaget notwithstanding, the imaginary companion usually is more than a cognitive stepping-stone on the way to mastering adult reasoning. The playmate may alleviate anxiety, as in the case of an elf who would chase monsters from under the child's bed, or the phantom sister blamed for the child's misdeeds.

The one common function served by the playmates, regardless of their form or sex, is that of *listening*. They corroborate the child's accounts. They provide a sympathetic ear and a validation of how unjust the adult world can be. They give *unconditional* support.

Sometimes the imaginary companion serves as a superego, filling the gap between the period when the child depends entirely on the parents to control his behavior and the time when the child has developed his own conscience and social judgment. The imaginary playmate may counsel the child against the impulse to do something forbidden. The child sometimes turns the tables by scolding the companion and instructing it in the proper way to behave.

In *Calvin and Hobbes*, we can see how the tiger serves the classic functions of the imaginary playmate. Calvin is really too old for an imaginary playmate; nearly all children abandon theirs by age five. Yet, Calvin is not a typical child; he is continually rebellious, although imaginative and innovative. His favorite pastime is "Calvin Ball," a physically exhausting game in which the rules are changed with the game in progress and no two games are played in the same way.

Hobbes, for all his genteelness, is physically aggressive, frequently pouncing on Calvin and leaving him in disarray. Hobbes sometimes jokes about humans' chief purpose being food for tigers. He usually supports Calvin in evading parental restrictions, tormenting Calvin's female neighbor, Susie, and outwitting their harassed baby-sitter. Yet Hobbes often warns (usually unheeded) Calvin against ventures bound to end in disaster. When the hated Susie invites Calvin to a dolls' tea party, Hobbes tempers Calvin's masculine outrage by wondering what kind of cookies will be there.

The popularity of *Calvin and Hobbes*, particularly among college students, lies in our acknowledgment that we all want to rebel against the restrictions of society but fear the penalty of alienation and isolation. Hobbes is that portion of our psyches that encourages us to pay the price, that tells us we can stand alone without being lonely and that we are not as alone as we think.

Imaginary playmates are not limited to the two-to-five age group. While they are much less common, a second wave of such beings are generated around the age of nine. This is not surprising, for around that age children have achieved a considerable degree of independence from their families, are very needy of peer support, and begin to have an increased awareness of sexuality, even though not physically mature.

Boys are especially vulnerable at this age. They have learned some of the rules of manly conduct, such as never crying, never showing fear, never running to a parent, and daring to match any accomplishment mastered by a peer. Girls have a profound advantage in that they are allowed to be vulnerable and to share vulnerability. They are allowed to spend time with their mothers and to imitate them, since their goal is to become women. They can confide longings and disappointments to girlfriends, even cry on one another's shoulders.

There is far less information about the imaginary companions of older children. One of the characteristics of early imaginary playmates is that they are foisted upon reluctant adults, who are informed of the playmate's existence, demands, and activities, even to the degree of having to provide extra food or accommodations for the invisible intruder. Older children do not spontaneously share their companions, so their prevalence may be much greater than we think.

Boys no longer limit their imaginary companions at age nine to males, as they did when younger. The dream girl certainly can come to consciousness this early. She can appear as soon as the boy develops any sort of concept of romantic love, which, as Charlie Brown demonstrates, can occur very early, sometimes even in kindergarten. Perhaps this growing awareness of a higher emotional interaction between two people of opposite sex helps to eradicate the horde of male-sexed, fanciful creatures who form the first generation of imaginary playmates.

Kindred Spirits

By now, you are probably objecting to so much attention to a psychological phenomenon that seems limited to childhood. While the subject is not widely discussed, imaginary relationships, usually of a romantic nature and directed toward a celebrity, are extremely common in adults. Psychologist John L. Caughey, in the course of interviewing fifty male and female subjects, unearthed thirty-six "artificial relationships," about one-third occurring in men. The object of the attraction was almost always a celebrity the person had never met, 47 percent being actors or actresses, and 44 percent musicians. All the people interviewed were at least of college age.

The relationship usually involved a fantasized love affair with the celebrity, with the fan never losing contact with reality or imagining the relationship ever to exist in actuality. Rarely, the relationship may be with someone of the same sex whom the imaginer wishes to imitate. Caughey gave examples of a medical student who compensated for his fears of inadequacy by trying to act like James Bond, a young man who dealt with his feelings of alienation by forming a "friendship" with St. Francis of Assisi, and a young woman who fantasized about being the daughter of author Isak Dinesen, whom she finally met after she got a job in a publishing house.

This type of intense hero worship or identification is not as common as the fascination people develop with attractive celebrities of the opposite sex. The difference between simple appreciation and an artificial relationship is that the latter does not stop at watching a TV show or attending a concert, but proceeds to a fantasy of knowing the celebrity and even engaging in romance or marriage. There is a self-confessed obsession with the admired one, manifested by religious attendance at every personal appearance and collecting photos and other memorabilia in large quantities. The afflicted fan nevertheless knows that he or she is not known to the celebrity and that the relationship is one-sided.

Do such relationships sometimes involve a loss of contact with reality, where the pursuer comes to believe the relationship actually exists? Certainly. The case probably most familiar is that of the woman who repeatedly breaks into the Connecticut home of David

Letterman and claims to be his wife, a pattern that persists despite several arrests and brief psychiatric hospitalizations.

Once when I was on duty in the psychiatric emergency room of St. Luke's/Roosevelt Medical Center, the police brought in a woman they had picked up at a nearby television studio. She was a physician who lived in a different state, with a history of treatment for bipolar disorder (manic-depressive illness). She said she was in love with a prominent newscaster and was sure he was destined to be her husband. She had once apprehended him in the studio's lobby and he had cordially listened to her discourse about her life and literary ambitions. When she said she would like him to read some of her material, he said he would, after which she mailed him some of her writings.

Today, however, he had been less accommodating. When she approached and insisted on speaking to him, he called the police. The patient refused to be admitted voluntarily to the psychiatric unit and, since she was not suitable for commitment because she posed no threat of harm, I released her back to the care of her treating psychiatrist. I cautioned her that such an incident could have resulted in notoriety and seriously damaged her professional career, but I don't know how much that helped against such a powerful fixation.

A dramatic case of fan worship gone terribly wrong occurred in 1949, when an eighteen-year-old woman, who had developed a two-year crush on Eddie Waitkus, a major league ballplayer, shot him. This act, which was portrayed in the movie *The Natural*, was motivated by her realization that she would never get to know the player in a normal way and her decision that if she couldn't have him, nobody could. She checked into the hotel where he was staying, called him and asked him to come to her room to discuss "something important," and then accused him of bothering her for two years before she shot him in the stomach. Like Robert Redford in *The Natural*, Waitkus survived the bullet and returned to his productive playing career much more quickly than his fictional counterpart.

Men are even more prone to develop obsessive crushes and many become "stalkers." While we tend to associate stalking with very aggressive men who harm or even kill the object of their professed affection, the majority are passive men with a deep sense of inadequacy. They harass the woman by following her around, spying on her through windows, or making late-night telephone calls to check on her whereabouts. They may have succeeded in dating the woman briefly at one time, after which they become convinced that the woman loves them and will marry them. Protests by the woman are usually ineffective, since the man rationalizes that feminine coyness is expected and, with persistence and time, he is bound to win her heart.

Because of their sense of inadequacy, these men can frequently be stopped by a confrontation with a male friend or relative of the woman. While orders of protection or threats of legal action have little power under our system of justice, since penalties for such harassment are slight, a few hours in a holding pen among hardened criminals and the prospect of more of the same can terrify these pseudo-aggressive pursuers and cause them to abandon their quests. Unfortunately, they tend to find another unattainable woman and repeat the cycle.

Artificial relationships are most problematic when the object is in close proximity, as in the case of the stalker who becomes obsessed with a neighbor. A Hollywood star is less threatened by a fan than a Broadway actress is. Elvis Presley is still worshipped by legions, but is now immune from further misfortune.

Ardent admiration is not necessarily unwelcomed. Ann-Margret's chief fan, after amassing a museum-size collection of memorabilia and organizing fan clubs, eventually met his idol and now corresponds with her. He was able to maintain the real boundaries of a performer-fan relationship and did not delude himself into seeing it as a personal love relationship.

There is a problem with defining at what point the idolization becomes pathological. Until she attempted to murder Eddie Waitkus, the teenage fan's crush would have been considered normal by most, if for no other reason than so many other girls her age develop similar fixations, usually on show business personalities rather than athletes.

Dr. Caughey, during his interviews with men and women, was not surprised to uncover evidence of so many artificial relationships among apparently normal subjects. One reason was his having lived on a small Micronesian island in the Pacific, where he studied social relations in a primitive tribe. He found that the islanders' "social" contacts included not only relatives and neighbors but numerous spirits as well. The spirits appear to them in dreams or hallucinatory states of mind, giving them comfort and advice. Tribesmen imagine themselves to be in kindred, adversary, or even romantic relationships with these spirits. There are mediums who profess particular skill in contacting these spirits, and tribesmen use them to solicit advice, warnings, or knowledge from the spirits. The spirits have names and histories, which involve relationships with other inhabitants of the spirit world.

In modern society, the celebrities become the equivalent of the spirits. Through television, they enter the privacy of our homes. Newspapers and tabloids keep us abreast of their latest ventures, professional and personal. Like the members of the spirit world, celebrities are "known about" without being actually "known to" people. As sexually attractive role models, celebrities are adopted by many people as imaginary friends. Television stars with daily shows become part of a fan's regular routine, offering more contact, however limited, than a sibling living miles away.

A Private Audience

Many years ago, I started treating a young woman who feared that she was crazy because of her imaginary relationships. (Psychiatrists are usually faced with the opposite problem, that of patients with psychosis who think there is nothing wrong with them.) She had suffered considerable trauma as a child and had married young, then spent most of the day alone in her apartment. She would imagine herself surrounded by various people, usually actors, to whom she would speak about her plans and goals, sometimes aloud and sometimes in her head. Her favorite listeners were members of the *Star Trek* cast (the "first generation"), including William Shatner and Leonard Nimoy. She perceived them as the actors, not the characters whom they played (Kirk, Spock, et al.).

These imaginary figures were essentially an audience. She never thought for a moment that they were anything other than imaginary. When they spoke to her, she imagined their replies and did not "hear" them. They did not interfere with her daily work routine and they did not convene when she was in the presence of other people.

Their psychological function was clear. They were validators. Their presence made her feel that her thoughts were sound and worthwhile. Their importance as celebrities gave importance to what she was communicating. Her husband, while supportive, was not much of a communicator and could not supply the reassurance she needed. As Trekkers, her supporters were competent and imaginative, living on the edge of fantasy, their mission to go boldly where no man has ever ventured before; as actors, they reminded her to keep the fantasy in check and focus on practical limitations as she pursued her dreams.

Years later, I would read that therapists were encouraging patients to develop self-assertiveness by imagining themselves giving a lecture to an audience that included one or more people they admired and whose ideas they valued. Patients were instructed to verbalize what they had learned in therapy and to describe their goals while the audience listened with obvious approval. My patient had intuitively realized that she could reinforce her own self-validation by recruiting fantasy allies.

In this case, my therapeutic task was not to help her dispel her imaginary friends, but to reassure her that she was not crazy and that there was more health than pathology in her secret companions. When I told her about the studies that showed how frequently people adopted media stars as secret confidants, she was pleasantly surprised and relieved. She went on to complete college and a master's degree while raising a child and now is an art therapist.

Julian Jaynes, psychologist and author of *The Origin of Consciousness in the Breakdown of the Bicameral Mind*, believes that prehistoric man "heard voices," much as schizophrenics do. He claims that at least half the people who recall their childhood imaginary playmates could hear them speak. Dr. Jaynes feels that our society becomes too easily upset if imaginary playmates persist too long and children are encouraged to get rid of them. In a less restrictive society, the playmates might develop into full-fledged personal gods, and serve as guides into maturity.

I recently was asked to evaluate a fourteen-year-old boy who spoke of having an imaginary friend, named Ali, who lived in his bathroom and usually stayed in the tub behind the shower curtain. The only part of Ali that the boy could see was his pigtail, but he could hear his voice. Ali usually gave him good advice on how to conduct himself and stay out of trouble.

There is nothing like a good hallucination to panic teachers, parents, and novice mental health professionals. They jump to a quick diagnosis of schizophrenia and hope the psychiatrist can medicate the experience out of existence. I have learned that there is little connection between the frightening, disorganized voices that torment schizophrenics and a well-structured, (partially) visible entity like Ali. He was a source of support, and I was more interested in helping my young patient keep him in proper perspective than in exterminating him. The patient confided that Ali would disappear for many days at a time and had warned him that he would not always be with him. I knew that, just as much younger children discard imaginary playmates when they have outlived their psychological usefulness, so, too, would the day come when my patient could not see Ali's pigtail floating above the bathtub.

This discussion of imaginary playmates in children and artificial relationships in adults is meant to emphasize the little-recognized prevalence of turning to fantasized supportive figures throughout life. At first glance, they seem to be a defense against loneliness, but they are not fabricated only by isolated individuals. Children with siblings have them and married adults have them. Their main function is to provide *validation*; that is, to supply, in fantasy, someone who understands your innermost thoughts and emotions and, despite your foibles and inadequacies, accepts and likes you for what you are.

To some degree, this is a defense against loneliness, not necessarily social isolation, but the universal knowledge that no one can ever know us completely. There are parts of our minds that we cannot even articulate, much less share.

In the opening scene of Shaw's *Caesar and Cleopatra*, Julius Caesar stands alone at night before the Sphinx and says, "I have found flocks and pastures, men and cities, but no other Caesar, no air native to me, no man kindred to me, none who can do my day's deed, and think my night's thought."

Caesar implies that it is his greatness that has isolated him from other humans, but *anyone* could make such a statement.

There is no other John Doe or Jane Roe, either. People may match or exceed our deeds, but never duplicate them in the exact same way; as for the thoughts that drift through our consciousness at night and form our dreams, they will never occur in identical form to another person.

This sense of alienation is attained relatively early in life. Infancy usually begins with a sense of security; a cry will usually bring prompt gratification in the form of food or cuddling. Not long afterward, we start to experience frustration, as certain wants are denied to us or unpleasant demands are made. The child's emotional response is the conviction that the parent does not understand the importance of getting one's own way. Soon the child enters a wider world where he is often scolded or disciplined for not complying with demands that seem to be against his own interests.

Dog Days and Puppy Love

The antidote for all this frustration is love. Generally, we think of love as a relationship that ideally involves equal amounts of giving and taking, but in the parent-child bond, the child is nearly always on the receiving end. Mother love gives a sense of security, the confidence that even if she does not understand the child completely, she will do her best to make him happy.

Boys and girls count on mother's love equally during the first years of life, but by age five boys begin to lose that source of support. Freud, in formulating the Oedipus complex, said that boys experience rivalry with the father for mother's affections, develop castration anxiety, and resolve the dilemma by identifying with the father and detaching from the mother. Girls, because of penis envy, turn from the mother and form a strong attachment to the father.

Girls actually get the better deal, since they still are primarily dependent on mother for their physical and emotional needs, while their affection for father is encouraged as cute and wholesome. Boys, for whatever motive, are encouraged to develop patterns of independence and to resist their natural impulses to run to mother and cry in her lap whenever they are traumatized. Mother still picks up their clothes and prepares their meals, but there is less physical affection (which fathers rarely replace) and sharing of confidences.

The phrase "Daddy's little girl" elicits approving sighs. The term "Mama's boy" is a challenge to a fight.

School causes an even wider degree of separation from mother, and perhaps this explains the early appearance of puppy love in children as young as five. The malady seems to affect boys more severely than girls, in degree if not in prevalence.

Having vivid memories of my own kindergarten infatuations, I am reminded of the joke about an elderly woman whose aged spouse constantly attempted to flirt with young women. Asked why she wasn't more upset by his behavior, she replied, "Shoot, my dog is always chasing cars, but if he ever caught one he wouldn't know what to do with it!"

What, I ask myself, would I or any five-year-old boy have wanted from a five-year-old girl? The longing was clearly presexual. Even if kisses were fantasized, they were the kind of cheek pecks Mother gave. The goal (never achieved) was that the girl would be as interested in me as I was in her, would talk to me, spend time with me, and consider me special. If I had to put that all into one word, I'd have to say "validation." It never occurred to my five-year-old mind that a girl my age was as immature as I and completely incapable of giving me what I needed. Little girls, as the nearest available substitute, are expected to step into the role normally assumed by a mother.

There is a second type of elementary school crush, one that usually develops in slightly older boys—the strong attraction to an adult teacher. My mother always contended that my younger brother's entire class went down the tubes in the fifth grade when the elderly nun who taught them took ill and was replaced by a beautiful, blond "lay teacher" in her early twenties. Mother was right. While the boys did graduate and for the most part went on to college and successful careers, there was a dark period when they deteriorated from disciplined, studious youths to mush-brained, rowdy slackards. They misbehaved in the hope of being kept after class. If that didn't work, they volunteered to clean blackboards and clap erasers. They joked and snickered about their teacher's attributes, but they were incorrigibly smitten with her. Even we older students, raised in an atmosphere of bonneted, long-skirted asexual nuns, glimpsed the blond angel with a sense of wonderment, but we were too distant to fall under her spell.

It must be remembered that these boys were only ten. Their knowledge of sex (this was a generation ago) was rudimentary and their bodies prepubertal. I recall that when we entered puberty, we suddenly experienced a new appreciation of our young, buxom art teacher, but this was uncomplicated lust and we knew it. At ten, my brother's classmates had abandoned their simple attractions to their undeveloped female peers for an infatuation with an older, wiser adult woman. They had found in the flesh the dream girl that the average ten-year-old must create from thin air—and often does.

The blond angel was particularly deadly because she afforded a real relationship, free from the incestuous taboos that would accrue to any female kinswoman. She was part of their everyday life, spending six hours of every weekday with them. It was her job to care for her students, to contribute to their development, and, with enough effort, a student could become a true favorite, a teacher's pet. She was a validator; what could be a more precise measure of validation than a report card?

In the average modern public school, where young female teachers are the rule rather than the exception, boys are less likely to focus collectively on one teacher. Although the crushes are more disseminated, they nevertheless occur, and a considerable degree of boisterous misconduct is merely a frantic attempt to be noticed.

A need for love arises before the emergence of a strong sexual drive. One might ask why boys cannot fulfill it from its most available source, the extended family. Part of the answer lies in the incest taboo, the danger of forbidden thoughts or libidinous feelings that might be directed toward an aunt, sister, or cousin. This is certainly true by age eleven or twelve, but younger boys probably are more deterred by another obstacle.

Boys' games deal with aggression and achievement, either on playing fields or battlefields. They aspire to becoming men, not average workaday men but potent supermen. In their fantasies, they do not teach a bully a lesson with a well-placed uppercut, they wipe out battalions singlehanded, like Rambo or G.I. Joe. They do not aspire to advancing a base runner to second with a grounder to the right side, they drive in all the runs with a towering homer. Girls' play tends to be noncompetitive, without fantasies of impossible goals.

Now, a boy does not expect any woman to believe he is a superhero, but he does want to be given his due. He is gradually becoming braver and more assertive, gaining acceptance from his peers. The problem is that female family members remember every embarrassing thing he did as a child and continue to view him as "Little Johnny," unaware of his psychological maturation.

Shaw's John Tanner, the descendant of Don Juan, said that his tailor was the only man who behaved sensibly when he was growing up because the tailor took his measurements each time he saw John, while everyone else went on with their old measurements and expected him to fit them. He warns his future wife that when she gets her wings in heaven she will seek a new circle of acquaintances who will not remember her as she was in her earthbound days.

So, although a boy is surrounded by potential female validators, they are useless to him, because they will see him as he was and is, not as the future man he is becoming. Girls of his own age are not good sources of validation, although their attention is often sought. Boys relate either by "showing off" or by hostile teasing. Since boys are usually at a disadvantage academically, they try to win admiration by physical stunts or athletic feats, with forays into the type of antisocial behavior that girls have the good sense to avoid. The pseudo-misogynistic teasing is a sure way to avoid being ignored and defends against rejection by feigning a devaluation of the girl and her approval.

Even if he wins a shy smile from his female peer, the boy is likely to be dissatisfied, because a man needs validation from a woman, not a child. In *Bye Bye Birdie*, the harried father complains to his adolescent daughter that he is given no respect. When his young son says, "*I* respect you," he snaps, "Who wants respect from a *kid*?" It is this paradox that confronts the frustrated boy, wanting validation from someone who lacks the maturity to give it.

The boy is like Tantalus in Hades, tortured by thirst and hunger, surrounded by sources of assuagement, but with relief always just beyond the tip of the tongue. Just as starving prisoners dream primarily of food, the boy turns to fantasy for what he cannot obtain from real females.

In the beginning, she may be sensibly imagined as someone existing in the future, the woman he will meet and marry when he is older and more accomplished. Soon, however, the dream girl comes to inhabit the present. She becomes more vivid than the object she presages. Unlike the women in the environment who can only measure the boy's change in inches, the dream girl is privy to every new thought and goal.

Even boys who have preadolescent romances often enter a period of asceticism in early adolescence when they withdraw from companionship in general and that of females in particular. John Tanner explains to Ann Whitefield why he suddenly broke off their childhood romance: "It happened just then that I got something that I wanted to keep all to myself instead of sharing it with you … It was something you'd never have let me call my own … My soul."

The growing need to make some sense out of life runs at cross purposes with the increasing sexual attraction to females that begins to crest in early adolescence. The male body is going through an awkward growth spurt, resulting in an ungainly, uncoordinated appearance. The mind is flourishing in the final phases of cognitive development. It even becomes a source of sexual gratification, supplying in fantasy what the boy is unlikely to be yet able to obtain from physical interaction with real women. With the exception of the occasional superjock, most adolescents endure a period of mistrusting their bodies and flexing their introspective minds.

It is then the dream girl, who was born when the body was smaller but more dependable, gains new power. The new sexual attraction toward female contemporaries is counterbalanced by a sense of suspiciousness and estrangement from the girls who might have once been buddies. A balance must be struck between desire and fear, attraction and repulsion; at the fulcrum stands the woman who promises that. In time, she will bring love and fulfillment without the agony of failure and rejection: behold the dream girl.

~ CHAPTER 3 ~

Sex Objects and Dream Girls

W hen I mention the concept of the dream girl to women, they usually nod knowingly and say, "Sure, men want the Playmate of the Month, Sharon Stone, Cindy Crawford—"

"That's not the dream girl," I interrupt. "That's different."

While a man might base the physical appearance of his dream girl on Cindy Crawford or Sharon Stone, he does not adopt a living fashion model or actress as the woman who will be exclusively his. And you could not pick a worse example than the Playmate of the Month; the dream girl is constant and the current centerfold is as ephemeral as you can get. The media figures that women think are dream girls are, to be blunt, sex objects.

To understand the concept of women as fantasy sex objects, you have to understand male masturbation, and there is probably no aspect of male sexual behavior that women understand less. Men simply do not talk about it, because while it is an activity engaged in by just about every male at some stage in life, it is regarded as shameful or sinful or, at best, puerile.

Joycelyn Elders, the first female surgeon general, lost her job because she said it *might* be considered as a fit topic for discussion in sex education classes. As soon as this statement was publicized, the commander-in-chief was on the phone to say good-bye.

Now, while Dr. Elders might have gone against public sentiment by advocating distribution of condoms in schools or the legal-
ization of drugs, she did not use her office as a "bully pulpit," which
some commentators suggested, to promote teaching masturbation
in the public schools. The offense that got her fired was the
inability to think quickly on her feet. The offending statement was
not part of her planned speech, but came as a reply to an unexpected query during the question-and-answer session.

A psychologist raised his hand and commented, rather smugly,
that masturbation still seems to be a taboo subject. He said that he
was going to do his part to combat this by admitting that he masturbates and asked how Dr. Elders felt about the subject.

The correct answer would have been a simple "Masturbation is
part of normal sexual behavior and, of course, should be discussed
like any other aspect."

Instead, the flustered surgeon general stalled for time by
launching into an irrelevant statement about how she supported sex
education in the public schools, a goal that usually won her much
acclaim and little opposition but was better avoided in this context.
By the time she figured out the "right" answer and said that masturbation was a part of sexual behavior, she had to tie it in with her
prologue and said *maybe* it should be discussed in school. Outrage
and disaster followed.

So, the onanistic psychologist was right: masturbation is the
last taboo. Defenders of Dr. Elders later pointed out that masturbation *is* covered in many schools' sex education classes, which makes
sense, since children (males, at least) are going to begin sexual
activity with it, not with intercourse. Why skip chapter one?

Most women, including female therapists, think they have an
adequate understanding of male masturbation because they can
draw parallels with female self-gratification. The feminist movement and the Masters and Johnson school of sex therapy brought a
downright respectability to the act. "Women are responsible for
their own orgasms" became the new axiom. For the enlightened
woman, skillful masturbation was a proud accomplishment, not a
source of shame. Men feel no more pride in masturbation than in
any other bathroom activity, so that is already one great intersexual
difference.

Masturbation has been variously called "self-gratification," "self-abuse," or even "self-love," depending on your moral stance. Psychological works call it "autoeroticism," again emphasizing its do-it-yourself nature. But most acts of masturbation involve a fantasy partner, which is the function of the sex object. This does not mean that a man thinks about certain actresses or models only when he masturbates, but their semiclad or nude images can easily provoke sexual excitement and invite release.

Consider the following list of unquestionably attractive women in the public eye: Madonna, Elle Macpherson, Maria Shriver, Kim Basinger, Diane Sawyer, Raquel Welch, Kathie Lee Gifford, Cher, Glenn Close, Michelle Pfeiffer. Which ones are sex symbols? Easy, wasn't it? Well, maybe there are a couple of borderline calls.

A man could find any of these women sexually arousing, but the sex symbol is one who habitually encourages this response by taking on movie roles that involve sexy behavior and/or posing for revealing photographs that are widely circulated. I say "habitually" because Glenn Close generally assumes demanding dramatic roles in which sexual activity plays a secondary part, although in *Fatal Attraction* she displayed enough sexual passion and body exposure to match the heat generated by her more notorious screen sisters, degree Fahrenheit by degree Fahrenheit.

Men can and do fantasize about attractive women they've never seen uncovered, but that much imagination is like work and the aim of masturbation is generally effortless release.

Pornography has been jocularly defined as anything that gives a judge an erection. Men know easily what has the capability of arousing them physically. Whether the material has enough artistic or educational merit to escape the label of pornography may be a tougher determination. Conventional men may respond to a wide, but limited, variety of stimuli. Men who are termed *paraphilic* today by psychiatrists who called them *perverse* a generation ago might find more excitement in the sight of rubber boots or leather slacks than in the woman who is wearing them. The female bodybuilder with massive muscles or the skeletal "waif" model may arouse some men as much as more endomorphic women, while other men may find them repulsive. Generally, the stronger a man's libido is, the less selective he becomes about his fantasies. Libido is high in the young, and when there has been a considerable amount of time since the last sexual release.

The videocassette has produced a minor revolution in masturbatory practices. For aficionados of the solitary art, it has moved the practice out of the bathroom and replaced the "one-handed" magazine as the primary visual aid. Of course, the teenage boy living with parents or the surreptitious spouse may find magazines a lot easier to stack and stash. Also, you can't say you rented a video "for the articles." Women in motion provide more variety than static photos and sex acts can be viewed rather than imagined, although male co-stars with unusual physical accouterments and stamina may arouse competitive anxiety and a sense of inadequacy in the viewer. This may account for the popularity of girl-on-girl scenarios. The popularity of the video medium has undoubtedly diminished the perception of famous beauties as primarily sex objects. The realm of pornography has generated a number of "star" performers, but most men prefer variety to singular devotion.

So far, none of what I have said will sound new or surprising to women, even though they have not given much thought to the subject. The one element of male sexual fantasy that women greatly underestimate or totally fail to perceive is the role of novelty.

One Alone

I myself never thought much about the connection between novelty and male masturbation until I read the opening chapter (and not much more) of a thick book about sex in America, written a couple of decades ago. Gay Talese had received a huge advance to write *the* definitive work on the topic at a time when the "sexual revolution" was in full bloom. What resulted was less an objective sociological treatise and more a highly personal odyssey. Titled *Thy Neighbor's Wife*, the book recounted the author's sexual adventures in massage parlors, sex clubs, and other erotic venues across this great land.

What impressed me was that this ambitious, erotic book opened with a curious anecdote about a boy's fascination with a model named Diane Webber, a rather obscure personality whose comely likeness I have encountered in pictorial histories of the pinup. In the pre-*Playboy* era, photographs of nude women were not easy to acquire in legitimate marketplaces. The prime source was *National Geographic*, which several times a year would include pictures of bare-breasted African or Polynesian natives. The other, less respectable, form of publication was the nudist magazine, which had the ostensible if transparent aim of promoting good health through exercise, sunshine, and eliminating the noxious effects of clothing. It was in such magazines, bearing titles such as *Sunshine and Health* ("sun" being the code word for nudity), that Diane Webber made frequent revealing appearances.

It was never clear to me why Talese chose to begin his long tome with a story about masturbation. Perhaps he was following Lewis Carroll's White King's advice to Alice: "Begin at the beginning." Fantasy and masturbation is certainly where it all starts. Maybe, for this particular adolescent, Diane Webber was one of those rare instances where the sex object does double duty as dream girl.

Talese made the point that the images of Diane Webber had the unusual ability to arouse the boy every time. Women in other magazines quickly lost their power to excite, unless they were put aside for a time and then reemployed.

Talese was right on target. *Playboy* would have been out of business once every male owned just a single issue if novelty was not such a potent erotic stimulus. It doesn't mean that men are completely disinterested in familiar images, it is a question of degree, much as a man who frequents prostitutes or has a mistress will still have sex with his wife of many years. Sex is always a positive experience for him, but it is obvious which type of partner he will find more exciting. A typical issue of *Playboy* will have four spreads involving several different unclad females: the Playmate of the Month; a "pictorial" featuring a different woman, usually a celebrity or someone aspiring to notoriety; a spread involving several different women with some common bond, such as attending the same college or belonging to the same profession; and a less formally posed hodgepodge, such as "The Year in Sex" or "Sex in Cinema." There are other scattered nudes, in ads, the letters column, and the issue-closing "Grapevine" and "Potpourri" melanges. Most males during a single masturbatory experience will flip from image to image, much as TV viewers channel-surf rather than focusing on one image. If one particular model becomes the focus (obviously, only one can prevail at the moment of orgasm) during one session, others will have their turns in future closed-door encounters.

Similarly, most men do not buy X-rated videos, they rent them. They prefer variety to the repetition of a proven-positive experience. This may seem illogical to many women, whose personal preference is to return to the same fantasy that has given them previous pleasure.

Even the old burlesque houses and the current bars that feature "table dancers" would never operate with only one well-endowed lady. The ads always proclaimed "12—Count 'em—12!" and quantity was emphasized more than quality. The expectation is not that the customer will select a favorite among the simultaneously performing women and devote his attention to her, but that he will partake visually of all the delights, just as someone at a buffet does not fill his plate with the single item he likes best.

The recognition (I cannot call it a "revelation") of the aphrodisiac properties of novelty and variety on the male libido is disturbing to sensitive men. Most of us like to think we are selective and monogamous and that only philanderers and cads naturally gravitate to new conquests. Yet the autoerotic experience, if we are honest, confirms what our natural proclivities really are. We can control our impulses, but we should not underestimate them.

The dream girl does not compete with other fantasies. She may be periodically modified by her creator, but she is not replaced at frequent intervals like the centerfold girl. The dream girl belongs exclusively to one man, which is why he keeps her carefully hidden.

The concept of the dream girl is scarcely a new one. Ovid recounted the classic myth of Pygmalion, a gifted sculptor who lived on the island of Cyprus, which was sacred to Venus, the goddess of love. Detesting the faults of women, he resolved never to marry and vowed to devote his life to his art. What he created, however, was a statue of a beautiful young woman, which he continued to work on until it was so lifelike that, except for its immobility, it appeared more like a real person than a marble form.

Pygmalion fell deeply in love with the statue. He not only embraced and kissed it, he brought it gifts of flowers, dressed it in pretty clothes, and tucked it into bed at night.

At the annual feast day when prayers and sacrifices were offered to Venus, Pygmalion beseeched the goddess to send him a maiden like his statue. Venus knew that what he really wanted, though he dared not ask such an impossibility, was the incarnation of the statue herself.

Venus reportedly decided to intervene dramatically because Pygmalion was a new type of lover, something the eternal goddess rarely encountered. Had Venus concerned herself more with psychological matters instead of her usual carnal domain, she might have come to the conclusion that the only thing that was different about Pygmalion was his exceptional ability to give his dream girl a tangible form that communicated to the world her desirability and the hold she exercised over him.

Venus signaled her favor to Pygmalion at the altar by making the sacrificial flame flare up three times. When he returned home and embraced his creation, she became warm and soft, a living woman who reciprocated his caresses and kisses. He named the maiden Galatea, they wed, and had a son, Paphos, who gave his name to Venus's favorite city.

In George Bernard Shaw's *Pygmalion*, a speech professor molds a coarse flower seller into a lady. The success of this popular play was far surpassed by the musical version, *My Fair Lady*. In Shaw's version, Professor Higgins and Eliza do not marry, both having the good sense to realize that the misogynistic bachelor was too mired in his solitary lifestyle; however, Lerner and Loewe could not resist at least implying that the modern Pygmalion would find marital bliss with the dream girl he molded from rags and dust.

The average man lacks the talent and patience to construct a full-scale model of his dream girl, which he knows would not make her any more alive, but most dream girls involve the use of a template, a type of mold or plan that uses some preexisting concepts of appearance or personality as a starting point. Even if the dream girl is named after and visualized as a familiar woman, living or fictional, she comes to assume an original identity that best meets the emotional needs of her creator.

One source of inspiration is the living actress. It is easier to envision someone whom you have never met if you give her an appearance that is attractive and familiar, borrowed from someone you have never met and are not likely to meet. It is possible for a man to find a certain celebrity's looks particularly attractive or arousing, yet not adopt that appearance for his dream girl.

Mike Myers and Dana Carvey, who portrayed a pair of goofy adolescents in the "Wayne's World" skits on *Saturday Night Live*, would often mention the name of a famous "babe" and allude to her effect on their libido with such comments as "She'd give a dog a bone!" or, simply, "*Schwing!*" while lifting their pelvises off their chairs. Madonna once topped their "babes of the year" list, beating out such rivals as Betty Rubble and the vice president's daughters. This was not a dream girl list. While the dream girl is, unquestionably, number one, she stands alone. She has no competition.

I was recently a guest at a wedding where I sat with an old acquaintance, a man in his mid-forties, and his wife. I started talking about dream girls and the wife said of her husband, "Oh, I know who his dream girl is—Sharon Stone."

I shook my head. "Can't be. She's a newcomer and he's too old."

"Well, it used to be Farrah Fawcett," she added.

"That's more like it," I said.

My nationwide survey for *Beyond the Male Myth* in 1977 included a question about dream girls, and Farrah Fawcett far outdistanced all other celebrities in frequency of mention. You could tell the age of the respondent from his choice of actress: Dolores Del Rio, Fay Wray, Ann Corio, Ingrid Bergman, Marilyn Monroe, Sophia Loren, Kim Novak, Raquel Welch. You will note that most of these nominees had charismatic personalities as well as physical beauty.

One middle-aged man, married for many years, initially said (as most initially say) that he had never had a dream girl, but after a moment's reflection, added, "Of course, I always had a thing for Audrey Hepburn."

Audrey Hepburn, in her many screen roles, had the uncanny ability to be simultaneously the vivacious urchin and the regal princess. It is not surprising that she beat out Julie Andrews for the film role of Eliza Doolittle, the audacious guttersnipe who became Professor Higgins's fair lady. The majority of men would not pattern their dream girl after her, but many would. She is a more typical template than Kathleen Turner or Pamela Anderson of *Baywatch* because her screen persona is more compatible with a man's idea of how a wife would be, and dream girls are for keeps.

Choosing an actress as a model for a dream girl is not the same as choosing a real person. While the celebrity's true-life personality may, to some extent, resemble the fan's idea that is drawn from her typical roles, the man cannot know her as an actual person—nor does he need to. The actress provides an outline; the man fills in the details.

Farrah Fawcett's admirers were abundant a score of years ago, and she probably inspired as many dream girls then as Marilyn Monroe and Rita Hayworth did at their peaks. Yet, I would categorize her not with the celebrity group but in the next group to be considered: fictional characters identified with specific performers.

Ms. Fawcett was the most popular member of the trio that comprised *Charlie's Angels*. The Angels were, collectively, true to the dream-girl ideal, because they were brave, cool, assertive and competent. Remember that the dream girl is first envisioned as a mature, supportive woman by an immature, insecure boy. Despite their prowess and take-charge bearing, the Angels were not in charge; Charlie was. Charlie was their boss and he gave them their assignments. In a curious reversal, the dream girls were seen and the man who masterminded them was not. His voice was deep, calm, with a tone of perpetual detached amusement. He seemed to be James Bond without having to put in the effort or face the perils. The dream girls made him what he was and continued to validate him.

Kate Jackson (Samantha) was the most experienced of the three when the series started and reportedly drew a higher salary. She was the intellectual and tended to keep her body covered, rarely donning anything more revealing than a pair of mid-thigh shorts. Jaclyn Smith (Kelly) was probably the most physically perfect of the lot, blessed not only with exquisite facial features but a body that called for her to wear the bikini whenever the Angels put out to sea.

Farrah (Jill) soon eclipsed the others. Her hair was blond, in the tradition of storybook princesses, and it was wild and tousled, suggestive of a nymph or other unhindered spirit. She was always flashing a set of perfect white teeth in a friendly, reassuring smile, except in those brief instants when, both hands clenching her revolver, she was ordering some perpetrator to "Freeze!"

Kate seemed to be the young mother, always level-headed and reserved. Jaclyn had an aloof "look-but-don't-touch" aura. Farrah was, at least in fantasy, thoroughly approachable and embraceable. She could make a man feel protective and unintimidated, while acknowledging that she could hold her own in any situation.

The poster that hung in every dorm was dominated by that wild golden mane and larger-than-life smile. She wore a conservative bathing suit, yet the outline of her right nipple made it naughtier than Jaclyn's bikini. It was the "Farrah" poster, not the "Jill" or "Charlie's Angels" poster and no other single picture of a dream girl ever matched its popularity.

But when Farrah flew from the heavenly Angel band, her popularity plummeted. Her dramatic talents were praised as she assumed roles of abused women who eventually confronted and bested their male assailants. She was still in her prime physically. But she was never the dream girl again.

It was not a question of aging. Too many legends, including Sophia Loren, Cher, Raquel Welch, Joan Collins, and Tina Turner, have been able to play sexy temptresses and vixens in their forties and beyond. These actresses are identified with a type of role, not one particular role, and as long as the roles keep coming, their dream girl status remains intact. Since *Charlie's Angels* was her first major success, Farrah, the actress, was equated with the role she played. Even today, if you ask people to name the three original Angels, many will say, "Kelly, Samantha, and ... uh ... Farrah." A generation was enchanted not by a beautiful actress, but by a perfect fantasy.

Several other actresses have become inextricably linked with the popular fantasy characters they portrayed on television, such as Lynda "Wonder Woman" Carter and Lindsay "Bionic Woman" Wagner. While *any* actress in a recurring role on a sitcom, soap opera, or dramatic series will be identified with her character, some are particularly prone to become dream-girl models, none more so than Barbara Eden in *I Dream of Jeannie*. Jeannie was a close cousin of Elizabeth Montgomery's Samantha, the spell-weaving wife in *Bewitched*. That TV show was probably inspired by the old Veronica Lake film, *I Married a Witch*.

The function of a dream girl is to validate and empower her man through her own desirability and competence, without ever overshadowing or competing with him. Ms. Eden's genie was the slave of her master, Major Nelson, who usually tried, unsuccessfully, to stop her from using her magic. Samantha's husband, similarly, tried to restrain her practice of witchcraft, but he did not own her, as the master of the genie did. At least for the first highly successful years of the show, Ms. Eden's character was provocative and flirtatious, but untouchable, just like any dream girl. (The writers eventually had Major Nelson and Jeannie get married, which begat *Bewitched II* and deserved oblivion.)

The bungling genie and the inhibited witch provided an imperfect solution to the dream-girl dilemma: how do you match up a superwoman with an imperfect man? Major Nelson and Darrin, for all their attempts to be masters of the house and the women therein, were chronic bumblers. If she lived freely with such a man, instead of a more worthy mate, her judgment would be obviously impaired, negating her status as a perfect woman. So the dream girl, though potentially omnipotent, is denied her full potential by her inferior master/husband, who strives to keep her supernatural attributes secret from his prying peers. Jeannie and Samantha would try to be subservient, then would yield to the temptation to release the magic, screw things up, and nevertheless make everything turn out right in the end.

The suave, accomplished macho man may get the girl, but not the dream girl. In the movies and TV shows, she is rightfully the prize of the klutz, the nerd, the guy who constantly trips over his own feet. She is created out of loneliness and desperation by the immature boy; she gives him the support he needs not only to succeed in finding a mate, but in any area of his life that demands confidence and self-esteem.

The third type of dream-girl model is drawn from the printed page, a woman portrayed only in words or ink, with no human actress to flesh out her image. The comic books, especially during the youth of men now middle-aged, were once a prime source of inspiration, because they featured beautiful women without the slightest flaw, and because many of these women exemplified the role of dream girl as validator. Lois Lane is the grande dame of this group of adoring females. Unlike the genie who gives her wimpy master new power, she does not appreciably assist Superman, but is there merely to be rescued from peril and then to express praise and gratitude.

Many of the major male comic-strip heroes had such a woman in their lives: Tarzan had Jane, the Phantom had Diana, Mandrake the Magician had Narda, Prince Valiant had Aleta, and Spiderman had Mary Jane Watson. The women tended to be rather passive and limited to the role of victim, saved by the hero in each episode. These women are not without strengths of their own. Aleta is queen of her own kingdom (the Misty Isles), Narda was princess of some nebulous realm, Jane helped to educate Tarzan and, to this day, Mary Jane supports her seldom-employed superspouse. But the accomplishments of these women only magnify the deeds of the men who preserve their precarious existences.

Other fictitious women would include goddesses, princesses, and any female that epitomizes the highest form of feminine perfection. A boy's first exposure to the idea of what a man is to seek in a woman is likely to be the fairy tales read to him by his mother. The heroine is invariably a beautiful princess, coveted by every male in the kingdom and surrounding environs, who faithfully waits for her one true love. The dream girl may draw her identity from the Sleeping Beauty, Rapunzel, Guinivere, or Tolkien's Galadriel. (In one of his films, Woody Allen confessed to having had a perverse early crush on Snow White's stepmother—but hey, the Wicked Queen *was* a close second to the fairest in the land and built a lot better.) In the movie *One Touch of Venus*, the bungling leading man aspired to a liaison with the love goddess herself, who materialized in living form from a priceless statue (and where have we encountered *that* plot before?). Vanna White, about thirty years later, reprised Ava Gardner's starring role in a TV remake, entitled *Goddess of Love*. Vanna is still spinning her wheel, Ava's spinning in her grave, but Venus continues to personify everything about the dream girl that elevates her above mortal women.

The fourth type of inspiration is a real woman, but usually someone barely known to her admirer, even if he has seen her more than once. The most famous example in this category was a woman named Beatrice, who smote Dante Alighieri like no man has ever been smitten before or since. Their closest encounter occurred when they passed one another on a bridge and she gave him a neighborly nod of recognition. Dante poured out his unrequited admiration for her in his writings and, in the *Divine Comedy*, gave her the main role in the *Paradise* section.

The main obstacle to a real relationship with this type of woman is usually an age gap. She is often an adult woman idolized by a young boy. She may be a neighbor, the mother of a friend, a pal's big sister, or a teacher. If she is a latecomer in a boy's life, she may be his own age, but deemed unapproachable because she is someone else's girlfriend, the junior prom queen whom everybody pursues, or simply too intimidating because of her overabundance of assets.

Again, bear in mind that the real woman provides the foundation on which to construct a highly individualized dream girl. Knowing the model too well would interfere with the fantasy, which will probably bear no resemblance to the model's personality.

Finally, many dream girls are concocted out of thin air. There is no conscious connection to any real person, living or dead, and no copyright infringement on any fictitious character. Her owner would not be able to draw a picture of her, even if he had the artistic skill, because he has no definite mental image of her physical aspects. He will probably have some idea about her hair color, height, and apparent age, but even that may be subject to change because it is really inconsequential.

You could ask a man a question such as, "If you had to spend your life with any famous woman, whom would you choose?" or "Who is your favorite female TV personality?" or "Who is the most fascinating woman in literature?" You would probably get a definitive answer, but it would not necessarily be the name of his dream girl. The answer might help you to understand the nature of his dream girl better, and that can be very significant. If someone asked you to describe the appearance of your best friend, you might compare that person to someone you both know and then add some qualifying remarks, such as "but she has long red hair" or "she's much heavier." You might even be able to approximate a personality that way, such as comparing the person to Danny DeVito or Meg Ryan. It helps, but it's a comparison, not an equation.

Finally, you may occasionally meet a poor soul who will say that his dream girl is a woman with whom he once had a loving relationship, but they broke up. That's not a dream girl. That's a torch. It usually burns out in time. The dream girl can burn you, consume you, or simply flicker in some recess like a vigil candle, but you can't extinguish her. She is the eternal flame.

~ CHAPTER 4 ~

The Movie Version

*L*et's see a movie! Visual aids enhance any good instructional program, and films are better than colored slides and pie charts.

But this is a book and has no moving images. It doesn't even have any pictures. Still, I like to use an occasional movie to illustrate my points. Films have become the literature of the masses, and the invention of the VCR has completely redefined them. A generation ago, you saw a movie once, or, if you were crazy about it, maybe two or three times. Then it was lost. Parts of it were preserved in your unreliable memory. With luck, you might see it occasionally on television, considerably edited and shortened. Rarely, a local theater, if you lived in a large city, would revive it.

Now, one can own a copy of almost any film produced within the last forty years or rent it at will. Films are now like books, to be opened anytime. The Pause button is your bookmark. You can replay a scene the way you can reread a page.

Films have more successfully captured the dream-girl theme than books, even though most of the dream-girl films are based on obscure books and stories. I'm not sure why this is so, but I suspect it is because a reader has to imagine all the characters in a novel, the real as well as the surreal, so the difference between them is less dramatic. Movies can use smoke, haze, lighting, and sudden fade-ins to emphasize the special nature of the fantasy characters. In a book, the looks of a human heroine are just as nebulous as

45

those of a superhuman one. On the screen, a mermaid or fairy becomes as distinct as her mortal sisters. This vivid materialization of the type of female previously relegated to the realm of the unseen can produce a powerful response in the viewer.

Weird Science, produced in 1985, is the quintessential dream-girl movie. I viewed it for the first time recently after my daughter, Rita, told me it was *the* movie. I doubted her and felt sure it would not compare with the more classical goddess/mermaid themes, but she was right! Other films may be more artistic and better written, but *Weird Science*, in its brief course, captures the psychological truths behind the dream girl's genesis and the resolution of the conflicts she causes, despite its implausible plot and stereotypical characters.

The film opens with Wyatt and Garry, two teenage boys, ogling their female peers in a women's gymnastics class. Garry is verbalizing a fantasy about their conquest of two of the lovely girls, when Wyatt protests that nobody likes them and nobody ever will.

"Why are you messing with the fantasy?" Garry says. "We know about reality. Why mess with the fantasy?"

The scene ends when Ian and Max, their "cool" adversaries, come up behind them and yank down their shorts, humiliating them in front of the girls. (One prominent sexual inequity is that a girl in her underwear is sexy and a man in his underwear ridiculous.)

Wyatt and Garry are "nerds." They are bullied by their peers and by Wyatt's older brother. They are timid and sexually inexperienced. Miserable as they are, they are merely at the painful point where male adolescence begins, a point that all boys turning into men must pass. Their rivals are not good role models. Older brother Chet is a caricature of the soldier/hunter who, despite his bravado, is never seen with a girl. Ian and Max humiliate their girlfriends with their boorish pranks, but the girls passively stick with them, expecting nothing better from males. Wyatt and Garry at least hold the promise of evolving into something better.

Garry is inspired by a Frankenstein movie on TV to build a girl—"just like Frankenstein, only cuter." Wyatt asks Garry about how his "girlfriend in Canada" would feel. Garry's stammering rationalization that "she's in Canada, she has no morals," makes it clear that he has already engaged in the fabrication of dream girls to cover his loneliness and inexperience.

Thus, at the stage where the average frustrated boy is constructing a dream girl in his mind, Wyatt and Garry are simulating one in a computer. Their input includes a motley variety of images, not only body parts from *Playboy* centerfolds and Kelly LeBrock's face, but a portrait of Einstein. A Barbie doll (yes, she of the anatomically impossible dimensions and deformed insteps) is somehow employed as a template and, in a steal from *War Games*, the boys obtain unauthorized access into the computer of a NASA-type installation to use its power. As torrential gales rip through the house, the terrified boys peer over a boxed game of Life, that simplistic childhood pastime in which wealth, success, and happiness (but not sex) are easily acquired in a matter of minutes.

If you buy the premise, you buy the bit. Well, the premise is so implausible that you never buy it, but the dream girl is so true-to-form that you go along with the fantasy. Kelly LeBrock materializes in a puff of smoke and not much else: the upper half of a sweater, bikini panties, and high-heeled shoes. "Before you made me, I didn't exist," she proclaims. Later, she adds, "You made me, you control me."

She is older (twenty-three) and wiser than her creators, as all dream girls are. They look to her for direction. If they even dare to desire sexual contact, they cannot express it, much less attempt it. She stands in the shower with them, unabashedly nude, while they cower in their sopping jeans.

She asks for a name and Wyatt comes up with "Lisa," a girl whom he once liked, although she responded to his tentative advances by "kicking him in the nuts." Dream girls always have a link to reality, however tenuous. Not all have names, but if they do, the name belongs to someone once admired but never attained. They are often amalgams; Wyatt's creation uses a magazine model's face and a past acquaintance's name.

Lisa is not only beautiful and intelligent, she is omnipotent. She states, "I can get anything I want," and provides the boys with fancy cars and hip clothes. This is stretching the fantasy quite far, but it makes the point that, although the dream girl is a slave, she is a powerful one. She is the genie of the lamp, popularized by Barbara Eden. Her greatest power is the ability to confer instant manhood, as Lisa does by handing ID cards to the boys and declaring, "You're twenty-one."

She takes the boys to a seedy bar and, in a scene of questionable political correctness, they drink with dangerous-looking black and Hispanic men, as Garry regales them with misogynistic tales about the bitch who dissed him. Lisa is all the validation they need to assert themselves as peers among the macho men. When they get home, she kisses her fourteen-year-old master, purring, "Are you sure you're only fifteen?"

The boys fall into a drunken sleep. When they awaken, one says it must have been a dream. "How can two people have the same dream?" the other asks. The irony is that all men have the same dream.

Wyatt, to his older brother's shock, is wearing the bikini panties that Lisa first appeared in. It's not clear why. Of course, Lisa, as the creation of Wyatt's imagination, *is* Wyatt. Whatever power she has is the power of Wyatt's own potential.

But Lisa is still on the scene and decides to throw a party in Wyatt's house to give him the popularity he craves. First she accompanies Garry to his house to get his parents' permission to attend. She confronts the father with taunts of an orgy ("chips, dips, chains, whips") and berates him for condemning the boy to a sex life limited to "tossing off" over magazines in the bathroom, which elicits shock from Mother and denials from Garry.

"I don't know who you are or where you came from ... ," the father challenges Lisa. We suspect he does know. He must have had a dream girl once, who enabled him to emancipate himself from his own parents. Lisa intimidates him with a realistic-looking water pistol, then casts a spell on him so that he forgets Garry is his son. "My dad's going to castrate me!" Garry wails on the way to the party, in an unrestrained Oedipal outburst.

The party, hosted by Lisa, goes into full swing, as the petrified boys hide in the bathroom. "What really galls me," says one, "is she's ours and we can't get close to her," even as Lisa is telling their rivals, "I belong to Garry and Wyatt. I do whatever they say." The paradox of the dream girl is that she is the exclusive property of her creator, but cannot enter into a *real* relationship with him. He can fantasize any situation, but there is no true gratification.

The boys have already encountered Deb and Hilly, the attractive girlfriends of their nemeses, Ian and Max, and flirted in the upstairs bathroom. Enticed by Lisa, the two boors propose a swap: Deb and Hilly for Lisa. To their chauvinistic minds, the girls are as much their possessions as Lisa is the computer whizzes'. Wyatt and Garry offer a compromise; they'll build a new Lisa on the computer. Hurriedly and greedily, they rush the process. Lisa's conception was motivated by a yearning for acceptance, but Ms. Frankenstein number two is the product of unadulterated lust—her breasts are enlarged to enormous size. In their haste, the hackers also forget to hook up the doll and the electrodes come to rest on a photo of a missile. What emerges from the wind and smoke is not a girl but an enormous nose cone that rises through the roof, ripping up floors in the process. It is the brainless phallus, an agent of destruction, the symbol of unbridled lust.

Lisa articulates the true purpose of the dream girl: "Those guys really need some self-confidence—something that will bring out their inner strength and courage." So she conjures up some more caricatures, a pack of macho mutants straight out of a Mad Max movie, who tear through the house on motorcycles. One leads a willing, leather-clad woman by a chain around her neck, the trophy of a real man. Lisa pauses to immobilize Wyatt's unexpected grandparents, eliminating the last threat of parental authority, then implores her frightened masters to intervene.

Wyatt and Garry finally rise to the occasion when the rifle-bearing villains begin to manhandle Hilly and Deb. Garry brandishes Lisa's pistol, postures and threatens, causing his adversaries to back down with apologetic whimpers. The macho men have been exposed as nothing but bluff and bluster, no more powerful than any self-confident man. Garry is startled when Lisa's water pistol, in his hands, fires a real bullet.

The dream girl has fulfilled her mission by helping the boys acquire the courage and sense of manhood they need to love real women. Wyatt is in love with Hilly, Garry with Deb, but Hilly is intimidated by Lisa. "I love her," Wyatt affirms. "It's a different kind of love—big sisterly." He is telling the truth, for the dream girl is a presexual object, too revered to be lusted after, too intimidating to be a true lover.

"What would I be, compared to her?" Hilly sighs.

Wyatt replies that Lisa was "everything I ever wanted in a woman before I knew what I wanted. If I could do it again, I'd make her just like you."

Meanwhile, Garry is confessing to Deb that the car, the clothes, and the friends came from Lisa and are not really his. Lisa knew everything about him; Deb knows nothing. "I want you to like me for what I am," he says. The dream girl validated him. He needs the same from the girl who is to replace her.

Deb meets the requirement. "Whatever you are, I like you," she says.

Lisa has repossessed the cars and completed her final task, that of turning the bullying big brother into a slimy monster until he promises to reform.

We see her wearing a demure, high-necked dress, instead of her usual provocative garb, primping before a mirror. We've watched this scene before. It's Mary Poppins preparing to take leave of the children. The boys begin to stammer the confession they presume will crush her. "You guys got girlfriends," she says simply. Mary Poppins would have added, "That's as it should be," but Lisa's tone says it all. The house, in shambles, is quickly restored to its former order, as the film of its destruction is run backward. That was the way Mary Poppins tidied up the nursery. The dream girl has accomplished her mission and leaves Wyatt and Garry.

In the final scene, the other boys at the high school are confronted by Lisa, the new phys-ed-instructor-from-hell. The dream girl never disappears. She just finds new boys who need help in becoming men.

Romancing the Stone Girl

The old myths die hard. In the film *One Touch of Venus*, made almost half a century ago, the dream girl is none other than the goddess of beauty and love, Venus. The plot is not very complex and the outcome is never in doubt.

The hero, Eddie Hatch, is an underpaid department store employee. In the opening scenes, he nails his tie to the wall and hits his boss, Savory Whitfield, with a ladder, thus establishing himself as the clumsy bungler all suitors to the dream girl must be (remember, the dream girl is created by the adolescent boy, when he has least control over his coordination and is unsophisticated). Nobody wants to see a suave, erudite man (like Eddie's boss) get the dream girl; such men have too much going for them already.

The boss has paid $200,000 for a "priceless" statue of Venus and has made one of the floors of his store into a small museum. Eddie, in fixing the curtains that surround the statue, kisses it, which brings Venus to life. Eddie's first response is terror, and he faints. As Venus cradles his unconscious head, she exults, "Oh, he's wonderful!" You would think a female with her experience would be more critical, but dream girls do love klutzes.

Molly, the boss's wisecracking secretary, thinks less of Eddie. When the boss accuses him of masterminding the theft of the missing statue, Molly snorts, "Hatch couldn't be leader in ring-around-a-rosy!"

Eddie does have a girlfriend, Gloria, a co-worker so marriage-minded that when she goes to a restaurant she will eat only rice. Eddie's problem is not that he can't get a woman; he wants someone so special that she will change his humdrum life—a dream girl.

Eddie is frightened by Venus's advances, wondering what she could possibly see in him. "I'm not famous, not rich, not even very bright," he points out.

Venus gives him the answer he wants: "You can be anything you want to be." The dream girl can elevate him to the status of a winner.

Her kisses intoxicate Eddie and he accuses her of putting a spell on him. Venus denies it—it's just simply falling in love. Eddie's abandonment of Gloria would be cruel, except that his best friend, Joe, happens to fall for Gloria. Both try to resist this strange new attraction, but slowly succumb, while Venus's song eerily enters their world. The song, "Speak Low," warns that time is a thief and everything ends too soon. It urges taking love when you can get it, not procrastinating in hope of something better.

Eddie's boss sees Venus and is determined to seduce her through his wealth and power. Eddie initially resolves to give up Venus and be "sensible, orderly, and practical—my life will be like it was before." He is not able to keep his resolution.

Mr. Whitfield, however, breaks up Eddie's romantic date in the park with Venus by having him arrested for stealing the statue. Venus meets Whitfield for an evening of champagne and dalliance, during which she intercedes for Eddie. Whitfield pulls a double cross by phoning Molly instead of the police. But when Molly becomes incensed by his duplicity and quits, Whitfield suddenly realizes how much the loyal Molly means to him. With encouragement from Venus, he charges out with the champagne bottle to woo Molly back.

By the time Eddie, released from jail, gets back to the store, Venus is once again a statue, her sojourn on Earth having expired. She has worked her magic for Joe and Gloria, Whitfield and Molly, and much of New York, which Molly reports ran out of marriage licenses while the statue was missing.

The ending is a happy one for Eddie, who not only gets a promotion, but who meets the store's newest employee, Venus Jones, who is a dead-ringer for the love goddess. The dream girl is an impossibility, but the hope is that someday her human equivalent will materialize to fulfill the promise she held.

A Fish Tale

While *One Touch of Venus* dealt with the dream-girl theme in a rather superficial way, with a problem-free ending for all, a more modern movie, *Splash*, probed deeper into the heart of the dream-girl dilemma.

The film opens with an eight-year-old boy suddenly jumping off a ferry to swim toward a pretty little girl. After he is pulled from the water, the girl cries, then dives to reveal her fish's tail.

The scene then switches to New York, twenty years later. The boy, Alan Bauer, is breaking up with his girlfriend, Victoria, because he cannot make a commitment. "She had everything; why didn't I love her?" he laments to his brother, Fred. "Something here is not working," he adds, thumping his chest like the heartless Tin Woodman.

There is obviously some connection between the first scene and what Alan has become. He became infatuated with the little mermaid at age eight, and although his memory of their meeting is like a vague dream, he cannot love a real woman. Depressed, he takes a taxi to Cape Cod, not knowing why. It is, of course, where he dove off the ferry.

Alan quickly establishes his credentials as a klutz, the prerequisite for getting the dream girl. He cannot swim, gets stranded in a small boat, falls overboard, and gets hit in the head. He is rescued by the mermaid, who appears on land as a naked biped woman. She kisses him and retreats into the water, where she redevelops her mermaid nether regions.

Alan does not remember the mermaid from his youth, but she remembers him. Fishing his wallet from the ocean floor, she gets his address and, with the aid of a map from a wrecked ship, finds her way to New York. When the police help her to locate Alan, she smothers him with kisses and their sexual relationship is consummated in the elevator. Although Alan complains that their marathon lovemaking will put him in the hospital, he ignores his business to stay for more.

Thus far, there is a lot of lust and not much grounds for love, since the mermaid can't speak a word of English. When she leaves the apartment in his absence and he frantically tells the doorman, "I'm looking for a girl," the doorman replies, "Two hundred dollars, same as always." Alan is still in the world of prostitutes.

The mermaid, with typical dream-girl omnipotence, becomes fluent in English after six hours among a store's TV sets. She chooses her name, Madison, from a street sign. She sees Alan's world with wonderment, delighting in the sound of music and finding beauty in the red and green glow of a traffic light.

Madison tells Alan he is the reason she is here, but warns him that she can only stay for six days or "I can never go back." Alan gives her the ironic gift of a music box with a dancing couple, which recalls the Hans Christian Anderson tale of the Little Mermaid who suffers agony when she has to walk on her legs and ultimately perishes.

Madison reciprocates with a grander gift, a huge fountain surmounted by a mermaid statue, saved from urban demolition. Alan had confided that it had always appealed to him and almost confesses something he saw at age eight when he was "just a stupid kid." He is finally able to say to Madison, "I love you."

Complications arise, because Madison, without her knowledge, is being pursued by Dr. Kornbluth, a scientist who knows her secret. When he is reprimanded by his old mentor for spouting such nonsense, Kornbluth reminds him that he was the one who told him the mermaid legends at the age of twelve. The older man scoffs that these were fairy tales to amuse a child. The dream girl must not be carried into adulthood.

Kornbluth sprays Madison with water, exposing her identity, as her legs become a tail. Alan is crushed and retreats, with broken heart, to his business, where the fish tank is a haunting reminder of his hidden fascination that predated Madison's arrival in New York.

Brother Fred chides him for abandoning Madison: "Some people will never be that happy!" This includes the often-divorced Fred, who once brought a date to his wedding. Fred, Alan, and the repentant Dr. Kornbluth conspire to rescue Madison. Pursued by soldiers and police, the chase ends at the pier. Madison obviously cannot stay on in Alan's world.

She tells him he can join her in her world. She reminds him that when he was eight "you were safe under the water; you were with me." When Alan talks of visiting Fred at Christmas, she tells him, "You can *never* come back."

Alan hesitates, then dives in after her. He starts to drown, but she finds him and kisses him. With her powerful tail, she vanquishes the pursuing frogmen and she and Alan swim off together toward a distant undersea castle.

This is a disturbing movie. Alan never finds love with a real woman. He will not grow old on earth with a beloved spouse, like the elderly couple whom he observes with envy at the skating rink. He gives up his loving brother and his work. Instead of finding an earthly equivalent of the dream girl, he chooses the dream girl herself, which means detaching himself from the real world. This is psychosis at best, death at worst.

The captive mermaid had wept, "You thought at least I was a human being." And Alan, trying to regain his freedom, had protested, "I am not a fish!" Madison had a good point. If a man is human, requisite number one in a partner should be membership in the same species.

There are many victims of the dream girl like Alan. They may not be able to escape completely from the world, but they either doom themselves to lonely bachelorhood or, more often, sabotage workable relationships by comparing them unfavorably with the dream-girl fantasy.

The mermaid is a fitting symbol for the dream girl. She is the siren that seems human, but is not. She dwells in a world man can visit, but not inhabit. And following the lure of her call invariably leads to wreckage and doom.

Siren Song

Where the mermaid in *Splash* lured a man out of his earthly existence and became the only person in his life, there is an older mermaid film in which the mythical dream girl guides a man through a psychological crisis and restores his self-esteem. *Mr. Peabody and the Mermaid*, made in 1948, is a touching parable about a man who is trying to cope with getting older and who seizes on a fantasy creature's love to fend off the erosive effects of aging and ultimate death.

The dream girl, as in *Weird Science*, exerts a strong influence on the adolescent, who is frustrated by his lack of achievements and sophistication that are needed to win the love of a woman. In the well-adjusted man, the dream girl yields to the woman he comes to love and marry, the one who will fulfill the needs that the dream girl could only promise to satisfy. When real life becomes unsatisfying, often through the man's own limitations and not the fault of his spouse, he turns again to the dream girl. He may perceive her in the person of a younger woman and throw himself into an affair or even a premature divorce. Or, like Mr. Peabody, he may resist the temptation of infidelity and take temporary refuge in a forgotten fantasy.

The film opens on a snowy day in the office of a psychiatrist, interestingly named Dr. Harvey, which reminds one of the large imaginary rabbit who became the most famous invisible character in theatrical history. Polly Peabody, an attractive woman who appears to be in her late thirties, tells the psychiatrist, "My husband is in love with a mermaid." Arthur Peabody, played by William Powell, is a handsome, distinguished-looking man, who assures the psychiatrist that he is *not* crazy, but will tell the doctor his story in order to please his wife.

The doctor's first eager questions are those of an avid fisherman: was Peabody trolling or casting when he caught her, what type of fishing line did he use, how much did she weigh? Intentionally or not, he establishes a sense of trust in his patient through the male bond of the sporting life.

Peabody then settles into his narrative and the story is told, without further interruption, as a flashback. He and his wife had rented a beautiful estate on the Caribbean island of St. Hilda's so he could recuperate from a bad case of flu he had contracted in the fall. They left their "youngster," Priscilla, in Boston with her grandmother. Peabody, while obviously well off (his occupation is never revealed), says the estate was more than they could really afford, but "if you can find a little piece of heaven, who cares what it costs?"

He is vulnerable from his recent illness. Polly adds to his insecurity by fetching his bathrobe, warning, "A man doesn't get his strength back so quickly at your age." She reminds him that he will soon turn fifty; Arthur says he is only forty-eight, but recalculates and realizes that fifty has sneaked up on him. Polly does not help by saying, "A wife doesn't really begin to feel safe until her husband turns that fifty curve."

"Fifty—the old age of youth, the youth of old age," Arthur muses. It is then that he first hears the sound of a woman singing. It seems to be coming from a small key, which he is told lies in "black water, filled with sharks and barracudas." He sails out to the island and finds no one, but spies a decorative comb, which he decides to leave in place.

At a beach club party, Arthur inquires of Mike Fitzgerald, the club's public relations agent, about the mysterious key and if anyone could swim there. While they are conversing, both men stare admiringly at the legs of a woman lying in the sand, her back toward them. It turns out to be Polly, talking to the island's lothario, Major Ronald Hadley. "Holy Moses! I've never seen her in a suit like that," Arthur exclaims.

Fitzgerald introduces Arthur to Cathy Livingston, a flirtatious young brunette whose avocations are swimming and singing. Arthur thus suspects she might be his mystery siren. Hadley, who has been said to be "taken" by Cathy, watches as Cathy sings for Arthur. He makes disparaging remarks about Arthur's age. Polly lies and tells Hadley that Arthur is forty-six. Driving home, both the Peabodys are miffed over their mutual flirtations, as Arthur thinks, "Polly had made a public spectacle of herself. I was making a few serious inquiries."

Arthur later confesses to the viewer, "I don't go for those all-around women like Cathy Livingston. They make me nervous. What I like is a woman who can't do anything very much."

This prelude to the appearance of the mermaid establishes the need for the intervention of a dream girl. The woman to whom he has been married for fifteen years is attractive and desirable, but Arthur literally does not recognize her at the beach party. Without realizing it, Polly is slowly emasculating him by reminding him of his age and vulnerability. Cathy provides the perfect opportunity for an affair, but Arthur is too timid to take on such an aggressive, accomplished woman. So, he or the fates must supply a dream girl to meet his needs.

He returns to the key where he spotted the comb and discovers its owner has reclaimed it. He sets sail for home, trolling his fish-line. He snags the mermaid by the tail and pulls her aboard, thinking he has landed a fish, until he sees her arm, raised behind the collapsed sail. She's a blonde, of course.

Initially, Arthur has no intention to hide the mermaid from his wife. He carries her into the house, her upper parts concealed by a towel, shouting Polly's name, but his wife is out. He places the mermaid on the bed and, noticing she seems lethargic, fills the bathtub for her. He carries her to it, saying, "Trust your Uncle Arthur."

Arthur drinks heavily, while drafting a letter to the Museum of Natural History where he briefly considers sending his catch. Polly comes home to find her bathroom door closed, with heavy emanations of her best perfume. She suspects "that Livingston woman" is in there. Arthur explains about the mermaid.

The incredulous wife bursts into the bathroom and sees only a huge tail emerging from a sea of bubbles. She orders her thoroughly plastered husband to get "that fish" out of her tub. As Arthur carries the mermaid, again covered from the waist up, down the stairs,

Polly is on the phone with Major Hadley, canceling the dinner date she had made for herself and Arthur, but accepting a lunch date alone with him.

Arthur means to return the mermaid to the sea, but as he passes the estate's aquarium, a huge outdoor pool, he decides to keep the mermaid, whom he names Lenore. He kisses her, explaining, "It's a symbol. It means 'I think you're very pretty and I like you very much.'" Lenore learns the lesson quickly and returns the kiss very aggressively before tumbling happily into the pool.

There are obvious contrasts between Lenore and her modern counterpart, Madison, who starred in *Splash* forty years later. Madison had legs when on land and she learned to talk in a matter of hours. She was sexually hyperactive.

Lenore cannot walk and never learns to talk, although she comes to understand what is said rather well. Obviously, she cannot be a sexual partner, given her anatomical limitations. (When I was a boy, I often admired a fountain in the Bronx's Joyce Kilmer Park. The stone mermaids at its base had tails that were split and began at mid-thigh, rendering them considerably sexier than the more conventional types. Rubens had taken similar anatomical liberties with the trio of sirens who grace *Marie de'Medici Arriving at Marseilles*. The three voluptuous nudes standing in the water have lower legs terminating in scaly tentacles, leading Delacroix to write: "The sirens never seemed to me so beautiful. Abandon and the most complete audacity alone can produce such impressions.")

Arthur is neither audacious nor abandoned. He has found the dream girl who "can't do anything very much," including commit adultery. He even goes shopping to buy Lenore a sweater for modesty's sake, and when the saleswoman suggests that a bathing suit would be more appropriate for swimming, Arthur tries to buy only the top half of a two-piece suit, to the great amusement of Cathy, who wanders into the shop and conjectures about the mystery woman who swims bottomless.

Arthur returns to Lenore, who has been feasting on the aquarium's rare fish. "My age means nothing to you, does it?" he says. "A man at fifty is at the very peak of his faculties. He can appreciate beauty like yours. It's the beauty of eternal wisdom and the beauty of a child, too. Simple, direct, uncomplicated—like your love for me. With such a love, no man could be anything but younger."

Lenore has not shown any indication of average intelligence, far less "eternal wisdom," but the dream girl, when she is first formulated in the mind of the immature boy, is endowed by him with the knowledge of the eternal mother. The dream girl is also childlike because she never ages. The aging man realizes how he has changed while his dream girl has not, and fantasizes that if he can cling to her as he did when a boy, he can stop the aging process. When Olympia Dukakis, in *Moonstruck*, theorized that men cheat because they are afraid of dying, she was alluding to the legacy of the dream girl.

Cathy pays an evening visit to the Peabodys and flirts with Arthur beside the aquarium while Lenore seethes with jealousy. Arthur, as he did in the swimsuit shop, gets flustered, in accordance with the rule that only the klutz (even if he's William Powell) gets the dream girl. Cathy, eager to see Arthur's alleged mermaid, strips off her gown and, wearing the two-piece swimsuit that was underneath, plunges into the aquarium to confront the dream girl. Clearly out of her element, Cathy is attacked by Lenore, who bites her on the leg.

The human bite mark is seen by Polly, as well as Arthur. In the confusion, Cathy's gown disappears from the side of the pool. This scene is important, because without it one could draw the conclusion that Lenore was nothing more than a large fish Arthur had snagged, around which he constructed a delusion. The bite and the missing dress contradict this interpretation.

Polly, still convinced that Arthur covets Cathy, has a bedroom talk with him, beginning with "Men go a little peculiar at fifty." She confesses her lunches with Hadley and says it is perhaps time "to pull ourselves together and remember who and what we are." She promises to give up all contact with Hadley if Arthur will do the same regarding Cathy. Arthur readily agrees, even playing into his wife's jealousy by saying, "With your strength and faith and help, I believe I can."

But at four A.M., he hears the siren song and goes downstairs to find Lenore sitting at the aquarium's edge in Cathy's gown. Polly, spying from the window, assumes he is with Cathy. As she descends, Lenore slips back into the water, leaving Arthur with the empty gown and Polly with visions of a nude escapee.

"It wasn't a woman at all!" Arthur protests, honestly. Polly drives off in a huff and, as dawn breaks, a ghostly chorus sings "Happy Birthday" as Arthur turns fifty.

Arthur, abandoned by Polly and the servants, is not unhappy. "There's much to be said for a woman—even an imperfect one—who lives, breathes, and exists only for the man she loves."

But Arthur cannot find peace. Polly's car has been found abandoned on the road and the police can find no trace of Polly on the island or evidence of her having left by plane or boat.

Mike Fitzgerald, the P.R. man, is sent by the very proper British police to make a discreet, unofficial inquiry of Arthur. Arthur confesses that Polly was right. "I did love someone else—this enchanting young creature I did and do love." Lenore, who has obviously acquired a thorough understanding of English, exults in a joyous underwater ballet.

Fitzgerald, who has become progressively nastier as the result of enforced abstinence from tobacco and alcohol, tells Arthur he is going to report the story to the police, who will probably claim the mermaid for the Crown and put her on public display. Arthur flees with Lenore in the sailboat, taking her out to the key where she had first been heard singing. He tells her he will take her to the Florida keys, build a shack on a remote island and spend his life there, away from newspapers and radios. (This is the ultimate escape, achieved by Alan Bauer with Madison, in *Splash*.)

But Fitzgerald and the police, riding in a motor launch, catch up with Arthur, who surrenders. They are not, it turns out, arresting him on suspicion of murder, because Polly has surfaced in Boston, Fitzgerald reports, having been given an airlift by a U.S. Army pilot in a bomber.

Sitting in the boat, Arthur hears Lenore's song. So do the others. The elderly police chief muses that the music is "like something I heard off Capri once, more than twenty years ago," when he was undoubtedly undergoing his own midlife crisis.

Arthur dives into the water to join Lenore, although he had told her earlier that water was "not my element." He struggles and goes under. As his limp body sinks, Lenore swims to him and kisses him, as they continue to fall together.

> *We have lingered in the chambers of the sea*
> *By sea-girls wreathed with seaweed red and brown*
> *Till human voices wake us, and we drown.*
>   —T. S. Eliot, *The Love Song of J. Alfred Prufrock*

But Arthur does not drown. He is back in the psychiatrist's office, concluding his narrative. Dr. Harvey does not think Arthur is insane, but he cautions him against telling his story to "children" like Mrs. Peabody and the office nurse, who have not hit the "air pocket" of the fiftieth birthday. The doctor confides that he was forty-nine for five years and confesses that he had a dream girl of his own, a tiny ice-skater who could skate through the air and into his room.

In the final scene, Arthur and Polly are alone together. He tells her about the crazy doctor and says he is through with Lenore "after she tried to drown me."

Polly says, "I hope next time you feel yourself slipping it's for something flesh and blood that people can tell me about." Arthur gives Polly a gift, the mermaid's comb. They decide to spend the night together instead of going out for dinner.

The wife has come up against the dream girl and won. In giving her the comb, Arthur lets her take the place of the fantasy lover. It is a classic tale about a dream girl, impossible but real, delightful but disruptive, rejuvenating and potentially deadly.

One wonders whether Polly would have won if she were as old as Arthur. One wonders whether, had the island police not intervened, Arthur would have rejected the world to live with his mermaid in that barren shack on a remote island. A real woman can beat the dream girl, but the battles are never easy, and the outcome never certain.

~ CHAPTER 5 ~

Prostitutes, Madonnas, and Dream Girls

The perfect woman is a virgin nymphomaniac whose father owns a liquor store.

—ANONYMOUS

*M*en, particularly the young ones, love sex and they want partners who are enthusiastic and who are skilled and knowledgeable in bed. They loathe promiscuous women, not because such females readily accede to sexual activity with them, but because they know these partners will indiscriminately offer the same favors to another man.

My patient, Professor Jeff, had been engaging in a series of transient love affairs, each of which would begin with high promise and end in disillusionment. When he told me that it was over with Ruth, I was surprised, not that it ended, but that it had ended so abruptly, because he had barely begun to move from the enchantment to the disenchantment stage.

When Jeff told me that Ruth had made an unwise confession, I understood perfectly.

Ruth and Jeff had not even made any sort of commitment to

one another, and Jeff was concurrently dating and bedding other less promising women, although he was seeing more and more of Ruth. One Sunday, Ruth had gone by herself to an art museum, hardly the place where one gets into trouble. There, Ruth met a very attractive foreign sailor, who was in port for only a few days. She invited him to her apartment and enjoyed the rest of the day in bed with him.

What Ruth did not understand was why Jeff got so infuriated when she told him about it, especially since she explained that the man meant nothing to her, she would never see him again, and it was purely "a physical thing."

What Ruth did not understand was men.

"What is she, some kind of slut?" Jeff fumed in my office. He had broken off the relationship immediately and did not regret doing so.

Ruth might have understandably protested that men frequently justify one-night stands, extramarital adventures, and the patronizing of prostitutes as "just a physical thing." Women are not happy about such behavior, but are surprisingly tolerant in many cases, as long as they believe their man has no true affection or regard for the woman with whom he dallies.

Men have no such tolerance. They would not be any happier to find their mate in a sexual relationship with a man she really loved, either. They may, however, be less threatened if their partner had a nonsexual close friendship with a man, provided they were convinced the relationship would stay that way. Women, on the other hand, are more likely to fret over a female who shares her partner's confidences and friendship, objecting that she herself should be able to meet all such emotional needs.

Is there a double standard that remains in effect, despite several decades of effort to equalize relationships between the sexes? Of course there is. Is it fair? No, but neither is life. Is it natural? That is about to be discussed.

The contempt men have for sexually uninhibited women despite their fascination and involvement with them is half of the prostitute-madonna complex, a fact of life that is by now familiar to the average woman who is repeatedly distressed by its prevalence. The other half is men's high regard for monogamous, maternal women, whom they cherish like their sainted mothers; the problem is that they cannot see such revered women as exciting sexual partners. Women whose husbands found them irresistible before marriage are doomed to practically celibate unions either after the wedding or after they bear children, while their husbands pursue less esteemed females.

So, is the dream girl the prostitute or the madonna? She is neither. She is a third archetypal figure, heretofore ignored, but just as potent in her effect on men's psyches as either of her two recognized sisters. She is, to some extent, a compromise between the two incompatible extremes, one who comforts the confused man but only aggravates the beleaguered woman.

But before we explain how this precarious compromise was reached, we should have a good understanding of what the madonna and the prostitute mean and how they came to be.

The Lou Grant Rule

"They want an experienced virgin," my co-author, Jacqueline Simenauer, muttered in amazement after reviewing some of the responses of men describing their ideal woman for *Beyond the Male Myth*.

Men are, basically, rational beings. Since most of them have sexual experience with a few partners before settling into marriage and since they prefer a partner with some savoir faire, they cannot logically expect to live in a world populated chiefly by virgins who have been awaiting their coming. They will allow a woman *some* sexual experience, preferably with men she cared about, as long as she is not a "slut," who is a person with too much experience.

The typical male attitude was expertly portrayed in one of the later episodes of the *Mary Tyler Moore Show*. Lou Grant, Mary's boss, had been through a divorce and was making a painful adjustment to the world of modern singles. He had been dating an attractive band vocalist and was happy until his buddies began teasing him about how much experience she must have accumulated in years on the road with an all-male band. Lou confessed his worries about this to the usually sympathetic Mary, who did not respond with her customary saccharine understanding.

"Oh? Just how much experience is a woman allowed?" she fumed. "How many lovers is she permitted to have before she becomes *that* kind of girl?"

Lou contemplated the question for several seconds and then replied, simply, "Five."

One of the men who responded to a question about what sort of sexual experience he would prefer in a wife for the male sexuality survey for *Beyond the Male Myth* volunteered that she should not have had more than five previous lovers. "Aha!" I cried in recognition, "The Lou Grant rule."

Oedipus Wrecks

The madonna has had no lover prior to marriage, except possibly her future husband. People scoff when you tell them that men today still prefer virgins, but such women are scarcely extinct, even if they may qualify as an endangered species. When Morton Hunt in 1972 surveyed American females, more than two-thirds of the younger half of his sample had engaged in premarital sex—twice the number reported by Kinsey a generation before; however, half of the experienced women had limited premarital sex to the man they married. Hunt also found that nearly half the men under age twenty-five disapproved of premarital sexual experience for women *unless* strong affection existed for her partner.

Men will never, in significant numbers, endorse women's engaging in sex for the sheer physical pleasure of it. They may find this type of free expression stimulating in pornography, but not in women they care about. Sexually indiscriminate women are called whores, although applying that term to someone motivated by a strong physical urge is inaccurate. Prostitutes are motivated by money, not by lust. They may not show much selectivity in accepting customers, as long as the man has the means, but attractiveness or lovemaking skill will not get a john a discount.

Rodney Dangerfield claims he gets so little respect that hookers make him say, "Please." That's a joke. As Julia Roberts tried to reassure a nervous Richard Gere in *Pretty Woman*, "I'm a sure thing."

The true prostitute, a tradeswoman, has little in common with the archetypal prostitute, who opposes and balances the passionless, if not virginal, madonna. Why do men have the tendency (perhaps *need* would be more appropriate) to make this psychological schism? There are two common explanations, the psychodynamic and the sociobiological.

According to Freud, little boys are reluctant to resolve their close ties to mother, since she has been, from their earliest remembrances, the source of love and nourishment. They become painfully aware that father has a more permanent claim and a special relationship with her, an intimacy that they can never know. Even if their understanding of the sexual relationship is a vague one, boys cannot deny that mother has engaged in intercourse with father.

The only way the boy can reconcile his desire for mother's exclusive love and his feelings of inferiority to father is by justifying mother's actions as something she is compelled to do. He rationalizes that mother's role of wife and mother entails an onerous duty to be a sexual partner, one that mother would not take on if she had a choice. As the boy develops strong sexual urges of his own and becomes exposed to portrayals of sexual conduct in the media, he concludes that marital sex is pure, dispassionate, and procreative, quite unlike the exciting, lewd realm of lingerie, nude displays, and perverse permutations of sexual interaction that inspire his own orgasms. He comes to expect his future wife and mother of his children to be the way he imagines his mother, even though this would not make marital sex an inviting prospect. If the mother of the second generation proves to be as libidinous and uninhibited as the women who engage in promiscuous sex, she would not only be a prostitute herself, but she would raise the unthinkable possibility that so was her mother-in-law, old Dad's presumably reluctant mate.

The second explanation for the dichotomy is psychobiological. Men have a strong investment in their offspring, an investment of tens of thousands of dollars, more if you consider college and graduate school costs, and two decades of precious time. A man would probably not want to devote nearly an adult lifetime of parental and fiscal responsibility to a child that was not his, and the only way to insure against such a misfortune is a wife who is absolutely monogamous.

The one excuse for an unwanted pregnancy that might work for the man but never the woman is "The kid isn't mine!" A woman who bears a child through conventional conception is assured of her 50 percent genetic input, regardless of whether her husband or someone else is the father.

People may well argue that men often marry women who already have children and willingly help to support these youngsters and often adopt them. Men also consent to their wives' being artificially inseminated with donor semen. It is rare, however, to find a sterile man who encourages his wife to have intercourse with another man and become pregnant. It may be because, in nature, there are many species whose males take precautions to guarantee it is their sperm, not that of a rival, that fertilizes the ovum. Other species know nothing of artificial insemination and paternity tests; these were invented after Nature laid down the genetic blueprint that governs instinctive reproductive behavior.

Male insects and a few mammals, including bats and rats, plug the female reproductive tract with post-insemination secretions, which prevents other males from copulating until fertilization is completed. Male mice can produce an odor that causes a pregnant female to abort and become available to be reimpregnated. If a male lion is able to usurp a harem by driving off the incumbent males, he kills all the cubs before starting a new bloodline. This type of infanticide by the victorious has been seen in Amazonian tribes.

Orson Bean tells a joke about a missionary trying to improve the English of a young male tribesman by pointing out and naming things as they walked through the forest: "Bird flying. Squirrel climbing. Fish swimming." Suddenly, they stumbled on a couple vigorously copulating in the grass. "Uh, man riding bicycle," stammered the flustered missionary.

The pupil whipped out his blowgun and promptly dispatched the man on the ground before he could rise. When the shocked cleric asked why, the young man snarled, "Man riding *my* bicycle!"

Such possessiveness may offend feminist sensibilities, but male demand for an exclusive sexual relationship with his wife (even if he has several wives) is so prevalent that it is difficult to view it as other than "natural." A study of marital systems in 849 societies found 709 permitting more than one wife to a man, but only four that allowed more than one husband to a woman.

Parental investment theory might explain why the madonna is monogamous, but why could she not have a strong sexual appetite that is directed toward only one man?

Men may dislike a frigid woman, but they fear a torrid one. Nymphomania was a diagnosis attributed by Victorian psychiatrists to women who preferred a number of sexual partners to monogamy and, while the term no longer exists in the official nomenclature of mental illnesses, the concept of nymphomania persists in contemporary mythology. While therapists still treat women who habitually get involved in ill-advised and catastrophic sexual relationships, these dangerous liaisons are motivated by emotional insecurity and the desire for love and caring, not by insatiable lust.

Men fear the nymphomaniac because of their own biological limitations. Any money-motivated prostitute could accommodate a series of customers for hours and hours, while even the most virile of men could not aspire to such endless indulgence. As a boy, I heard a joke about a nightclub performer who claimed he could make love to twenty-five women in rapid succession. When he collapsed and was booed off stage while engaging lady number four, he gasped, "I don't understand it! I was fine at tonight's rehearsal."

Masters and Johnson proved in the laboratory that, in the male cycle of arousal and orgasm, there ensues a refractory period during which the penis is incapable, temporarily, of rearousal. Now, I know that any number of women will give expert witness to men's consummating numerous acts of intercourse with rest periods shorter than a cigarette break. These marathons occur when the sexual relationship is a new one. Under the stimuli of novelty and wild infatuation, the man's refractory period seems to be reduced to a duration of milliseconds. There are also men who, voluntarily or naturally, have markedly delayed or no orgasm, enabling them to prolong the arousal (erectile) phase ad infinitum.

These exceptions do not overcome the rule that men have definite physiological limitations, of which they are keenly aware. They can imagine themselves perpetually aroused, but know it cannot happen. They can imagine a nymphomaniac being in a state of continuous desire and fear it *can* happen. They could not satisfy such a creature, so she would move on to a man who, for a while, could.

Uptight

My experience with couples in therapy has led me to conclude that a man would rather have a wife whose disinterest in sex leaves his desires unsatisfied than be married to a woman whose drive he was unable to satisfy.

Nick and Linda had been married for three years and were both approaching thirty. Nick complained that Linda's aversion to sex left him frustrated. She would become so tense that her vaginal muscles would contract, barring entry. She had premenstrual tension and, since her periods were irregular, this interval of physical discomfort and emotional irritability could last several weeks at a time. Prior to marrying Nick, she had been involved with a man who coerced her into oral and anal sex acts by threatening to tell her parents she had lost her virginity if she did not comply. (I never understood why Linda believed her suitor would be foolhardy enough to make a confession that would involve him in a shotgun wedding at best or a shotgun barrage at worst.) Sex had become an act of revulsion for her, which inhibited her range of activities with Nick, although he described her as a delightful "terror" during premarital acts of conventional intercourse.

Nick complained, although without much bitterness, that sex was 90 percent of marriage and that men cheated on their wives primarily because they could not get good sex at home (Nick apparently had been faithful). Linda viewed Nick as having an unusually strong sex drive and said, "He would love to have it twenty-four hours a day," although it was not uncommon for them to go two months without it.

The thing that made me suspicious of Nick's protestations was that when I asked the couple to keep track of their sexual activity, Nick reported four encounters during one week, while Linda only recalled two. If Nick really wanted more frequent sex, he would have undercounted. He had hardly been a satyr during their courtship; Linda said that one of the things that attracted her to him most was that he was such a nondemanding gentleman.

Although they were both employed and many years out of college, they both felt they were overly attached to their parents and regarded themselves as still kids.

Had Nick been married to someone without Linda's hang-ups, that wife would probably have been making the same complaints about him that he lodged against Linda. In Linda's eyes, however, Nick was the superstud, the marathon man, who was thwarted by the misfortune of being married to a sexually inadequate woman. Linda tried to atone for her failures as a sex partner by doing virtually all the cooking and housecleaning after they came home from work, a bonus benefit for Nick.

Nick and Linda's marriage endured and they went on to become parents. Their relationship improved when they stopped blaming their conflicts on the professed chasm that separated their interest in sex. John's dread of the prostitute had made him cast Linda in the role of the asexual madonna, as his own anxieties about his sexual adequacy elevated his wife's tension level, resulting in vaginismus and premenstrual syndrome.

Treacherous Triad

So is the dream girl more madonna or prostitute? She is neither. The dichotomy arises as early as age four or five, when the boy acquires some idea of mother's sexual nature and its evil effect on her exclusive commitment to him because of father's unique claims. The madonna restores the infant's oral-stage perception of mother as the unfailing nurturer and comforter by denying the sexual nature that interferes with his gratification.

Not long after the formation of this split, the boy enters a wider world beyond the confines of his family. He develops longings that he knows mother cannot satisfy. Identification with father and his male peers and role models has made him not only abandon his dreams of possessing mother for himself, but has made this desire seem infantile and undesirable. He does not want mother, he wants a woman of his own, one who will care for him as mother did, while allowing him the sexual fulfillment that has always been taboo.

The dichotomy is now a trichotomy. The dream girl, an adult woman like the madonna and the prostitute, completes a triangle more treacherous than the one around Bermuda reputed to swallow ships. Only this triangle sends heterosexual relationships to a mysterious end.

The dream girl, like the apex of an isosceles triangle, stands midway between the madonna and the prostitute, but not on the same line. While one could fantasize a continuous spectrum of women, starting with the altruistic, chaste madonna and progressing (or deteriorating) into the destructive, wanton prostitute, the dream girl is not exactly the golden mean. While more of a real woman than the two stereotypes, she is as much an impossible phantom.

The prostitute accommodates everyone and belongs to no one. The madonna belongs to her children more than her spouse, divides her love, and is possessed sexually by no one. The dream girl belongs exclusively to her creator. She will give him the love that the songs and poems and movies promise. The madonna infantilizes him and the prostitute abandons him for her next conquest, but the dream girl watches him turn into a man and approves that transformation.

Since the dream girl is the ideal woman, she is also imagined to be the boy's future sex partner. Yet she does not become involved, usually, in daydreams that accompany masturbation or even lead to sexual arousal. (Women can probably understand this if they relate it to crushes they had on actors or rock stars. Most girls have romantic reveries that involve embracing or kissing their idols, but not progressing to nudity and intercourse.) The need for love and esteem precedes puberty, so the dream girl is generally born before the boy experiences a sexual drive and need for release. When he does, he does not try to integrate his need for sex with his hunger for love. After all, he has had considerable experience in separating the two when he desexualized his mother.

Yearnings for love tend to be chronic, with the need initially unconnected to the object that might satisfy it. Sexual arousal is immediate, intense, and usually in *response* to a stimulus, rather than a de novo urge. It does not take much to arouse an adolescent. A drawing of Betty and Veronica in sunsuits might provoke as strong a physical reaction as a sexually explicit photo of a nude, well-endowed *Penthouse* Pet.

Boys have guilt about erections. (In later life, this is usually replaced by guilt over not having erections.) They are most uncomfortable when the physiological response is to the sight or casual touch of a woman in the vicinity, and when the woman is a relative, including sisters or mother herself, shame can be overwhelming. Here, the prostitute-madonna split that had its roots in childhood becomes reactivated. The prostitute becomes a target for all those troublesome tensions; she may not be good for much, but she certainly is good for one thing. Good women (madonnas), such as populate one's family, are filed under "Asexual." The monogamous dream girl tends to be classified with the madonnas.

There are other reasons why the dream girl gets desexualized shortly after the onset of sexual awareness. Visual images are usually the strongest stimuli for male arousal. The image may be directly viewed or recalled from a photo or movie or actual person once seen, but it is hard to visualize someone you have never seen. Vivid descriptions of women and sexual acts in pornographic books may be sufficient to create a mental image; it is this explicit detailing, as opposed to subtle innuendo and euphemism, that is the hallmark of pornographic literature.

The dream girl, of course, has never been seen. Some boys base her appearance on that of an attractive celebrity, but since she was formulated as an all-encompassing love object, not a sex object, she is more likely to have been based on mature, smartly attired artists such as Audrey Hepburn and Elizabeth Taylor than Madonna or Sharon Stone, who are more familiar when they are not disguised by clothing. Sex, for young boys, is masturbation. Fantasies of romantic preludes, employed by many women, are irrelevant to the already horny boy. The act, effected in secret, tends to be rapid, so as to avoid detection or even suspicion. The boy focuses his attention on the provocative female image and the physical sensations he is inducing, not necessarily an act of intercourse, which he may not have ever directly experienced.

This sordid scene is no place for a respectable dream girl. Just as Victorian men who had to delay marriage until they were financially secure kept their fiancées chaste by patronizing prostitutes, the boy spends his allowance on paper tigresses and video vixens, excluding the dream girl until he is mature enough to become a skilled and worthy lover. The phantom floozy in his employ changes constantly, for novelty is exciting and broadens his pseudo-experience.

The man's first real sexual experience will not be with the dream girl, because she does not exist. By the time he has the opportunity for real sex, enough years have usually passed to allow the young man to forget the dream girl entirely or to dismiss her as a childish fantasy. The woman he chooses as his lifetime mate will be, by definition, the dream girl, the woman who will bring what the imaginary companion could only hint at.

Men have been reputed to say, "The worst sex I ever had was pretty good." Don't believe it. Masters and Johnson divided sex into four phases: arousal, plateau, orgasm, and resolution. They neglected the fifth: aftermath.

When a man is in the throes of arousal, he is, by definition, responding in a positive way to his partner and his experience. Orgasms (all 3.5 seconds) are too brief to offer much of a range of variation. Even the resolution phase lasts less than an hour for the young and middle-aged.

But aftermath can encompass a long time and is not modified by the physical excitement that lets men ignore or minimize the negative psychological aspects during the act itself. In the aftermath, the male mind is free from the adrenaline rush that accompanies erection and orgasm. His logical, rational mind, with all its limitations, is emerging from the anesthesia to review what transpired during that frantic interlude when it was put on "hold."

The analytic mind hasn't much concern with pleasure; that's a feeling and feelings don't lend themselves much to logic. Any woman who has heard, "Was it good for you, too?" knows that it's validation time. The man will accept a simple nod and a reassuring hug, but what he really wants to know is *how* good was he? How did he fare in comparison to other men? (The elimination of this question is one big reason for the undimmed popularity of virginity.) Was he so good that the woman would never be tempted to take another man to bed?

I remember back when Donald Trump was muttering evasively about his innocent friendship with Marla Maples and the *New York Post* exploded a banner headline, over his picture, proclaiming:

"Best Sex I Ever Had," a quote attributed to his new friend. That day, I awarded set, point, and match to Marla and left Ivana's consolation prizes to the divorce lawyers. While The Donald's future wife did not supply data on the size of her sample and the margin of error for her conclusion, she had supplied him with enough validation to carry his ego through several fiscal recessions.

While any woman, even an honest one, can give a man enough validation regarding his sexual prowess to keep him coming back, there is another troublesome postcoital concern, which relates more directly to the dream girl, the issue of making a commitment to an exclusive partner.

This does not mean the man is reluctant to give up hope of an existence where he flits from one beautiful partner to another, like James Bond used to do. Most surveys report that the average man has had sexual experience with five women prior to marriage, which may include the woman he marries, prostitutes, one-night stands, and women of easy virtue, scarcely material to tempt Sean Connery out of retirement to recreate the exploits. Granted, masturbation is characterized by an infinite variety of fantasy partners, but the variety pertains to appearance, not any imaginary love relationship with the woman who is conjured up.

Even the inexperienced, immature boy can imagine a sexual union that provides both love and physical pleasure. Parents and clergymen, if they talk about sex at all, always place it in this context. It is this belief that such an ideal type of sex can be achieved that causes the boy to bar the dream girl from his coarse, uncomplicated masturbatory acts.

Choosing one sexual partner for life does not mean giving up all the sex objects in the world, it means giving up the dream girl. When the choice is made, the man is in effect awarding his partner the title of dream girl, whom he knew all along to be an imaginary projection of the woman to whom he would make the ultimate commitment. But the choice is fraught with doubts.

When the man begins to encounter any type of disapproval from his partner, any sort of response short of total contentment either in sexual or nonsexual areas, his thought is not "What is going wrong in our relationship?" but "I made the wrong choice! I should have waited!"

A Fallen Nightingale

Sometimes problems that seem to stem from a prostitute-madonna split really should be blamed on the dream girl. When Barbara and Gino came to my office after eight years of marriage, they complained of a sex problem. She was a twenty-nine-year-old nurse and he was a thirty-nine-year-old former merchant seaman now working for a maritime union. He had been trying to fan the dying sexual fires of their union by persuading Barbara to try new practices and techniques to increase excitement. While Barbara admitted that this helped, she felt Gino was abandoning the tenderness and declarations of love that had originally made their union a secure one.

They were an unusual couple, professionally successful after faulty starts. Barbara had met Gino when she was a college dropout, reeling from a broken engagement. She fled to Italy, a land idolized by her father, hoping to "find herself." What she found was Gino, a self-educated orphan shunted from one relative to another until he took to the seas at age sixteen. Their bicontinental courtship included frequent trysts in the port of New York City, midway between his native land and her home in Oklahoma. And New York is where they settled after they married, since Oklahoma would have been as inappropriate a habitat for a seaman as it would have been for a mackerel.

Gino encouraged Barbara to finish college. Then he supported her through nursing school. At first he took pride in her development, but with time he became less supportive. A nurse is like the archetypal madonna, unselfishly caring for the infirm. "Nurse" has, after all, the primary meaning of nurturing through one's own body. The woman in white was traditionally the unquestioning hand-maiden, carrying out the orders of the male doctor.

Gino was less enthusiastic about Barbara's advancing past that stage. When she wanted to take courses in computers, he protested that it had nothing to do with nursing. Barbara argued that, on the contrary, there was a computer at every nursing station, conveying information on patient census, laboratory results, medication, and numerous other aspects of patient care.

Gino became increasingly critical of Barbara. He sneered that she never read a newspaper and wouldn't know if California fell into the sea. Barbara countered that all he cared about was business and that they had no friends or social life.

The fatal blow to the marriage came when Barbara went to spend an evening with a recently divorced male friend in Greenwich Village. They went to a small nightclub, drank wine, and listened to folksingers while the hours slipped away. When Barbara finally got home, Gino exploded, accusing her of having sex with her friend. In subsequent therapy sessions, he berated her for having been promiscuous prior to marriage, and that once she had lost her virginity—to a man she hardly knew, while very intoxicated—she had adopted a lifestyle of casual sex with little inhibition.

Strangely, Gino proclaimed that he had wanted to marry a virgin. When asked why he then married Barbara, Gino shrugged and said some men marry "hookers from the street" and said he was in that category.

At first analysis, one might see Gino as the victim of a severe prostitute-madonna split. He never forgave his wife for her premarital experience and was quick to believe that she was still a prostitute at heart. He could love her as the madonna in white who nursed the helpless, but could not relate to her sexually unless he could get her to engage in more and more unconventional variations. He wanted to keep her socially isolated from others to meet his needs for nurturing and naughty sex.

Yet, what did not make sense was why Gino, if he really wanted a virgin bride, was willing to overlook Barbara's confessed history of loveless liaisons. When Gino said that some men marry hookers, I was reminded of a comment written by a respondent to the sexuality survey, who said that, while a prospective wife should be experienced, he wouldn't marry a whore "unless I really feel she would become a good wife."

Barbara was not so much an archetypal madonna lapsed into prostitution as she was a failed dream girl. Like Galatea, she was created by Gino. When she met him, her life was in a shambles. She had no direction and had come to Italy to "find herself." Gino supported her evolution into an educated, competent professional. While Henry Higgins had Colonel Pickering to proclaim, "You did it!" Gino needed no such confirmation. Barbara's success was not only a validation of his value as a mentor, it gave stature to his own rise from an unschooled orphan to an accomplished man of the world.

While most dream girls are older and more mature than their masters, Gino was probably too busy crossing oceans to be distracted by siren songs until he was nearly thirty. But can a prostitute be a dream girl, if exclusive possession is one of the virtues? Curiously, yes, because the prostitute is generally perceived as a woman who engages in sex for profit and, if not a frank man-hater, is incapable of love. (This is a fallacy, since prostitutes do, for the most part, fall in love, marry, and become mothers.) The man who truly wins the heart of a prostitute and converts her to monogamy is, in his estimation, more validated than the bridegroom of a virgin, for he has succeeded where scores of men have failed.

From Phyrne, the Greek courtesan who posed for statues of Venus, to the prostitute in *Pretty Woman* who becomes the Cinderella bride of a rich and handsome john-turned-suitor, our tradition abounds with tales of the hooker with the heart of gold. Why? Probably it is our stubborn protest that mother was *not* a bad woman, even if she engaged in those hateful sexual acts for the sake of financial security.

Barbara lost Gino when she stopped being whatever he wanted her to be, the way a dream girl does. When Barbara extended her personal frontiers beyond the field she had comfortably occupied, she moved out of the realm of Gino's dream girl and out of the marriage.

Paradise Lost Again

Some men think they've married the dream girl, get disillusioned, and start looking for the dream girl again. Others marry someone they know is *not* the dream girl, come to regret that decision, and start looking all over again.

Leonard was referred to me by his brother, a doctor I knew. The patient was also a doctor, a specialist in gastrointestinal surgery who, by the time he was thirty-two, had established a successful practice.

The brother asked if I could see Lenny right away, because he was apparently on the edge of a mental breakdown. His brother had found him trembling and crying, saying his life was ruined and even saying that life wasn't worth living. When I asked the brother if Lenny had indicated what was bothering him, his answer was that Lenny and his wife had just closed a deal on an expensive house in the suburbs. Lenny had finally yielded to the pressure from his wife to move with their two daughters from their comfortable apartment into a more spacious home of their own, but now he was not sure whether he wanted the responsibility and expense that such a home involved.

Now, buying a home may give one second thoughts, but it does not drive a previously stable and wealthy professional to the described degree of panic and despair. "Principle Three," I noted to myself.

In the course of my life, I have identified certain rules that bear remembering at all times, since they are so simple that people often overlook them and become perplexed by apparent paradoxes.

Principle One is Freud's pleasure principle, which he plagiarized from Aristotle: people like to do what is pleasant and try to avoid what is unpleasant. If someone says, "Our sex life is great, we just never seem to have the time," their sex life is not great. If someone says, "I hate meaningless, casual sex, but I always wind up with one-night stands," he or she doesn't hate it.

Principle Two is what this book is based on: satisfaction depends not on what you get, but on what you expected.

Principle Three, which I just invoked with Lenny, is that if things don't add up, you're missing one or more pieces of information.

When I met Lenny for the first time, I got the missing pieces. For nearly a year, he had been in an affair with his young office receptionist. It had started with apparent innocence when he took her to lunch for her birthday. He took her to the type of restaurant and ordered the type of meal and wine that young office receptionists and their usual dates cannot afford. Rachel, the receptionist, liked the lifestyle. There were other lunches, after-hours talks, little gifts, growing affection and the inevitable hotel trysts and weekend "medical conventions." It was always easy for Lenny to tell his wife he had to visit the hospital late at night to see a post-operative patient with complications.

Lenny insisted that he had never led Rachel to believe their affair would be anything more. While he loved her and the sex was terrific, he did have a wife and two children and he did not want the mess of a divorce. But he certainly didn't discourage Rachel from her flights of fantasy in which she playfully encouraged him to run off with her to a Pacific island and spend their lives in erotic dalliance.

When Rachel learned that Lenny had bought the house, she got very upset. Not only did she become hysterical, but she talked of killing herself, and that was what threw Lenny into a panic. Rachel realized that this new commitment to property meant Lenny was not about to leave his wife soon. It made me wonder whether Lenny had not encouraged her more than he claimed in fantasizing about a future divorce.

Concern for Rachel's safety did not last long. More quickly than Lenny would have wished, she decided there was no future with a married man and told Lenny their affair was over. Suddenly, Lenny was no longer so casual in his regard for their former union. He was losing the best sex he had ever experienced and the idolization of an attractive young woman. The situation was doubly awkward because Rachel continued to work for him and he had to see her every day.

Lenny could have fired Rachel, but partly because he did not want to lose her completely and partly because there was the vague fear that she might sue him for sexual harassment, he did not. Rachel even asked if he wanted her to resign, but she was not about to leave on her own. She was well paid and unlikely to command that sort of compensation elsewhere.

Rachel even came to my office once, at Lenny's request. I told him that I had no objection to seeing her, if she wanted to come, providing he would respect the confidentiality of anything she said.

Lenny was not the first bad object choice Rachel had made. She had a pattern of getting into relationships that never seemed to go anywhere. She lived with her widowed father, long after all her other siblings had moved out, and it was probably the ambivalent tie to him that attracted her to men who would not lead her into a life apart from her father. Rachel had tried therapy a few times, but always terminated after a few sessions. She was a thin, pleasant young woman, modestly dressed, with nothing seductive about her—nothing, it seemed to me, that would make a man take a second leer.

She reiterated her decision to break off the sexual relationship with her boss, although she was feeling some guilt over his obvious distress. She made perfect sense and, had she been my patient, I certainly would have advised her not to get reinvolved.

At the end of our meeting, she smiled and said, "I guess I'm not at all like what you expected."

"On the contrary," I said, honestly. "You're pretty much what I expected." No blue-angelic Marlene Dietrich, no fatally attractive Glenn Close, no flint-hearted Sharon Stone to unearth a man's base instincts. If the wife is not the dream girl, neither is the mistress.

So, in therapy, we focused on Lenny's wife, Marcia. And those who preceded her. Lenny had met Marcia a continent away, about fifteen years earlier. She was studying at a college in California. Lenny wasn't doing much of anything. He had fled to California to spend his hours surfing and drinking, except for the time he had to eke out a living at an unchallenging sales job. The reason he took this unproductive hiatus from life was the loss of a woman. He and Brenda had been high school sweethearts and had dated throughout college, even though they attended different schools. Then, at the beginning of senior year, Lenny got a letter from Brenda, saying that she had become involved with a classmate and was ending her relationship with Lenny. He muddled through to graduation, but never applied to medical school as he had intended.

Marcia rescued him. She was not as pretty as Brenda, and rather passive sexually, but she made Lenny feel secure. They got married, returned to New York, and with financial help from his family, Lenny went to medical school and established himself as a successful doctor. He found his marriage dull, but filled whatever little leisure time he had by developing a talent for painting and following his stock investments. Then Rachel came along.

Lenny recovered from Rachel, even though seeing her each day at the office slowed the healing process. He came to understand that buying the house was motivated by his guilt over the affair and showed that the marriage must have meant something to him. Then, he dropped out of therapy.

According to the old rules of therapy (by which even the old patients rarely played), termination is supposed to be an important, difficult phase of treatment. I have found, since I started in this business, that most patients come when they're hurting and leave when they're not, just as people stop going to the dentist when their teeth no longer hurt. They then come back when they get into trouble.

And Lenny came back—in big trouble! He was in the middle of another affair and Marcia was pregnant. He was over the pain of Rachel and under the spell of Helen, who was a radiologist in her mid-thirties.

As always, things had started out innocently enough, with a cup of coffee in the hospital cafeteria. One casual cup led to others, and conversations veered from case histories to gossip about the staff and hospital politics. Then, one day when Lenny noted that Helen seemed upset, she spilled her guts to the gastrointestinal repairman.

Helen had been in a five-year affair with a divorced man and they had just broken up for the fifteenth or twentieth time. The pattern was that Helen would give her boyfriend the marry-me-or-stop-wasting-my-time ultimatum, he would move out, she would fret, he would make overtures, they would reconcile, he would come back and, after a few months, the cycle started anew. Lenny was sympathetic and said all the right things. He told Helen that such an attractive and desirable woman should not be wasting her best years on such a cad. He began to make half-serious jokes about how he would be pursuing her if he were not married. She made half-serious jokes about how she would take him up on it.

Then, the joking stopped. They made a motel date for the weekend. Lenny was flying. Two days later, Helen canceled the date. She was trying to reconcile with her boyfriend. Lenny was hit, spiraled downward, and burst into flames of anger. He went home, and Marcia took the heat in an uncharacteristic burst of conjugal ardor.

Within weeks, Helen's reconciliation had fizzled. Lenny and Helen had their rendezvous at a two-day "convention" for two. Helen reached new heights of arousal, Lenny achieved a new pinnacle of self-worth, and, back at the homestead, Marcia missed a period.

During the weekend idyll, Lenny and Helen were already planning a serious future together. Helen was synchronizing her biological clock against the chronological progression of Lenny's separation, divorce, and marriage. Helen took the news of the pregnancy with only slightly more aplomb than Rachel had demonstrated when she found out about the house. It is an ill wind that blows no good, and Helen shifted her sails and took a new tack. She confessed the affair to her old, recurrent boyfriend who *finally* asked her to marry him, provided she never spoke to Lenny again.

Lenny crashed. He was in a major depression, crying when he was not sleeping, abstaining from food, and spending more and more time home "sick," asking colleagues to cover his patients. He had lost the great love of his life. He was about to have another child in a marriage he was trying to leave. He was now frankly telling his wife everything he hated about her and the marriage, which didn't make things any better at home, where he was trying to isolate himself from the sight of Helen and the sounds of rampant rumors about them.

Which woman was to blame for Lenny's misery? Marcia? Helen? Rachel? No, I concluded, it was Brenda. I would have taken Helen more seriously had I not watched Lenny play the exact scenario before with Rachel. In both cases, he felt the pull of temptation and reacted by doing something that would cement his relationship with his wife. At the same time he professed to find sexual bliss and true appreciation from exciting, desirable women, he was frantically chaining himself to the picket fence in suburbia.

With Lenny alternately threatening to leave his wife or this vale of tears, Helen trying to cope with Lenny's despair and her own long-shot chance of marriage, and Marcia (who did not, except intuitively, know about Helen) faced with a child on the way and a husband on the way out, it might have seemed strange for me to take the focus outside this turbulent triangle and chase after Brenda, a phantom from two decades ago. But Brenda was where things had started to go wrong, so I wanted to go back to the starting point.

In asking Lenny to review his first love, I found out that the romance with Brenda was two-thirds anticipation. They had never had sex together. Brenda had been raised by religious parents and gone to Catholic schools. She was determined to remain a virgin until her wedding night. In high school, there had been some hand-holding with Lenny, a few warm kisses, and reassuring professions of love. When Brenda went upstate to college, the romance heated up on paper, as fervent letters were exchanged, but the lovers rarely saw each other. Even the summers were largely spent apart, as Brenda's family took her off to their distant summer home. Lenny threw his energies into his premedical studies and put his passions on hold.

Brenda was, then, essentially a dream girl. She was based on someone Lenny knew well in many ways, but never as a lover. She, like any dream girl, would bring happiness in the future and in the present was little more than a hope and a promise. When Brenda snatched the dream away, Lenny dropped out of life.

The average man either thinks of his fiancée as the dream girl who has finally arrived or dismisses the original dream girl as an immature fantasy and accepts the pleasant reality of human love and marriage. Lenny was in the unusual situation of knowing his wife was not the dream girl and the dream girl was not a fleshless fantasy. He had lost the dream girl and was settling for less, which was better than nothing.

As time went on, Lenny learned that there was better than Marcia. What did the other women give him that Marcia did not? I suppose you would call it validation, the dream girl's stock in trade.

"You know what I enjoy most in sex?" Lenny said. "Making a woman get excited, making her feel good. I did things to Helen that her boyfriend never did and, even after she made up with him, she told me she couldn't stop thinking about me. She got so excited, she had to give herself an orgasm."

This did not surprise me. Twenty years ago, Shere Hite wrote a bestseller that accused men of caring only about their own orgasms and being insensitive to women's desires. She could not have been farther off the mark. Most men can reach orgasm with little effort with a variety of women—or by themselves. They don't have to focus on their own gratification. What makes one sexual encounter better than the others is how the woman makes them feel about themselves.

I told Lenny that the core issue was whether he was going to stay with Marcia and try to improve the marriage or divorce her and move on. He protested that the pregnancy had posed a big obstacle to divorce; I pointed out that he already had two daughters, who knew him as a father, so while the children were an important consideration, the newest one had not really added much to the dilemma.

The other women were undoubtedly nice people, but they were not goddesses. Rachel was no closer after all these years to marriage. Helen could not let go of a man who had been resisting her proposals for five years. Neither was worth killing himself over. If he did divorce Marcia and Helen were still single, he might not be so eager to rush in where his rival had feared to tread.

Good sex was another issue. If it were that important to him, he and Marcia could work on making their sex lives better. If not, he was doomed to a series of brief affairs and long searches for satisfaction. Affairs were essentially honeymoons; even his honeymoon with Marcia had been pretty good. When affairs and marriages go bad, sex tends to follow the same downhill course.

Half the couples in America divorce, I reminded him. That doesn't make the process any less painful, disruptive, and expensive, but at least he had the income that would allow him to maintain two households in relative comfort.

Great loves, tragic losses, suicidal ruminations—heady stuff! It's the cloudy realm of the dream girl. When Lenny came back to earth and realized that Helen was just as human as Rachel, he and his human wife entered marital therapy to work on their long-neglected relationship, one that had begun when he tried to bury Brenda. We hope Brenda has finally been laid to rest.

Endless Beginnings

Carlos said he was looking for a wife. He had been looking since he got divorced a dozen years ago and he was still alone, which was why he came into therapy. It was soon apparent to me that what Carlos was searching for was not a wife—it was the dream girl.

Carlos had the appearance that men immediately dislike, but women seem to go for. In the middle of a snowy New York winter, he looked as if he had just left a Miami Beach disco. He patronized tanning salons to bronze his wrinkles. He avoided ties so he could keep the top of his shirt unbuttoned, displaying a graying patch of pectoral hair. He adorned his neck and wrists with thick gold chains. He combed his thinning hair over the denuded areas of scalp.

"People tell me I look thirty-five," he said. People lie. He looked nearly ten years older than that, which he was.

He had never been monogamous. He had been briefly married to a flight attendant. When her transatlantic flights resulted in European layovers, Carlos had sleepovers with other women. When she became pregnant and gave birth to their daughter, Carlos was grounded temporarily. He soon returned to his extramarital adventures, which led to a divorce. His wife and daughter moved to New England, and he became a bachelor, his communication with his child limited to support checks.

He was now proprietor of a profitable "girl trap," as he termed his business establishment. He ran an art gallery in a fashionable neighborhood. It attracted a stream of upscale women, who came to browse and were charmed by the suave owner. Once in the trap, they were shortly thereafter transported to one of Carlos's favorite restaurants, where he was assured of V.I.P. treatment, and then to his apartment, which was an extension of the gallery.

Carlos used his business connections to furnish his love nest in breathtaking luxury. The centerpiece was the circular bed that women "just fell into." There was an expensive wooden bar, mirrored walls, and statues and paintings that managed to balance on the fine line between eroticism and good taste.

The ladies seemed to lack the flawlessness of the decor. Few received more than three invitations to the apartment.

There was one exception, a divorced woman with whom Carlos had been involved, off and on, for several years. Every time they seriously considered marriage, there would be a heated quarrel and a breakup.

Anita, the divorcée, had surprised him with a new look when they last got together, after a separation for several months. She had gotten her nose shortened and her breasts augmented. Was Carlos delighted? On the contrary, he was angry that she had undergone plastic surgery without consulting him. He said her chest was so hard, it was "like screwing the Venus de Milo." He complained that Anita was like a different woman—not that the original one had pleased him that much.

What was he looking for in a woman? Everything, it seemed: a beautiful face, a great figure, an intelligent mind, a wonderful personality. What puzzled Carlos was that his standards were difficult but not impossible to meet. He had, in fact, met women who passed the checklist and seemed eager for committed relationship, but he had backed off. What was he doing? Was he deluding himself about really wanting to get married?

So, I told Carlos the shaggy dog story. There are many shaggy dog jokes, silly tales involving animals, many of whom are not even dogs, but this was the one from which all the others got their name. A king has lost his precious pet and offers a fabulous reward to whoever finds it. He tells the searchers that they will know his dog because it is the shaggiest dog imaginable. The story drags on interminably as one devoted subject undergoes hardships and trials, finding a series of dogs and exchanging each one for an even shaggier specimen as the quest goes on. He decides he has succeeded when he finds an incredibly shaggy dog, its face and legs obscured by hair, resembling a walking mop.

The battered, exhausted man returns to the palace to claim his reward. The king, however, looks at the dog and exclaims, in dismay, "Good heavens! He wasn't *that* shaggy!"

The problem with finding an impossible dream is that even if you find it you can decide that, in retrospect, you were looking for something entirely different. Whenever Carlos found an ideal wife, it seemed he was actually searching for something else.

So I asked Carlos about his childhood. It had not been a happy one. He was the youngest child, born when his mother was almost forty and tired of children. He, alone, was sent to boarding schools while the others stayed at home, because his father abandoned the family about four years after Carlos's birth and the mother could not cope with going to work and raising a young child.

It was in boarding school that he escaped into fantasies. He would imagine himself to be a prince in a huge castle with high turrets and winding staircases. There were spacious ballrooms. And there was a beautiful little princess. Carlos would wend his way through the corridors until he found her. He would then take her in his arms and they would dance together. This little dream girl would make the rejected orphan a loved prince.

Validation. Giving worth to a man who considers himself otherwise without value. The hallmark of the dream girl.

This was the key to why Carlos had not reached the goal of marriage despite endless promising starts. When I asked him why he always abandoned a woman after no more than three dates, he did not say it was because they failed to meet his expectations.

His answer surprised me with its frankness: "Don't you see, Doc? I show them the art gallery, I take them to my favorite museums and restaurants, show them my great apartment, and they think I'm great. But I don't know what to do next! If they continue to see me, they'll know me for what I really am, not the guy they think they met. I'm nowhere near that good!"

Like a man caught in one of those old *Twilight Zone* time warps, Carlos was doomed to repeat a series of beginnings with no endpoint. The world of the prince and princess in the castle was timeless, but the clock runs in the real world and Carlos was aging fast.

Carlos seemed vain, but his self-esteem was still that of a rejected child, exiled from home and imprisoned in a boarding school. The escape, then, was to fantasize the princess who would make him a prince. The therapeutic task was to help him recognize and escape from the dream girl, so he could be content with the love of a real woman for an ordinary man.

The Young and the Restless

Sometimes in the course of my work, I see court-mandated cases, defendants who are referred for psychotherapy by a judge in lieu of harsher penalties. They come only because they must, are rarely motivated to change, and leave as soon as they can.

Marty, a forty-year-old lawyer, was a wife-mandated case. He had lived with a girlfriend for five months until his wife, Tricia, told him to come home or get a divorce. She also told him he must see a therapist to help him straighten out his life. Since the girlfriend, Betsy, had reached the stage where she was issuing a similar ultimatum, divorce your wife or get out, Marty decided to keep the wife he had and seek less-demanding girlfriends.

Tricia had told me that this was Marty's second affair during their fifteen years of marriage. She was apparently counting only the ones during which Marty spent some time living away from home, because Marty confessed to me that he had been involved in six "serious" relationships and countless trifling ones. He never wants to be without a girlfriend and sometimes overstocked his supply, resulting in as many as three extramarital sexual encounters in one day.

Like an addict, he found the highs to be terrific and the lows miserable. He referred to his wife as his "anchor to reality" and was now threatened by the strains of "Anchors Aweigh." He loved Tricia, but she was now thirty-six and he never went after a woman over thirty unless she looked "exceptionally young." Tricia was described by Marty as having heavy legs and a fat rear, not exactly the dimensions of a prospective Miss Teenage America. Not that Tricia exactly repulsed him—she had been his fourth sexual encounter the night he had earlier bedded his personal-best trio of partners.

So, Marty was a cheater. So are a lot of married men, at least a third and perhaps as many as half if you include those who start at midlife. He had the resources for it. "I'm a lawyer, I make my own hours," he explained when I asked him how he arranged so many daytime trysts. He had actually taken girlfriends to Europe, telling his wife he was going there to ski, a pastime she avoided. There were company accounts that provided the funds for his expensive pursuits. In his situation, maybe cheating was to be expected.

Still, there was an unusual driven quality to Marty's philandering, and the usual outcome was dissatisfaction rather than happiness. He never got what he wanted—a virgin. He wanted an exclusive commitment from his girlfriends, although he could not reciprocate.

Rhapsodizing about Betsy's beauty, describing her long, silky blond hair, he said, "She's twenty-seven, but she looks thirteen." I felt my ears sticking upward, like those of a German shepherd in response to a familiar whistle. Who the hell wants a thirteen-year-old girl, other than maybe a thirteen-year-old boy? Marty was searching for a thirteen-year-old virgin who he knew did not exist. The search had probably begun so many years ago that he had forgotten its origin and now he could not stop.

Marty's interest in girls started at an early age. At seven, he had fantasies of dressing (not undressing) little girls in pretty clothes, like living cut-out dolls. When he was nine, a friend told him there was an older girl in their building who was sexually adventurous, and before long she had introduced Marty to petting. She had a female cousin, who added to Marty's sexual experience.

Marty enjoyed the attention of these older girls, although what they did to him would be regarded under the law as child abuse. He didn't have intercourse until he was eighteen, but by age eleven, he had collected all the attractive women in his building into a mental harem. Maybe it was the feelings of inadequacy that generated a fantasy wherein he was with all those attractive women on a remote island, where he was the only man.

Premature sexual activity with a pair of women had engendered so much confusion that he would never equate sex with monogamy. As an adolescent, his favorite movie was *The Captain's Paradise*, which was about a sea captain with separate wives and lives in two different ports, each woman oblivious to the existence of the other. Even at that young age, Marty thought this would be the ideal sex life.

It was never enough for Marty to have women available; he wanted to be in charge, the captain, the master of the desert island. The thirteen-year-old girl who initiated him into sex when he was childish and unsophisticated would become the dream girl of the rich and experienced Marty when he grew older. She was the virgin who had saved herself for him, waiting patiently for him to reach manhood and reverse their roles.

So Marty looked compulsively for her and found only women who looked like adolescent virgins but were really experienced adults. He did not hang around junior high schools, trying to seduce real teenagers. He knew he was pursuing illusions, just as the man who patronizes prostitutes often buys the pretense of love.

Marty loved his girlfriends for the illusion they provided and simultaneously hated them because he could not forget it was only an illusion that he was the one man in their lives. Finally, he began to buy the services of "young, high-class" call girls; it was probably less expensive than taking women on European ski trips and just about as emotionally fulfilling.

Marty had grown up too fast. But by the time he was old enough for an adult relationship, he had hardly grown up at all.

CHAPTER 6

Encore La Différence

"**W**ell, I've got your sequel!" my daughter, Rita, announced. She had been talking to a psychologist whose practice consists chiefly of female college students, most of whom bitterly complain that they were brought up with stories of Prince Charming and none of the men they meet come close. So it would seem that there is a dream man as counterpart to the dream girl, who causes just as much havoc with real male-female relationships.

Wrong! The very term "Prince Charming" underscores the difference from the dream girl. Prince Charming is known to all of us since childhood; the dream girl is secret and personal. Prince Charming isn't even one man, he's two different guys, the one who kissed Snow White and the one who chased after Cinderella with the glass slipper. In *Snow White*, all he did was ride around the forest looking for girls, and in *Cinderella*, he didn't do anything more glamorous than try to fit a shoe on a lot of female feet, something that Al Bundy or any other shoe salesman can do.

Sleeping Beauty's prince, named Phillip in the Disney version, was much more heroic, hacking his way through thorn forests and slaying a huge female dragon. According to one old version of the fairy tale (hopefully not for children), he took advantage of the comatose princess during their first encounter. Between that sort of behavior and kissing girls in glass coffins, there seems to have been a trait for necrophilia in the royal bloodlines.

So, what does any woman really know about Prince Charming? Only that he is handsome and rich. If he marries you, you probably will not need a job. Donald Trump would also fit that description, although Donald might not have gone door to door all over New York with his beloved's shoe in hand (despite the powerful attraction such shoes have been reported to exert on certain men). There is no point in my recovering the territory explored in the best-selling *Cinderella Complex*—that women may envision a future husband as the answer to all their emotional and financial needs, at the cost of their own self-development.

The campus psychologist's disgruntled patients probably didn't take the fairy tales literally; what they meant was that they had grown up expecting to find at least an occasional man who had more virtues than faults, resulting in severe disappointment with contemporary men. Again, this seems to be a standard against which men fail to measure up, rather than a fantasized individual.

In their playrooms filled with Barbies, doll houses, and baby dolls, little girls can fantasize about weddings, homes, and children without any involvement of a male figure. Before Ken, you could go through countless nurseries without encountering a single male doll, except for an occasional Raggedy Andy. Even now, Andy is always acquired after Raggedy Ann, Ken after Barbie's extensive wardrobe; the males are humanoid accessories.

While little girls have imaginary playmates during their preschool years, often male in form, they do not resurrect them in mature, seductive form as they enter puberty, the way that boys form the dream girl. I recall one (unsuccessful) movie about a woman's imaginary playmate, *Drop Dead Fred*. Phoebe Cates played a young woman on the verge of divorce who was revisited by her old imaginary playmate, the elfin title character. Unlike the goddesses and sirens that have been featured in the many dream-girl films, Fred did not arouse romantic feelings in his mistress or outshine her estranged husband. He simply got her into mild trouble with his mischievous pranks. The lesson he had come to teach her was to loosen up and not take life so seriously. Nobody took the movie seriously.

The one phenomenon peculiar to girls is the hysterical worship of actors and musicians. Rudy Vallee, Frank Sinatra, Johnny Ray,

Frankie Avalon, the Beatles, the Rolling Stones, Axl Rose, and Jon Bon Jovi were all besieged in their turn by hordes of swooning, screaming and weeping women, most of them nubile minors. Clark Gable, Tyrone Power, James Dean, Marlon Brando, Paul Newman, Tom Cruise, Eric Estrada, Jason Priestley, Luke Perry, Hugh Grant, Mel Gibson, and Ethan Hawke drew women to the silver screen and cathode ray tube like moths to a bug-zapper, where the adulation is much more silent but just as intense. It is a good thing that most rock musicians are not conversant with Greek myths, since the hordes of young women who pursue them down the street, screeching and wailing, are uncomfortably reminiscent of the frenzied Bacchantes who caught up with Orpheus, the earth's greatest musician, and disassembled his body.

Men, despite their reputation for rowdiness and uncouth behavior, do not act that way. They do not scream and storm the stage at Madonna concerts. They do not go to a theater six times to watch the same Kim Basinger film (although when it comes out on videocassette, they may rewind a particular two-minute segment six or more times). If their local tavern holds a bikini or wet T-shirt contest, they may whistle and applaud in a near-gentlemanly way. But they do not simulate loss of control the way that women do.

It seems that the communal adulation that young women display toward particular idols is actually a form of ritualistic bonding with members of their own sex. A woman who begins to scream and swoon when Merv Griffin sings would probably be carted away for psychiatric evaluation; this is not to denigrate Mr. Griffin's pleasant voice, but he lacks the popular consensus that he is in the swoonable category. (I had an otherwise normal classmate in high school who had a crush on Princess Margaret, while the rest of us expressed quiet admiration for Marilyn Monroe, Gina Lollabrigida, and, my own amazing discovery, Anita Ekberg. Princess Margaret did nothing to enhance male bonding.)

Girls share their idol worship. Boys do not share dream girls. (The sex objects who are ogled and rated are *not* dream girls.) Girls have the curious ability to idolize a quartet or entire band with equal enthusiasm for each member, almost the way a woman might express separate but equal love for each of her brothers. The average teenager does not have sexual fantasies about her idols, although there are the "groupies" who are quite accommodating in this regard, to the stars and even their sidemen and "roadies." If a boy has sexual fantasies about a female performer, he knows it will never be a reality and does not waste much emotional investment in it. Dream girls may borrow attributes from famous women, but the celebrity is not the dream girl who promises a real relationship someday.

Girls can talk about attractions and crushes with their friends, sisters, and even their mothers. Boys cannot. The only communication about the subject that is permitted to boys is boasting about how far a certain girl (often fictional) lets you go. All the stories are war stories and they all must end in victory.

Fantasies grow best in dark, undisturbed places. Sharing a far-fetched dream risks having someone dissipate it by pointing out its impossibility. A dream girl who is given time to grow becomes more complex and realistic as the years pass. When girls titter about a mutually adored idol, they are acknowledging that *none* of them will have a real relationship with him, so it is all make-believe. When boys salivate communally over a gorgeous celebrity or the most desirable cheerleader on the squad, there is camaraderie because there is no rivalry over such unattainables. The dream girl is unshared precisely because she belongs to one man alone, her creator.

Paradoxically, the strong drive of pubescent males contributes to the development of the austere dream girl. It may surprise women that men are ambivalent about the powerful sexual urges that distract them from intellectual pursuits and impair their social judgment in many ways, from turning into awkward buffoons in the presence of women to destroying childhood friendships out of jealousy or rivalry. While even the pleasures of fantasy and autoeroticism are potent, they cannot be the basis of a man's entire existence. And they certainly are transient; with orgasm comes detumescence and a corresponding deflation of the tension and energy that was so dominant just moments before. If adult men have a tendency to terminate a casual sexual encounter abruptly in the postcoital phase, adolescents are no less disenchanted with their guilt-ridden simpler pastimes once physical relief has been achieved.

Adolescence, for males and females, is a time of introspection and soulsearching—dare we say, soul *creation*. There tends to be a quest for moral values and a repudiation of the existing order that was established by the previous generation, a preoccupation that often leads young men into a period of seclusiveness and self-denial at a time when their physical appetites and need for peer approval are strongest. It is what George Bernard Shaw's John Tanner termed the birth of the moral passion, a passion strong enough to override all the others. ("Is the devil to have all the passions as well as all the good tunes?" he exclaimed.)

If the boy has difficulty reconciling his base, indiscriminate attractions to women with his concept of himself as a controlled and rational man, it is understandable that he would turn to help from the dream girl. She is the hope of being able to merge lust and love, to be the recipient of his physical urges who will make him feel proud and worthy, not ashamed and insecure. The dream girl is his way out of his enslavement to the tyrannical demands of his hormones.

Girls do not have the problem of spontaneous genital arousal and the need for sexual release. They may have sexual fantasies and urges, they may masturbate, but never with the physiological urgency experienced by males. Human females do not come into heat periodically the way most other mammals do. If this means that they can be sexually responsive at any time, it also means they can be unresponsive, freed as they are of biological imperatives. In the male, spermatozoa are continuously produced, clogging the seminiferous tubules and then the efferent ducts, while the seminal vesicles and prostate gland swell in anticipation of ejaculation. There is a literal pressure that builds, and male libido, at any age, is increased as abstinence is prolonged.

Both women and men want to get married. The difference is that women plan and effect it. If a young woman starts thinking seriously of marriage, her conception of her future husband is less a fantasy image than a job description. She knows what she wants in a man and what she will settle for. She will encourage suitors who are promising and discourage those with limited potential. She has a time frame within whose limits she will marry and, if time runs short, she becomes more aggressive in questioning where a relationship is going and terminating it if the man is unwilling to make a commitment. Women are pragmatists. Shaw contended that it is a woman's business to get married as soon as possible and a man's business to stay single as long as possible. Perhaps, today, it would be more accurate to say that it is a woman's business to marry as well as possible and that men are no more in the business of marriage than prey are in the business of hunting.

Now, here we have an apparent contradiction. If men envision marriage to a dream girl as their manifest destiny, are they not just as interested in marriage as women are?

Men are interested in the girl first and marriage second. On an intellectual level, he knows the dream girl is imaginary, so obviously he cannot marry *her*, much as he would like to. He therefore consents to marry a woman who meets his needs for nurturance, validation, and sexual gratification, since this was what the dream girl was to provide in marriage. If the woman fails to meet these needs adequately, the man is less likely to conclude that his needs are unrealistic and more likely to feel that he betrayed the dream girl, who *did* meet those needs (in fantasy), by marrying someone so different from her.

Women, in choosing a husband, almost always include in the equation his present and future ability to provide for her and their children, his consideration for her, and his emotional strengths. While a man is projecting a woman's capacity to *respond* to his needs, a woman is assessing her man's current level of accomplishment and action. The biggest mistake she can make is selecting a man she knows to be deficient with the idea that she can change him. Generally, women make better objective choices than do men. The one factor they will always underestimate is the susceptibility of the man to his dream girl and the hold she continues to exert on him, even after marriage.

~ CHAPTER 7 ~

Blueprint for a Dream Girl

ictional females are only one of the sources from which dream girls are drawn. Yet, since all dream girls are fictitious, I would consider this category the most important source. The real-life lady worshipped from afar, the glamorous actress or model worshipped from even farther, or the dream girl who is pure imagination are not well known to their adorers; their personalities and fantasy trysts must be mentally scripted, just the way a writer would bring them to life.

The comic strips have been, for generations, the best source of inspiration for the dream-girl relationship. While competition from television has probably decreased the size of the average child's comic book collection, the heritage of the comics remains with us, often serving as the basis for the television series and films that were to have replaced them.

Most of the comic book buyers are male. The few comics that appealed almost exclusively to girls were the romance books and possibly *Katy Keene*, who was little more than a cut-out fashion book with plot lines as skimpy as Katy's underwear before her fashions were fastened on.

Comics had several advantages over novels, movies, and radio shows in their heyday. They say one picture is worth a thousand words and a picture of a beautiful, voluptuous heroine was more likely to enkindle preadolescent passions than the printed word or sounds on the radio. Movies also had visual impact, but the images were evanescent in those pre-VCR days. The guarantee of successive adventures on a monthly basis (or, daily, in the newspaper strips) gave the characters an ongoing life; there was no beginning and end, as there was in the movies. A comic book was to be kept, collected, reread, perused by flashlight under the bedcovers.

The superhero often had a main woman, the prototypical dream girl, whose primary function was his validation. She had no superpowers herself and was rarely of help while the hero was saving the universe; in fact, she usually complicated things by getting herself captured or otherwise imperiled and temporarily diverting the hero from his major mission by requiring a personal rescue service.

For the sake of brevity, I am going to refer to these women collectively as the sidekicks, although few of them actually accompanied the hero on his adventures. Male sidekicks assisted, with considerably less skill than the master, as in the case of Batman's Robin or Terry's co-pilot, Hotshot Charlie, or provided comic relief, such as Smilin' Jack's Fat Stuff or Roy Rogers's Gabby Hayes. The closest to a female equivalent was Dale Arden, who was usually aboard whatever spacecraft Flash Gordon was flying to his next mission, but she wasn't much of a fighter.

But validating, not fighting, is the function of the female sidekick. Lois Lane is stronger than ever, now being incarnated by Teri Hatcher and getting top billing in TV's *Lois and Clark* after Margo Kidder portrayed her in a run of successful movies. Why has Lois grown in popularity, while Mandrake's Narda and the Phantom's Diana are dim memories? No, it is not because Superman is a great hero and she is riding along on his superpopularity. Tarzan's Jane was usually in the movies, but did not have a role in the comics.

Lois is popular because she epitomizes the nature of the dream girl and the dilemmas she poses. She is adored by Clark Kent, the bespectacled, mild-mannered reporter, but she feels he is not man enough for her. Lois is pretty without being gorgeous, shapely without being voluptuous, competent without being overwhelming and occasionally sarcastic without being bitchy. The dream girl is a plausible future wife and, as such, is not to be confused with the sex object, who is usually a blonde and often villainous. Lois is a sidekick to Clark and they do share assignments, where she matches or supersedes him until she blunders into a situation that requires rescue by Superman. She is no pushover. She is more experienced than Clark—as a reporter and, we presume, otherwise.

Lois adores Superman. (Perhaps she loves him, although we should recall Cleopatra's caution about Caesar: "Can one love a god?") She is a super*validator*, because, as a star reporter, she spreads his praises and recounts his exploits to millions of newspaper readers.

Comedians and even small children ask the obvious question: since, except for the glasses and necktie, Clark Kent looks exactly like Superman, why doesn't Lois realize they are the same person? Lois's obliviousness mirrors what the average young man encounters in women. He feels they cannot see him as he really is, cannot appreciate his exceptional virtues. They are more impressed with fame, power, and muscle, not with sensitivity and imagination. Clark wants Lois to love the whole package, the human frailties as well as the superpowers, and she occasionally gives him the tiniest bit of encouragement to let him pursue that goal.

Occasionally, the media experiment with the idea of Superman and Lois becoming lovers, but then retreat to the status quo. In the movie sequel, the cost of sex with Lois is the loss of his superpowers. The memory of this encounter is obliterated from Lois' mind, so that they can pick up their usual triangular relationship in the next film.

In a comic-book story (*The Adventures of Superman*, 1991), Clark confides his identity to Lois, they marry, and she becomes pregnant. But the half-Kryptonian fetus kills her through an intrauterine superkick. The episode is resolved by the plot device of having this all happen on an alternate time line, villainously caused, and when the time-space continuum is restored (see *Back to the Future II*), the marriage, pregnancy, and death were all like a bad dream (cf. *Dallas*, the Bobby Ewing resurrection).

The consolation in such plot deviations is in the reassurance that you don't have to be a superman to get the dream girl. She is terrific, but not superwoman, and what she really needs is a human, wonderful man, one whose merit is probably vastly underestimated by the world in general.

There has been some ill-fated experimentation with companion superheroines, most notably Supergirl and Batgirl, who are active and powerful, but still wind up playing second superfiddle to the hero. Their invention was probably motivated by the prospect of selling more comics to girls than in attracting more males to the market. Supergirl was generally relegated to the prequel *Superboy* series, dealing with Clark Kent's adolescence, so as not to interfere with the Lois and Clark relationship, and she never matured into Superwoman. She was eventually killed off and then resurrected as some sort of audioanimatronic superrobot, which did not involve much change from her original personality.

Generally, the superhero stayed chaste and unwed, much like the comic-book buyers, but some of the dream girls crossed the marital, or cohabitational, barrier. Jane was Tarzan's "mate" and Boy the proof. The Phantom's Diana knew his secret, which was shared by his loyal pygmy tribe and was not a very deep one: that "the ghost who walks" was not an immortal spirit, but merely the latest in a line of Phantoms who inherited a purple bodysuit from their fathers. The rest of Africa never figured that out. The jungles in which they lived provided a metaphorical setting for the realization of the dream-girl relationship: the hero and his mate isolated from civilization, the only members of their race, except for the good and evil explorers who came and went, either being rescued or thwarted in their evil plots.

The one comic-strip dream girl who made the transition from naive part-time girlfriend to fully informed wife was Mary Jane Watson Parker Spiderman. For years, Mary Jane dated Peter Parker and was rescued by Spiderman without noticing that she never saw the two of them together. Mary Jane was different from the average sidekick in that she had a premarital independent streak, was very beautiful and sexy, and even had a fling as an actress in a bikini-beach movie. Other women entered Peter's life briefly, but comic-strip heroes, unlike James Bond, are not allowed to be promiscuous. Since the semi-employed Peter was not a co-worker of Mary Jane's, just about the only way to keep them in proximity was to marry them. Peter confided his secret identity and, while they still don't know whether their children will have two legs or eight, their marriage is still in the honeymoon stage.

But can the hero marry his dream girl and still keep the magic? There was an amusing movie entitled *How to Murder Your Wife*, in which the leading man was a cartoonist, your typical bungling average guy, who drew a strip about a tough private investigator. When the cartoonist fell for and married a gorgeous blonde who popped out of a cake at a party, he was so delirious that he married his comic-strip hero to a similar creature. Predictably, the strip deteriorated into a marital comedy, like *Blondie* or *One Big Happy*. The dismayed cartoonist had no choice but to have his private eye kill off his wife, so he could return to his previous exciting lifestyle. (This has unfortunate personal complications. The angry wife leaves the cartoonist and he is accused of murdering her by the same methods employed in his comic strip. He manages to convince twelve angry married men to acquit him on grounds of justifiable homicide before his wife reappears and reconciles.)

Spiderman may succeed because married life hasn't changed Mary Jane's role much. She frets when he is out fighting crime, fusses over him when he returns, gets jealous when he helps ladies in distress and gets rescued herself on occasion, since living in New York makes her a crime victim every few months.

There was a second class of comic-strip dream girls, who had less staying power than the sidekick: women who were the stars of their own strips. Either they were jungle girls or patriotic spy/crime fighters. Living in the jungle gave the former leading ladies a good excuse to be minimally clad during all their adventures. Sheena was the best known, but others included Tiger Girl, Nyoka, Rulah, Lorna, and Camilla. Sheena had a steady boyfriend, Bob, but contrary to most strips, she was invariably the rescuer, not him. The others routinely got themselves captured, and either escaped through their own powers (Tiger Girl had a magic amulet and her devoted big cats) or through the kindness of male strangers. The heroines who lived in more temperate climates (e.g., Phantom Lady, Yankee Girl, Sky Gal, Rio Rita) either stripped down to more revealing crime-fighting uniforms or wore skirts that conformed to the advice veteran cartoonist Milt Caniff was given by his mentor: "Always leave a few inches above the stocking for the old man." Phantom Lady, in her everyday identity as Sandra Knight, had a male friend who escorted her. Since he couldn't recognize her when she took off a few clothes to become the superheroine (the Lois Lane syndrome), we can surmise that the two had not been very intimate. The others were rather independent ladies, who were sometimes assisted by men in their adventures, but belonged to no particular male.

Outside of their erotic appeal, the leading ladies appealed to young men because they were not enamored of a particular hero, especially one with superpowers. Like all dream girls, they were mature, competent, and good, with just enough vulnerability to require help from an average guy occasionally.

Wonder Woman should be cited as the only superheroine to carry on without interruption since her inception, although her incorporation into the male-dominated Justice League of America has diluted her independence. She has an alter ego (Diana Prince), a boyfriend who cannot recognize her without her glasses and skirt on, and superpowers that emanate from her magic lasso, magic bracelets, and own Amazonian hard body. Her birth on an island inhabited only by females and her early cohort of female cadets have always made one wonder about Wonder Woman's sexual preferences, but that may have enhanced the daydream of being the first man in her life for the reader.

The theme of boy meets girl, boy rescues girl, boy marries girl is not a new one. We find it in the fairy tales, where the prince breaks the evil spell that has immobilized the maiden. We find it in the tales of chivalry, where the damsel is rescued by the knight from the dragon or ogre. We can go back further and find it in the Greek myths, which originated as tales told and retold.

Perseus rescued Andromeda from the sea monster, as she waited, chained and helpless, to be devoured, then married her. Hercules married Deianira after killing his rival, a river god who took the form of a bull for the fight. Hercules later saved her from being raped by a centaur, although that act would eventually cost him his life. Deianira used the blood of the centaur years later, thinking it was a potion to ward off a potential rival, but contact with the blood caused Hercules such unending agony that he killed himself. Ironically, the rival Deianira feared was a princess captured as a result of Hercules's exploits in battle.

Sometimes the dream girl is a passive spoil of war. Sometimes she is a grateful victim rescued from death. Occasionally, as in the case of Theseus and Hippolyta, the woman is herself a powerful warrior, vanquished in battle. But the common thread in these stories is that the man has obtained the woman by excelling in feats of prowess usually considered the province of males, such as fighting or physical strength. The woman, usually quite willingly, becomes his trophy, his validation. Does the story go back even before the start of written history? We are all familiar with the cartoon images of the caveman who, with club on his shoulder, is dragging a woman by her hair back to his lair. Is there some truth in the joke? Well, since the concept is not intrinsically hilarious, we can assume that brute strength, whether used for vanquishing rivals, becoming a better hunter and provider, or subduing ambivalent mates, had some advantage in the days before there were Cadillacs to drive and diamonds to bestow.

The dream girls who populate the world of fiction, from comic strips to movies, are a pretty fantastic lot, ranging from the exotic to the inhuman to the divine. They rarely marry the hero and, if they do, either the marriage occurs at the end of the book or film so we don't know how it turns out or they continue the nondomestic role of validating sidekick that occupied all their time prenuptially.

Are there no dream couples, people who are in realistic marriages and who share exciting lives as co-equals? Probably the closest we can come are the amateur detective teams.

The originals were Nick and Nora Charles, portrayed by William Powell and Myrna Loy in the Thin Man films of the forties. Note from the titles, however, that the male got all the billing. Nick and Nora had the advantage of being rich, which made life quite enjoyable between murders. They were witty and attractive, flirted with one another, and celebrated their successes with martinis, which also made crime-solving lots of fun, as it would grave-digging.

~ CHAPTER 8 ~

Newer and Less Improved

Several years ago, I learned a lesson about female fantasy figures. I was trying to acquire a plastic flexible Jessica Rabbit figure (if you want to know why, Jessica will be discussed later). I had spotted several of the characters, Roger Rabbit, Judge Doom, and the boss weasel, in a toy store. On the back of the cardboard cases were pictures of the five male characters and Jessica with the exhortation, "Collect them all!" The problem was that wherever I spotted these figures, Jessica was never among them.

I called LJN Toys, Ltd., the manufacturer, to inquire about Jessica some time in late November. The woman who took my call politely explained that Jessica was a female figure (I knew that) and female figures are made in smaller numbers (I did not know that). The reason is that little boys are the main purchasers of action figures and collect mostly male figures. I was assured that when the toy stores received their Christmas shipments, Jessica would be included. No, I could not order one directly from the manufacturer.

I never found a Jessica. Years later, my wife bought one for me through a collectors' specialist, paying about five times the $4.99 price tag affixed to the case.

This is a book about men's dream girls, but I am going to digress a bit into boys' early exposure to female characters in the pre-dream-girl stage. They are underexposed.

Television's earliest days coincided pretty much with my own childhood. While animated cartoons make up most of children's shows today, puppets predominated back then. Male characters greatly outnumbered the females, although this imbalance was sometimes adjusted by using an attractive young woman to interact with the puppets, as Leslie Caron did in *Lili* and Fran Allison did with Burr Tilstrom's puppets in the forties and fifties. The few female puppets that existed were ridiculous dowagers or half-batty witches.

I realize now that this was not sexist discrimination. Puppets, like clowns, are supposed to be funny. Women, at their most feminine, are not funny; hence the circus has few female clowns and they are overmatched by the male clowns in drag. In the puppet world, a male, whether humanoid or beastly, can be funny and endearing at the same time (think of Ernie or Cookie Monster on *Sesame Street*). Females can be only one or the other, so they usually wind up grotesque. If you want sweet and pretty, you're better off with a real woman.

I can think of one exception to this practice. On the *Howdy Doody Show*, Princess Summerfall Winterspring was originally played by an attractive actress, Judy Tyler. Ms. Tyler died prematurely and the Indian princess was, thereafter, played by a marionette. Since she was not a funny character, she fell short in the charm and beauty departments compared with the original; her performance had a wooden quality.

Sesame Street has usually had a token female puppet, such as Prairie Dawn or Betty Lou. They resemble animated socks (think of Lamb Chop after shearing) and have as much character as your laundry items after the spin-dry cycle. The human supporting cast always had a good representation of women in maternal counseling roles, but the childlike characters (puppets) the immature audience most identified with were male.

The first made-for-TV cartoons, chiefly those by Hanna-Barbera, followed the lead of the old Disney and Warner Brothers movie cartoons, employing male animals in the lead roles. Females did not crack the line-up until Hanna-Barbera moved their cartoons into the prime-time, adult-viewing hours with *The Flintstones* (yes, it was originally billed as adult entertainment). The wives, Wilma Flintstone and Betty Rubble, took second billing to the males, just as their human counterparts, Audrey Meadows and Joyce Randolph had on *The Honeymooners*. Animated art imitates sitcom life.

Miss Piggy was an undoubtedly strong female character among a male-dominated puppet contingent on *The Muppet Show*, another attempt to move a format designed for children into the realm of adult entertainment. A minimum of superficial female supporting characters was eventually added, notably Janice, the flower child, and Camilla, Gonzo's kinky chicken girlfriend, but only Miss Piggy rated a star on her dressing room door. The problem was that, with her voice supplied by a male puppeteer and her exaggerated mannerisms and flamboyant garb, she gives the impression of being a drag queen rather than a true sow.

The male-female imbalance in the fantasy world of children was best exemplified in the world of the Smurfs. No one is sure how many males there are in this tribe of blue elves, but the number of females is certain: one. There is a grandfatherly Smurf, a brainy one, a clumsy one, an inventive one, a handy one, a gluttonous one, each character type portrayed by a male. And then there is Smurfette (note the diminutive suffix): blond, cute, coy, and sweet.

Why include a female at all? The Smurfs have an arch-enemy, Gargamel, the wizard, who created Smurfette and threw her into the male milieu with the predictable aim of fomenting discord. (See ancient misogynistic tales of Lilith, Eve, and Pandora for precedents.) The brotherly Smurfs became hot-blooded rivals for the then-brunette temptress, but Smurfette changed sides, became a blonde and now shares the love of all the little celibate men, who remain quite blue.

The above situation has been rightfully decried by feminists as detrimental to little girls' self-image formation. In the ego-formative days when Barney precedes Barbie, girls tune in to a universe where any significant small person is male. Does it matter that the males are chiefly mice, dogs, bears, and fuzzy monsters, rather than humans? Not really, because these characters overcome the same problems as their human counterparts, outwitting bigger opponents, coping with frustration, and achieving new levels of mastery. The girls can only watch, like cheerleaders on the sideline.

This unseemly imbalance has less obvious adverse effects on boys. While those blessed with sisters may have a healthier concept of a two-sexed species, boys are not encouraged to think of girls as peers who are struggling with the same problems of growth and accomplishment as themselves. In the cartoons, if a female strays into the action, she is usually a seductive, adult caricature whose function is to distract the hero by charming him; his eyes bulge, his chest pounds, and his head spins as he pursues her. Bugs Bunny has donned dresses and padding many times to befuddle Fudd, the game but gameless hunter. In the puppet shows, the females are maternal adults.

In his real life, the boy depends, appropriately, on his mother for nurturance, protection, and guidance. As he grows older, he becomes more aware of and involved with boys his age and they mature together, comparing their progress with one another. Their tastes change from the harmony of *Sesame Street* to the mean streets of the adventure shows. The transition from childhood to boyhood to manhood is not always smooth, but it is continuous.

There is no such continuum in the perception of women. In the world of fantasy, the supportive mother is replaced by the supportive sidekick. In the real world, the little girls play apart, segregated from boys' action as they were in the first television shows. If men pose the paradox as adults of wanting to be in charge, yet needing the support and validation of women, it is easy to see how this pattern was set.

In 1995, public television launched a new puppet show, *The Puzzle Place*. Half of the six major characters were girls. Each of the puppets represented a specific racial or cultural group and the half-hour plot lines dealt with gender issues (e.g., you can't assume what a person's major interests are by his or her sex), as well as prejudices others may have about ethnic groups. It is unlikely that network shows will become sensitive to gender issues and follow suit on a large scale, but this is a start toward correcting the gender imbalance that has characterized children's shows for the past half-century.

About thirty years ago, Marvel Comics began to unleash a stream of female superheroines from a new mold. They were not little-sister versions of established superheroes, like Supergirl and Batgirl, their evanescent predecessors. They were always members of groups, an innovation that apparently had begun with the *Justice League of America*, which included Superman and Wonder Woman.

These new superwomen were affiliated with newer leagues, such as the X-Men (later redubbed X-Factor to reflect its female membership), Excalibur, and Avengers.

They were all drop-dead gorgeous, with conventional proportions—Firestar is 5'1" and 101 pounds and Elektra is among the tallest at 5'9" and 130 pounds. Marvel has been printing an annual swimsuit special issue for several years and this is one area in which the female characters get considerably more exposure than the males.

Their weapons were invariably of the "bio-energy" or "telekinetic" type. While possession of this energy enabled them to move heavy objects or unleash devastating blasts of heat or light, they did not have more than average power in their muscles. Some, like Phoenix, were born as mutants with the unusual powers. A few, like Dagger, acquired their powers; Dagger was injected with an experimental drug by criminal drug manufacturers. Elektra is exceptional in that she relies on ninja fighting skills, not superpowers.

Some of the heroines, like Scarlet Witch and Elektra, began their careers with bands of evil mutants or common criminals, then changed sides. And, of course, there are plenty of super villainesses to add spice to the drudgery of combat. Calypso uses voodoo magic in her vendetta against Spiderman. Maxima is a powerful outer-space empress who has waged a love-hate relationship with Superman. One of the most formidable of the evil clan is the Enchantress, who can make any man she kisses a love-stricken slave to her will. She is described as a ravishing beauty who stands 6'3" and yet weighs 450 pounds (a sort of early Anna Nicole Smith), is immortal, and is bent on defeating Thor, the only man who ever stood her up on a date.

While most of these women fight beside their male teammates, there are no romantic liaisons. They, like their male counterparts, have a vulnerability not observed in their forebears, who won every encounter. Their adversaries are no pushovers and they lose, by Marvel's official statistics, about one-third of their battles, but always survive to fight in another issue.

Some of the new breed, such as The Wasp and Marvel Girl, have already survived three decades or more. Yet if you stopped a group of men on the street, chosen randomly, the majority probably would have some idea of who Superman, Wonder Woman, and Spiderman are, but few could identify Phoenix, Firestar, or Dagger. The old characters, male and female, may have been less vulnerable in battle, but they could fall in love and were more affected by human emotions. You did not have to buy a new comic book each month to remember them; they crossed the print barrier into films, into TV, and into the collective unconscious.

The later superheroines were aloof and enigmatic, like the centerfold sex objects. Their mysterious powers, generated mentally, were little more than an exaggerated expansion of the feminine intuition myth and the uncanny ability to compensate for less height and muscle mass through cunning and seduction. They do not validate men. The Scarlet Witch wound up marrying a synthezoid, an artificial man, christened Vision because he was a vision of the best mankind is capable of becoming. The old female sidekicks made men feel good about themselves; the new superheroines make them feel superfluous, if not obsolete.

The latest of the female superheroines, aimed at the affections of the elementary school set, are even more mechanical and anonymous. I refer to the Mighty Morphin Power Rangers, an assemblage of television teenage superheroes to which most of the country's children have become addicted. I had to develop a nodding acquaintance with them because virtually every child I evaluated at a clinic where I work named *Power Rangers* as his favorite television show. Many wore "Ranger" watches and brought "Ranger" figures with them. "Rangers" were what they wanted for Christmas and birthdays. They showed me their "Ranger moves," a series of karate chops and kicks. Even the girls watched them.

Lest you think that only emotionally disturbed children are *Power Ranger* fans, the theater critic for the New York *Daily News* brought the nine-year-old daughter of a friend to a Ranger show at Radio City Music Hall to assist him in his review. The girl announced to a peer that she watched the television show every afternoon and was silenced by a boy in the row ahead, who sneered, "*Everybody* does."

I have watched the show and am appalled, not because it leads children to relate to their peers by trying to kick and punch them into insensibility (which has led some schools to ban Ranger apparel and toys), but because of the dehumanization of heroes and villains.

The plotline is absurdly simple. A group of six high school students has been recruited by some sort of intergalactic guru to fight the enemies of the universe. There are six kids, two of whom are female. Three are permanent cast members, while the other three, including one female, are periodically replaced. When danger comes, they change into the Power Rangers.

Here is the part that scares me. When they change, they wear helmets and goggles that render them faceless, so they can be identified only by the colors of their uniforms. Their enemies are essentially monsters that look as though they are made of plastic. When a Ranger needs to rev up his or her power, he or she calls on a personal animal spirit, from a mishmosh menagerie of extinct, real, and mythical animals, including a tyrannosaurus, dragon, white tiger, unicorn, and pterodactyl. This creature merges with the Ranger as a Zord—part human, part animal, part machine.

You realize that what you are watching is a half-hour toy commercial, interrupted by other commercials. When you watch a tiger Zord, you don't say, "I'll bet I can buy a toy like that," you know you can buy *that* toy (if it's not sold out). The Zords and the Rangers themselves are elaborations of the old Transformer toys, which can be manipulated or built into new shapes, from man to robot, from robot to vehicle.

If you have ever watched one or more children play with toys, that is the equivalent of a *Power Ranger* episode. Villain approaches saying he will destroy the Rangers and the earth. Teenagers flip down human heads and transform into helmeted Rangers. Then, "kick, pow, take that!" Wheel the Zords into action. Rumble, roar, crush. "Curses! You've won this time, but we'll be back!" "We'll be ready for you!" Yay, Rangers!

That's about as complex as it gets. It's never clear how a few ballet pirouettes and ill-directed kicks can have such a devastating effect on armor-plated monsters, but they fall like compliant tenpins. It's also not clear how an intelligent race of would-be universe conquerors cannot calculate their fuel needs so they don't run out of energy just as they are about to pulverize our planet.

A generation ago, the villains were more complex. Lex Luthor, the Penguin, the Joker, and the Riddler did not profess to super-strength, but they were clever. They forced the heroes not only to outfight them, but to outwit them. The heroes, the villains, and the girlfriends all had their vulnerabilities, which made their triumphs more satisfying. It was, I like to think, a training for life.

How does the dream girl inhabit the *Power Ranger* world? She doesn't. The female Rangers relate to their male classmates as bud-dies, without the slightest hint of infatuation or sexual attraction. When the girls become Rangers, their bodies are encased in pink or yellow jumpsuits, a plasticized breastshield the only subtle indica-tion of their sex. Their hair and eyes are covered. They cavort with the same kicks and punches as the White and Red Rangers.

There is a major female villain, Rita Repulsa. Surrounded by inhuman henchmen and garbed in the robes of a mad sorceress, she is vaguely reminiscent of Disney's Maleficent, the Sleeping Beauty's nemesis. But Rita Repulsa has none of Maleficent's class or grace. With her slim torso, long fingernails, and smoldering eyes, Maleficent used her femininity as a silent threat, implying that being a woman made her powers doubly dangerous. The cackling, hysterical Rita Repulsa lives up to her surname.

The Power Rangers are already being imitated in other time slots by the V. R. Troopers and Superhuman Samurai Syber Squad. The format is so similar that there is little point in describing the minor differences between each competitor and the Rangers. The kids automatically tune in to each, just as adults came to watch *Melrose Place* after *Beverly Hills 90210* ended.

Does it matter if preadolescent boys are exposed to a fictional world without intersexual tensions? Are they not, in fact, better off to regard girls with sex-blind vision? Should they be getting their validation as males from sources other than helpless, grateful women?

Men will always need women. When they no longer need women as mothers, they will need them as lovers and wives. Adult love, as opposed to maternal love, must be earned, and the sooner that lesson is learned the better. Granted, the lessons taught by the knights, cowboys, warriors, and superheroes were rather simplistic, but then, children cannot absorb the complex. If the dream girl once taught that sometimes you have to put the welfare of another above your own, even if you endanger yourself, and that the love of a good woman is part of the reward for virtue, perhaps she deserved an apple for her effort.

In the new world of plasticized Rangerettes and electrified mutants, will the dream girl go the way of the tyrannosaurus and the triceratops? Unlikely. Just as, through the power of imagination, these extinct creatures are as familiar to children as circus lions and zoo elephants, so will the dream girl live on in the imaginations that originated her. Like most endangered species, she may find her habitats shrinking, but the final sanctuary, the male imagination, will be available.

Venus lost her temples, her priests, and the artists who sculpted her form and sang her praises, but she is as familiar today as she was two thousand years ago. The dream girl is older ... and more endurable.

CHAPTER 9

The Toontown Backlash

*I looked up and saw that tall, beautiful blonde striding
across the room. At long last I was face to face with
SHEENA! Face to face with a life-long dream girl who
suddenly had become a flesh and blood reality instead of
just a paper and celluloid fantasy! Irish readily admits
to having just turned 64 (Christmas Day, 1992) but her
features deny it.*

—BILL BLACK, *GOOD GIRL ART QUARTERLY #11*

$\mathcal{B}$ill Black is describing his first face-to-face meeting with
actress-model Irish McCalla at a collectibles show in Tampa,
Florida, which he attended with other comic-book artists and
writers. Ms. McCalla, who had starred in the *Sheena* TV series
during the fifties, was making a personal appearance there, selling
copies of *TV's Original Sheena, Irish McCalla* and photographs of
herself from her days as a young model and actress. Recovering
from a cancer operation and tiring radiation treatments, Ms.
McCalla had planned to take long lunch breaks and rest, but "the
stream of fans was neverending."

Black describes sitting with her and his friends at breakfast in
the hotel: "We all had a grand old time. This was pretty amazing

considering the age spread: Chic is in his mid-seventies, Irish in her early sixties, me in my late forties and Paul in his early thirties."

This is the backlash. Comic books have replaced the vulnerable dream girls with a horde of indistinguishable hard bodies spurting laser rays. Television has given us masked, vinyl-encased fighting machines. Movies have given us cynical, independent, man-baiting career women. Magazines have replaced provocatively clad temptresses with unclad, blasé freestylers.

So, men are going back to the days when dream girls ruled the media. Those who have memories are resurrecting them. Those too young to have them are being introduced to them.

The November 7, 1994, edition of *New York* magazine features a six-page layout of model Eva Herzigova posing in swimsuits against a background of old war planes. "With swimwear suddenly looking Betty Grable-esque," the magazine unnecessarily explains, "there's no better place to explore (okay, exploit) bathing-beauty iconography than the flight deck of a World War II aircraft carrier."

The bikinis are definitely postwar, but the golden curls and bright red lips juxtaposed against propellers, fuselages, and cockpits evoke a strange sense of peace and security. The model is there to be admired, not seduced. If you turn the page, she will not be wearing anything less. She is there to inspire the mind, not to arouse the body.

Maybe if the year were 1944, not 1994, the photos would not be so innocent. The string-bikini bottom, the expanse of abdominal flesh between navel and rim of stretch-satin would probably have been considered scandalous-to-obscene back then. But men are returning to images, both the originals and the recreated, that were once considered "sexy" out of hunger for the erotic, not the libidinal.

Just as people will argue about what constitutes pornography, they may have difficulty defining erotic. But the distinction between the erotic and the libidinal is precisely the difference between the dream girl and the sex object. If an image results in sexual arousal and leads to a goal of sexual release and nothing else, that is libidinal.

The erotic will usually involve some sexual feelings, but the goals are more complex. It evokes feelings we associate with romance and love. It heightens our senses and our appreciation of beauty. It makes us hunger for emotional intimacy and it encourages us to develop our own creativity.

On some level, we can say of erotic material what Alice said, when she first read *Jabberwocky*: "Somehow it seems to fill my head with ideas—only I don't know exactly what they are!"

Libidinal and erotic feelings arise in boys at about the same time and are usually clearly distinguishable to the subject they influence. Libidinal feelings can be quickly gratified physically. Erotic feelings, in the absence of a suitable love object, can only be incompletely satisfied in fantasy.

What is libidinal to one person can be erotic or neutral to another—or even to the same person, depending on time and circumstances. If we try to define the libidinal objectively, by its tendency to provoke sexual arousal, how do you classify explicit images that some find very sexy and others find repulsive? The fetishist may find fur or leather by itself arousing, while most would consider it mere apparel. A horny youngster may find the summer edition of *Betty and Veronica* comics as stimulating as the corresponding edition of *Playboy*, while most would find the lightly clad cartoon figures no more sexy than Daisy Duck.

In the May 1993 edition of *Esquire*, Demi Moore was featured in a photo and story feature entitled "The Last Pinup." In the photos, as in days of yore, her breasts and pelvic area were covered, in this case by artificial butterflies and flowers. In less revealing photos, posed with a tiger, she bared only her midriff above lacy harem pants.

"I like looking at the duality of male/female, and kind of playing with stereotypes," Ms. Moore explained, esoterically. "Playing a sort of sex kitten in the movie [*Indecent Proposal*], then doing this exaggeration of the pinup, is a way to wink at the whole business, to show I don't take it seriously. I mean, look, these aren't come-fuck-me shots."

The writer of the article, Michael Angeli, recalls his adolescence and says, "The pinup was contraband and secret knowledge, an undeclared sovereignty, a glimpse of how we would be ruled by imagery that denotes freedom, liberation, fulfillment, a dream date. There was no stopping the surge of vitality it sent to the flower at the center of the brain."

Ms. Moore says, bluntly, that her photos are not an invitation to sexual interaction. Mr. Angeli, too, sees the pinup as a *date*, not a quick bathroom encounter, and defines its target organ as the brain, not the genitals, clearly the province of the erotic.

Yet Angeli says that as adults we are shamed by the politically correct world and envy the "lout who insensately pages through the girlie magazines." He confides that "Sneaking a peek" is our "dirty little male secret, like crying at the movies."

What provokes guilt? Is it the looking at the naked or half-clad bodies that women willingly display? Is it the experiencing of sexual feelings in a society that belittles passive and modest men, and tries to reach our psyches and wallets through libidinal stimulation? Or is the dirty little secret that men continue to covet the dream girl they idolized as boys and know they can never obtain?

We concede that the pinup of the forties was a mixture of erotic and libidinal elements, but as she evolved into the *Playboy* centerfold, the lust increased and the romance died. It may never have occurred to Hugh Hefner that by revealing not only the measurements of the Playmate of the Month, but the name of her high school, her father's occupation, her hobbies and turn-ons, she became completely demystified. Dream girls do not come, like the old Cabbage Patch dolls, with a name already attached.

It is not surprising that the year after Demi Moore's "last pinup," *Esquire* decided to revive the Varga girl that it had popularized half a century earlier. Under the heading "1994: The Pinup Returns," the magazine ran a photograph of a "famous model and budding actress" recreating a Varga girl pose. Perhaps out of deference to the late artist, her swimsuit was painted on. Although the subject was technically unclothed, the overall effect was comparatively wholesome. A pinup is not a centerfold.

Esquire writer Jamie Malanowski touched on the erotic-libidinal dichotomy when he commented about the World War II Varga girl, "It's also hard to think of her as sexy. Of course she's *sexy*, if only in an academic way, if only in the way one can accept as given that Jean Harlow was sexy." He goes on to lament that the surfeit of nudity and graphic sexuality in our culture has robbed the sex objects of their power to excite and left the Varga girl looking "quaint."

Camille Paglia says she adores the Varga girls and considers them sensual, not quaint. "The women appear to be swimming, their large breasts are buoyant, and they seem to be inviting the man to dive right in. This is prefeminist eroticism, and it's universal. It's the essence of femaleness—*why men are attracted to women*—and the obliteration of this kind of eroticism by the Anglo-American feminist establishment is one reason for the sexual crisis we're in."

Ms. Paglia's comment makes one reevaluate what the feminists, purposefully or unconsciously, were fighting. We think of them protesting the employment of women as sex objects, but it was the dream girl who fell to their slings and arrows. She was, after all, a more appropriate target. The sex object offers only the promise of sex and, since the human race must and will go on, no one has tried to eliminate sex. The centerfold may be air-brushed and cosmeticized but she is a real woman who lays her physical assets on the table (or hearth rug or haystack or whatever) with nothing concealed.

The sex object may have a body and face that are hard to match by conventional standards of physical perfection, but to compete successfully against her (if she wants to), a woman only has to offer a real and available body. Sex has never been a hard sell.

On the other hand, the dream girl offers a comprehensive fantasy, the genie's lamp that will give you *whatever* you require in the way of emotional satisfaction, love, and self-esteem. Sex is part of the burgeoning package, too, but not of the uncomplicated, down-and-dirty, quick-fix variety. The dream girl's face and form are only the wrapping for the package; it is the contents that neither the feminist nor any other woman can hope to match.

The ability to fire the imagination is the essence of eroticism. The woman who leaves nothing to the imagination can be sexy but not erotic.

Why, in a world where photos of nude women in uninhibited poses are available at every newsstand and videos of such women in explicit motion are available for nightly rental, does *Sports Illustrated* manage, year after year, to sell triple its usual number of copies for the swimsuit issue? One obvious answer is that more than sex is being sold. The pitch is that you will get the most beautiful women, revealingly (un)dressed, in America. One skeptical female columnist wrote that if the photos were shot on a vacant lot in Cleveland instead of an exotic setting, the issue would sell just as many copies.

I think she's wrong. The setting is part of the package, just as is the waterbed in the honeymoon suite.

Then, the magazine features supermodels. A decade ago, there was no such profession. Models were anonymous, attractive hangers for clothing. I was secretly pleased when the *New York Times Magazine*, in its periodic fashion layouts, began to credit the model in the minute type that ran laterally along the border, after it had credited the fashion designer, the makeup artist, and the accessories supplier. It seemed the legs deserved as much acknowledgment for the overall look as the sandals. But this was an exception. Occasionally, a Lauren Hutton or Christie Brinkley would become known just from chronic overexposure, but most of the models bloomed and faded in obscurity.

The supermodel is, I suppose, one whom most people can recognize by name. This is not as easy as it sounds. I have figured out that Cindy Crawford is the one with the beauty mark and Claudia Schiffer looks like Kim Basinger, only younger, and Stephanie Seymour has an "outie" navel. But Linda Evangelista keeps changing her hair color and Elle Macpherson never looks the same way twice and I thought I could recognize Vendela until Eva Herzigova came along.

The problem with supermodels is you can only identify them by their looks. Actresses make films and music stars cut albums, but supermodels just *exist*, unless you keep track of their love affairs and divorces in the tabloids. This makes them, to some extent, suitable dream-girl templates, because if a man likes their appearance, he can attach any personality or psychological attributes to them. They provide the blank slate on which to draw the dream-girl blueprint.

Another reason that men buy the swimsuit issue is the same as why they watch the Super Bowl. It is not because it is such an exciting game; most are dull, one-sided blowouts. It is not because it matches the two best teams in pro football; more often than not, the two best teams are in the same conference and one has been eliminated in the playoff games. Men watch the Super Bowl because it has become an annual ritual, something that men are expected to do even if they have not the slightest interest in who wins, something they are expected to discuss with their peers the next day, even if only to say, "What a lousy game!"

Similarly, a man is almost expected to be able to discuss intelligibly the relative merits of Kathy Ireland's dimensions versus the attributes of Rachel Hunter, even if he still hasn't figured out who was on the cover this year.

Above all, the swimsuit issue offers a chance to retreat to a more innocent era, where the girls went just so far and your imagination had the pleasant task of going the rest of the way. Often, you never made it past that beautiful tropical beach back to the hotel room with the dream girl, because a pair of sensuous eyes and tanned legs were all you needed.

Even today's supermodels fail to fill the void left by the dream girls of a generation ago, so their images have been summoned out of retirement for a booming business on the nostalgia circuit. Irish McCalla, for example, was a coveted swimsuit model even before her *Sheena* days, and not all of her best outfits are leopardskin. Tempest Storm was a stripper whose voluptuous body became familiar through magazine photos to thousands of men who had never been inside a burlesque theater. Among the "starlets" who were beautiful enough to have posed for hundreds of "cheesecake" photos and talented enough to have made one or more B-movies, some, such as Jayne Mansfield and Mamie Van Doren, are as prominent in collectible stores today as they were at newsstands when their careers were at their modest peaks.

Many of these images were gleaned from the sensationalistic but comparatively innocent magazines directed at men. One group of small magazines with one-word titles, such as *Wink* and *Titter*, consisted of sexy photos interspersed with risqué cartoons. The second group featured adventure stories that usually involved rescuing bands of lingerie-clad European girls from Nazi or Japanese torturers (illustrated, of course), photos of women in swimsuits or underwear, and sexually informative stories, such as "The Lesbian Epidemic—Our National Shame" and "Call Girls on the Campus." These magazines always contained one common word in their titles: *Men Today, World of Men, Real Men, Man's Adventure, Man to Man,* etc.

It should be pointed out, from the perspective of an aging male, that these magazines did *not* enjoy the widespread readership that *Playboy* and *Penthouse* acquired among the current generation, although they had their share of devotees. They were published in more restrictive times and, while sold openly, most newsstands did not carry them and young boys felt guilt about buying them. They were geared to the less sophisticated young adult. It should also be pointed out that, while these magazines were sexually titillating, it does not take much to titillate a fourteen-year-old, and a photo of Esther Williams wearing a swimsuit in *Life* was just as inspiring as Tempest Storm's G-string.

Lest women become alarmed, these men's magazines are not being reprinted in their entirety nor are they going back into business. The sadomasochistic tales of heroism and the pseudosociological exposés of sexual deviates and vice rings undermining our great nation now seem too ludicrous and transparent for actual reading. What has survived mostly are the illustrations and photographs, probably the prime sales motivators even then. Not only are the models being rediscovered, but glamour photographers such as Bunny Yeager, and artists such as Gil Elvgren, "The Norman Rockwell of Pinup," are gaining new recognition.

The most interesting phenomenon is Betty Page, an attractive brunette with trademark bangs, whose image was ubiquitous in the early fifties. She never aspired to film and was never more than a model, but she left a legacy of perhaps thousands of swimsuit photos in the "skin mags" of the day, culminating in a 1955 *Playboy* centerfold in which she knelt beside a Christmas tree wearing only a Santa Claus hat. (For the information of purists, her name was originally spelled Bettie, but the bulk of material today refers to her as Betty.) She was notorious for her underground (now widely surfaced) bondage photos, none of which were shot nude. Pre-*Playboy*, she did pose for nude photographs, most of which stayed in private collections until the easing of censorship in the late fifties.

But the most amazing thing was how many artists used her as a model, even those, such as Olivia DeBerardinis, whose paintings in the nineties relied on old photographs. For decades, her whereabouts was a mystery, and it was rumored that she had found religion and repudiated her past. Betty has finally decided to resurface and is receiving royalties from the plethora of photo collections and *Betty in Bondage* adult comics that continue to roll off the presses.

Dream girls or sex objects? Well, Betty, Irish, Tempest, et al.

were probably sex objects in their youth, but when men revere those images after age and death have ravished and decimated the originals, we have apparently moved into the world of fantasy and dreams. Why reminisce about young women who no longer exist when there are so many eager to replace them in men's fantasies? Obviously, they, or their era, must have had something that cannot be replaced.

And, while television's Sheena cannot stay the hand of time forever, the comic-book jungle girl who inspired the show is back. AC comics has been re-inking and reprinting strips from the forties and fifties under the rubric "good girl art." The "good girls" were all heroines on the side of good against evil and they were gorgeous, with the costumes to prove it. Unlike the ray-emitting mutants who succeeded them, the old heroines rarely had more than a dagger and their wiles. The jungle girls are so numerous that not even a comic of their own can include them all: Tiger Girl, Rulah, Tegra, Zegra, Camilla, Nyoka, Cave Girl, and Wild Girl among them.

In other magazines, the World War II heroines reassemble to relive their reprinted adventures and even launch some newly created ones. Phantom Lady, Sky Gal, Miss Masque, and Yankee Girl are back, sexy but virtuous, heroic but vulnerable, eternally feminine.

What we have seen is that you cannot completely eradicate the classical dream girl. You can offer alternatives. You can fill the book pages and TV screens with more androgynous women, women unattached to men, women who are closer to the real world. But if they do not meet the psychological needs of men, the men will return to the old dream girls, even ones who existed before the men were born.

If desperation can conjure up fantasies of mermaids and goddesses, a few decades is not that much of a throwback.

Rabbit Fever

In 1948, in the film *Mr. Peabody and the Mermaid*, a man on his fiftieth birthday, falls in love with a mermaid. In 1988, the year of my fiftieth birthday, I fell in love with a rabbit. She was only a rabbit by marriage, you understand. Otherwise, she was quite human in appearance, endowed with a beautiful face, a sultry voice, long red hair, and a spectacular body. On the down side, she was a toon, an animated drawing, pure fantasy.

Her name was Jessica and she was (at least, as far as I was concerned) the star of *Who Framed Roger Rabbit*. At first, I didn't worry about my admiration for her. I've always been a Disney fan and for many years carried a plastic Tinker Bell around as a luck charm. I still have a silver-plated one on my key chain. I had a job that let me budget my time as I saw fit, so I saw fit to take a few two-hour lunch breaks to watch the film about four times at a local theater.

When I got worried was when I saw a small plastic figure of Jessica in a card store. I didn't buy it immediately and when I went back, it was gone. I found myself going blocks out of my way to visit every local card shop and toy store, hoping to find one, until I could no longer deny that I was in the throes of an obsession.

I now have about six of that particular figure, in addition to the most extensive collection of Jessica memorabilia in New York (probably), including pins, greeting cards, books, mugs, figurines, and watches.

Once, when a female patient admired my Jessica wristwatch, I explained that I had a fascination with her.

"How does your wife feel about that?" she teased.

"*Very* safe," I replied.

Initially, I thought maybe my infatuation with Jessica was a safe way of dealing with an actual or feared turning-fifty mid-life crisis. I had seen *Mr. Peabody and the Mermaid* several times on TV as an adolescent, back in the days when *Million Dollar Movie* would show the same film every night for a week. It had made a profound impression on me and, needless to say, I watched it on videotape on my fiftieth birthday after everyone was asleep. Jessica was a lot safer than an affair or a flirtation.

But the more I watched Jessica on the big screen, the more I realized that here was the ultimate dream girl, an imaginary woman moving among real men. Until Jessica, we either had real women who could not sustain the illusion or imaginary women who could not enter the real world. Jessica broke the barrier.

Suddenly I realized I was not the only one to fall under her spell. *People* magazine (December 26, 1988) included her among its twenty-five most intriguing people of the year and named her the movies' top leading lady of 1988. "Jessica is typecast forever, burdened with a lusciousness that, even more than for most beautiful women, exists mainly in doodling male noodles," *People* proclaimed. "She's too good not to be bad, and for a bad girl, she's made good."

Us magazine (February 6, 1989) announced tersely: "IN: Jessica Rabbit. OUT: Dolly Parton."

England's *Tatler* magazine (November 1988) had a full-page drawing of Jessica wearing about $300,000 in real diamond jewelry on its cover. "Siren of the times Jessica Rabbit confesses to a weakness for small men who are big fun," it said in the space reserved for comments about the cover girl. "'It's not easy being a girl and looking like this,' she sighs."

But the biggest shocker was the cover of *Playboy*'s November 1988 issue, which featured a redheaded Playmate made up to look like Jessica, wearing that red sequined dress with the thigh slit and the purple gloves. The cover advertised: "Sex in Cinema (Starring That Torrid Toon)." In the article that reviews the year in cinema, Jessica is mentioned on the same page as Jamie Lee Curtis, Jennifer Jason Leigh, Sherilyn Fenn, and Barbara Hershey.

In *Playboy*'s very next issue, Jessica led the "Sex Stars of 1988." *Playboy* proclaimed: "The fact that the sexiest female on screen this year is a curvaceous cartoon character may tell us something about the state of cinematic erotica. Nevertheless, Jessica Rabbit is definitely *it*."

So, here was a surreal joke played on a nation, with its good-natured cooperation. In the movie, Jessica was a "toon" who walked among human beings, captivating the men she left in her wake. Now she was doing the same thing in the real world, receiving accolades reserved for the sexiest of flesh-and-blood women.

Nothing is accepted on a wide scale, be it a joke or book or movie, unless it contains a truth that nearly everyone can relate to. Jessica was dream girl, the imaginary woman adored by all men who distracts them from real women by being and promising the impossible.

It took three talented women plus countless animators to bring her to life. Kathleen Turner supplied her seductive, breathy voice.

Amy Irving (surprise!) sang her torchy admonition "Why Don't You
Do Right?" and Betsy Brantley, a diminutive actress, was Jessica's
performance model, a stand-in who walked her way through scenes
to guide the animators' later work. Ms. Brantley (who played the
mother in *The Princess Bride*) was a strange choice for the tall,
voluptuous Jessica, but no human female could have measured up;
Jessica's waist was so thin and her bosom so large that, like Barbie,
she was an anatomical impossibility. Most of the performance
model's body was screened out and only her arms and hands were
covered with artwork, while the animators filled in the rest of
Jessica's body without concern for true corporeal geometry.

From the start, Jessica dominated her co-stars, human as well
as animated.

What probably made most men subconsciously identify Jessica
with the dream girl was not her dreamy proportions, but her relationship with her husband, Roger Rabbit. (If the concept, even in a
wacky fantasy, of a beautiful woman being blindly in love with a
zany rabbit doesn't seem to add up—it doesn't. In the novel on
which the film was based, Gary Wolf's *Who Censored Roger Rabbit?*,
it is discovered that Jessica fell in love with Roger after he unwit-
tingly made the wish within earshot of a genie-containing teapot.
The movie offers no explanation for this strange union, other than
Jessica's "He makes me laugh.")

Jessica looks and acts like a femme fatale, but she speaks the
truth when she says, "I'm not bad, I'm just drawn that way." She
cooperates with the bad guy to save her husband's job. She knocks
Roger unconscious to get him out of harm's way. When she is finally
rescued, she praises and kisses Roger, rushing blindly past the true
hero, Eddie Valiant.

And, for all her seductiveness, she is sexually innocent. When
the private eye catches her "playing pattycake" with an admirer in
her dressing room, she is literally playing pattycake—with her
gloves on, yet.

True to form, the ultimate klutz gets the love of the dream girl.
Jessica implies to Eddie that, in the sexual area, being a rabbit may
be an advantage. When Eddie sneers on observing Roger's wrecked
car, "A better lover than a driver, huh?", Jessica jabs a gloved fore-
finger and snarls, "You'd better believe it!" Roger's baggy trousers
may be more necessary than comical.

One comedian commented on Jessica's status as the ideal mate: "She's loyal, she's got big tits, and she has a steady job." The dream girl is not only beautiful, she must stand by her man and take care of him. She is tough, streetwise, wily, and, even though vulnerable, she doesn't lose her composure when things are darkest. She takes a klutz, turns him into a hero, and makes him believe he did it all by himself.

Although after 1988, her film career was limited to cameo roles in three animated Roger Rabbit-Baby Herman shorts, Jessica's hold on the imagination is still strong.

My brother teased me about buying the issue of *Playboy* featuring Jessica, saying that I hoped to see some nude shots of her. I scoffed that I was reality oriented and knew that any pictures had to be frames from the familiar film.

Shortly thereafter, my brother mailed me a color picture of a bare-chested Jessica, clad in bikini panties, garter belt and stockings. It had been clipped from *Celebrity Sleuth*, where it was part of the pictorial on Kathleen Turner, chosen by the magazine as the sexiest woman of 1990. The text explained that the single topless frame of Jessica was one that the artists tried to slip by the Disney executives as a practical joke.

To appreciate the irony of this, you must know that *Celebrity Sleuth* specializes in revealing photos of famous people, but these are not the carefully posed shots that you might see in *Playboy*. *Sleuth* gleans its pictures from videocassettes and occasional candid shots, with the result that most of its offerings are blurred and grainy, as though shot off a TV screen with the aid of a VCR Pause button. Thus, we have been treated to out-of-focus shots of Anne Archer's panties from the fight scene with Glenn Close in *Fatal Attraction* and an isolated nipple said to be extracted from *Lifeguard*, which contained her only seconds of topless exposure during nearly twenty-five years of films.

Even though Jessica was only a toon, *Celebrity Sleuth* had managed to unearth the one shameful secret photo that had embarrassed so many members of the Screen Actors Guild in the past. Animation imitates life!

Few people got to see the topless picture, but in March 1994, poor Jessica was involved in a sex scandal of major proportions. It was discovered that *Who Framed Roger Rabbit* contained a scene in which Jessica's crotch was exposed, with no covering undergarments. She is thrown from an out-of-control taxi and flies through the air, as her skirt rides up her spread legs. It was conjectured that the animators (aren't these guys supposed to be paid professionals?) inserted the scene as an inside joke that could not be detected when the film ran at its usual twenty-four frames per second.

It was claimed that laserdisc technology allowed viewers to advance frame by frame through the action, which led to the discovery. When the story came out, people rushed to buy the expensive laser discs as collectors' items. (This laser talk is nonsense, by the way. Any decent VCR will allow you to run the standard VHS tape at slow motion and stop the picture at any frame. What is exposed is a pink area between her thighs with a vertical line bisecting it. What did you expect to see on a toon, the clitoral hood and the labia minora?)

One befuddled video store saleswoman said of the run on the laser discs, "I don't understand this. Frankly, we have a really good selection of porno. Why don't they want a real woman?" (I hope she reads this book.)

I ached a little for Jessica. When Sharon Stone claimed she had been duped by the director into removing her panties for the interrogation scene in *Basic Instinct,* I did not cast the first stone but neither did I feel she had harmed her career by not keeping her legs crossed. But Jessica had been victimized by those to whom her welfare was entrusted, the decent girl subjected to eyes peering down her bodice or lifting her skirt from behind.

Just when I think Jessica's well-deserved adulation has died down, she's back in print. *Playboy* in May 1994 included her in a feature about "Bad Girls," grouping her under the heading "Bad Girls, Good Choices," with Sharon Stone, Drew Barrymore, Heather Locklear, and Rebecca De Mornay. Among photos of La Toya Jackson, Madonna, and Tonya Harding was a drawing of Jessica, not in her familiar red sequined gown, but in the abbreviated, tight-fitting forest ranger costume she wore in the latest animated short. There are no small parts for large dream girls.

If imitation is the sincerest form of flattery, Jessica would have been extremely flattered when Kim Basinger, one of filmdom's sexiest actresses, played a toon in *Cool World*. In the nightmarish counterpart to Toontown, toons were called "doodles" and humans "noids," but the boundaries between the two worlds were as distinct as they were for Roger Rabbit. Frank Harris is the only human inhabitant of *Cool World*, having escaped to the fantasy world after his mother's tragic death. The imprisoned Jack Deebs has created Holli Wood, who is beautiful and bad (not just drawn that way).

Holli, the dream girl, lures the freed convict into Cool World. Her goal is to have sex with him, the only way a doodle can become a real woman. But Harris, who loves an equally pretty doodle named Lonette, warns Deebs that sex between noids and doodles is forbidden, because it will cause the dissolution of the boundaries between the worlds and destroy everything.

Deebs succumbs to Holli's seduction and the illustration becomes Kim Basinger in the flesh. There is chaos in Las Vegas as humans become grotesque cartoon figures and everything crumbles. Harris battles and defeats Holli, but is killed by her in the process. Fortunately, when a noid is killed by a doodle, he becomes a doodle. The animated Harris embraces Lonette, at last able to consummate their love.

The message of *Cool World* is that the boundaries between real life and fantasy must be strictly maintained, especially where dream girls are concerned. Holli Wood begins as the imaginary creation of a man denied access to real women, but she comes to take control of him. Harris understands the danger; his flight into Cool World after his mother's death was a virtual suicide, and his heroic return to the real world results in the death that should have occurred decades before.

Even in *Who Framed Roger Rabbit*, the barriers were respected. The Ink and Paint Club where Jessica worked was a place where toons were performers and employees, but the customers were human. It was the intersection of the two worlds. Toontown was dangerous; toons were invulnerable to bullets and falling boulders, but humans, like Eddie Valiant's brother, could be killed. Judge Doom plotted to destroy Toontown by extending the human world through it, via a freeway. The worlds of reality and fantasy can exist side by side, but they cannot mingle.

But Jessica keeps intruding on my world. In the summer of 1994, the *New York Times Magazine* ran an amusing essay on the many complimentary (often sexist) words to describe women. The illustration in the corner of the page showed four women placed in the shape of a square. The first, with her bouffant hairdo and long lashes was unmistakably Elizabeth Taylor. The second was a dark-skinned woman in an evening gown, probably Diana Ross. The third looked like a nightclub singer, possible Ann-Margret. There was no mistaking the fourth: long red hair half-concealing one eye, huge bosom, red sequined dress and long violet gloves. Jessica Rabbit.

I pondered for a few minutes over why the artist would have included my favorite toon in this group of legendary women. Then I thought of Liz having celebrated her sixtieth birthday at Disneyland, her body scarred by operations and her hair undoubtedly graying under the color; Diana Ross, still svelte and classy, but never again able to be Dorothy seeking the Wiz down the yellow brick road; Ann-Margret, who had rounded the "fifty" curve with me and Mr. Peabody. I recalled her as a vivacious, incredibly beautiful teenager, belting "Bye Bye Birdie." I—and the artist—recalled them as the dream girls they were, not what they had become, although grateful that they had made efforts to preserve those images.

Yes, I decided, Jessica had as much right as any of them to be included. Their images were no more real than hers. That's the nature of the dream-girl business. Jessica would never age, never change, and that's the *real* nature of the dream girl.

Keats never saw a movie, but he found the dream girl on a Grecian urn:

> *Bold lover, never, never canst thou kiss,*
> *Though winning near the goal—yet, do not grieve;*
> *She cannot fade, though thou hast not thy bliss,*
> *For ever wilt thou love, and she be fair!*

~ CHAPTER 10 ~

A Fragile Bond

My best friend wanted an appointment at my office.

I should say my former best friend, since I had last seen him twenty-five years ago. Jerry had been my closest buddy during eight years of elementary school. We chose the same high school, but wound up in different classrooms and, although we usually rode the subway to school and home, we were never together that much.

After not so much as a Christmas card for a quarter of a century, Jerry looked me up when he needed a psychiatrist. Seeing a psychiatrist can be scary, especially when you are raised in a family that would not dream of seeing a therapist, much less a psychiatrist, unless you were hallucinating Satan in full color and stereophonic sound, so maybe I seemed safe.

Before I became reacquainted with Jerry and even more so afterward, I thought about our childhood friendship and I realized how little we had actually shared then about our personal feelings and experiences. Here was a kid I saw every day at school, spent every Saturday playing ball with or Sunday playing cards, but whom, in some ways, I hardly knew. Yet I don't think our friendship was that atypical. I think that all boys, regardless of how inseparable they may seem to be from their buddies, never really are able to communicate well.

As a kid, I thought I learned a lot about women from Jerry, but what I chiefly learned was to stay away from them as much as possible. Jerry probably set my psychosexual development back four or more years. Maybe, by inadvertently teaching me to look (and look and look) before you leap and then not leap, it headed me toward a lifetime of analyzing situations as an impartial nonpartici-pant. In the office, at any rate.

Jerry was always popular. He was shorter than average, but handsome, with large brown eyes, a dimpled smile and wavy hair. Usually, shorter kids tend to be bullied, but Jerry was a good athlete and that always counted for a lot. By the time we entered puberty, the girls were even more susceptible to his charisma than the boys had been.

Jerry was the first boy (at least in our school) to date the uncontested dream girl. She was twelve at the time, one grade below ours. I know that, in retrospect, it sounds absurd to be talking about great romances between thirteen- and twelve-year-olds, but the intoxication we felt around the opposite sex then was certainly as great as anything that came later, even if the opportunity and action were more advanced.

I'll call the girl Coronis; she had one of those unique names that I have not encountered in actuality or fiction or newspapers since, and if I used her real first name here, a middle-aged woman in America and all her friends would know whom I was writing about. She was stunning. I know this is not a romanticized impres-sion stemming from infatuation, because I remember being with my family for Midnight Mass on Christmas Eve and Coronis walked into the church. She was wearing a blue overcoat that set off her blond hair to perfection and she had a wide-brimmed hat that framed her face like a halo. Every head, adult and child, turned to look at her and my mother whispered, "Who is she?"

If Coronis had a flaw, it was a jawline that was just a bit too strong. Otherwise, every feature, facial and bodily, seemed perfect. Still, I am sure that it was her hair, a sparkling golden blond shade, that made her seem unreal. I was incredibly disillusioned when, as a group of us sat sipping Cokes at our hangout, I teased her about coloring her hair. She blithely admitted that she did. It had never occurred to me that a twelve-year-old would be allowed by her mother to dye her hair, so I had assumed Coronis's hair had to be natural. (Her mother was a blond divorcée who had achieved moderate fame in burlesque, which might have explained it.) To this day, every time a blonde tempts me to a second glance, I tell myself, "Painting your head yellow does not make you beautiful." I married a brunette.

Jerry had won Coronis. Now, what that means, I'm not sure. They walked together after school, had Cokes, went to the movies on Saturday. Did they kiss passionately? Did they pet in the movies? Did he go to her house and did her mother leave them alone? I didn't ask and Jerry didn't tell me. They eventually broke up (I don't know why) and Jerry effortlessly moved on to the second-best girl (my rating) in the school.

Only once did I see Jerry in action and that, with its frightening aftermath, formed my earliest attitude toward women.

One of the girls in our eighth-grade class hosted a graduation party. It was held several weeks before school actually ended and it was unusual in several respects. First, it was the only time we had all been at a social event together. We all had friends and cliques among our classmates, but no sense of class unity. Second, the boys and girls were not close at all. At recess, we played or talked apart. Any peer-directed sexual interest from the boys had been exclusively directed at Coronis and the seventh-graders.

As a group, the seventh-graders were prettier and at least as physically developed as our classmates. I also suspected (when I studied psychology) that nine years in the same classrooms with the older girls had ingrained an Oedipal taboo, the type that accrues to sisters. But here we were (without the seventh-grade sirens) together in a social gathering and someone (I imagine it was the hostess, Marilyn) had decided we would play kissing games.

The games themselves were simplistic and rather tame. Usually, a girl would go into a secluded hallway and a boy would be sent out to join her. They would kiss, then the girl would go back to the group and send another girl out to take her turn. Some probably chickened out and made conscientious-objector compromises to abstain secretly. Christina, a proper classmate who had a slight British accent, offered me such a compromise, but I was seized with a sense of obligation to fair play and would condone no such cheating.

Back in the main group, most of us drank soda, listened to records and chatted, but a few had decided to extend the games. Christina was passionately pairing with Jim, a wild-spirited kid whose reputation as a charmer rivaled Jerry's. Jerry was kissing and rekissing Marilyn, the hostess. This surprised me, not because Jerry was so engaged, but because he was with Marilyn. Marilyn was one of the least attractive girls in our class and definitely the fattest. I had never envisioned anyone dating her and certainly not doing anything physical with her. The kisses seemed to be very passionate, since Marilyn was sitting with her legs extended and ankles crossed and, with each kiss, she would raise her crossed legs off the ground for the duration.

The shock for me came the next morning, Sunday. Jerry was my best friend, but Nick was probably his best friend. Nick lived in the same building as Jerry and his parents were friends of Jerry's. Nick went to a different school, which gave me a slight edge in weekday contact, but Nick was always available nights and weekends. After church, Jerry and Nick came to my apartment, as was our custom, to have breakfast cakes and coffee and shoot pool on my undersized table or play poker with my father. Jerry, however, was literally dazed. He looked sick, as if something terrible had happened. If the party had been weeks ago, instead of hours ago, I might have surmised that Marilyn had told him she missed a period—it was *that* kind of a look.

I pulled Nick aside and told him about the party. Nick decided to tease Jerry out of his funk. He started asking about Marilyn and what she had done to Jerry. Jerry was visibly getting angrier and put his coat on. Nick and I followed him into the hallway. Nick continued the teasing, moving directly in front of Jerry.

Then, Jerry punched Nick hard in the chest. Nick was twice Jerry's size and could have beaten him easily, but retaliation never occurred to Nick. Jerry's punch had never occurred to us a second before it was thrown. Jerry walked down the stairs and into the street, unfollowed.

In less than twenty-four hours, I had witnessed my best friend's brain turning to mush. He had seemed to be in a hypnotic trance. He had assaulted his lifelong buddy. If this had happened after a necking session with Coronis, I might have accepted it. Witchcraft from supernatural creatures I could understand. But fat, homely Marilyn? Women were obviously like weapons, I reasoned; Coronis was a sleek automatic and Marilyn was a battered blunderbuss, but either could destroy you if you got too close.

My terror was reinforced the following week in class. Christina, uncharacteristically, approached me after school and asked to talk to me. She poured out her heart, about how mixed up she felt after her necking session with Jim. She had never done anything like that before and wasn't sure whether she was in love with him or had just had her brains scrambled. I was only thirteen, with no psychiatric training. Okay, I got good grades, but why don't you ask me something about chemistry—preferably inorganic? I instinctively gave Christina some reassurance about her reputation and what a nice, sensitive girl she was and how complex love is. And I resolved to stay away from brain-scrambling activities.

Jerry made a rapid and uneventful recovery. We never talked about Marilyn. We never talked about *anything* meaningful. We talked about the Yankees and our teachers and our families, but not really about *us*. I don't think *any* of the guys did.

And now, Jerry was coming back, twenty-five years later, to tell me about himself. He hadn't been able to reach out to me as a kid, the way Christina, who barely knew me, did, and I hadn't been able to make the overture.

Jerry was still handsome, though heavier, but his face showed the erosion of years of hard living. He opened by saying he was "uptight about a lot of things" and that his home life "stinks—it's probably my fault."

I already knew about his first marriage, since it had been common gossip in the neighborhood. He had gotten married at twenty, been drafted into the army and sent overseas for two years. His young wife quickly found a boyfriend and the marriage was annulled on his return.

His current marriage had lasted eighteen years and he had three children, two sons and a daughter—seventeen, fourteen, and eleven. He "ran around a lot," he said, adding, "I always did that." He said his "real problems" had started six years ago when he was fired from a high-paying executive position in an investment firm because he "abused the code of ethics." He took a bank job at less than half his former salary, quit, and took a similar job.

But Jerry was a big spender, even when he didn't have it, so he got involved in a criminal operation, picking up and delivering cash. When his boss was killed for welshing on a deal and he himself was threatened, he got back into legitimate, low-paying work.

There followed a cycle of borrowing, some with the help of former business associates, some with less discriminating loan sharks. He bought a diner, which his wife wound up managing while he opened an employment agency. They both were working long hours, trying to pay off debts and raise their children.

His wife was critical and, Jerry said, he had a "tremendous ego" and didn't take criticism well. His wife would tell him that he had made every major decision on his own and it was usually the wrong one. She yelled at him, the way his mother used to, and he was the sort of person who rarely raised his voice. When she wasn't attacking him, she would show her displeasure by not having dinner ready or by picking him up late from work.

Jerry said he hated his kids. He felt he was always chauffeuring one or another to a game or an appointment. Meal times were chaotic and he tried to persuade his wife to arrange having dinner as a couple once in a while. He described his wife as from "the old Catholic school," rather inhibited sexually, and suffering from menstrual complaints.

One constructive outlet for Jerry was his love of sports. For years, he had coached children's baseball, football, and basketball teams, which often included his own youngsters. It had brought him closer to his children and won him esteem in the community.

As for the women, of whom his wife had never given an indication of awareness, they were never "serious," but always there. Lately he had been recycling, looking up at least two former extramarital partners during the past month. "I'm afraid of getting old," he told me. "Maybe it's a mid-life crisis." Except I had seen it begin at age twelve.

As I look over my notes for the three sessions we had, I note that they are marked "no fee." If he had insisted on paying, I would have accepted, but he didn't. He never came back and I didn't pursue him. I never heard from him again.

Had he gotten anything out of our contact? He had been trying to get his wife to do more with him, such as taking a trip to North Carolina with their oldest son to look at colleges, leaving him in a dorm for a few days while they went off alone. He was trying to include her more in their children's sporting events. He was joining her in non-athletic volunteer work at the schools.

Maybe he had realized, even before he came to see me, that he wasn't going to find validation in the singles bars and Parents Without Partners meetings where he had been seeking it. Validation, as always, was what all the questing was about. Charm the lady, win a smile and a few favors, then get out before she learns too much about you.

It was strange, I thought, that psychiatrists usually spend so much time trying to get their patients to recall and relate their early experiences and, in Jerry's case, I had been there at the start. If he hadn't always had a girl, maybe he wouldn't have always needed one later. If he hadn't always been so admired, maybe he wouldn't have bent so many rules to live in princely style. Maybe he peaked at thirteen when he had the love of Coronis and it was all downhill from there.

Some years after my brief reunion with Jerry, someone gave me an update on Coronis. There is only one woman with her name, so there was no mistaken identity. She was engaged to a doctor after two, or perhaps three, divorces. I don't want any more updates. I want to remember her as she was that Christmas Eve, a stained-glass window filtering in light from a streetlamp, illuminating her golden hair. Before I knew she used Lady Clairol "Canary Diamond."

Conspiracy of Silence

The girls talked and the boys played. That sums up my recollection of preadolescent and adolescent interaction. Once they outgrew jump rope and hopscotch, the girls simply walked together and talked, sat on benches and talked, sat in eateries and talked.

For the boys in the city, there were no manicured playing fields, but there was stoop ball and touch football and wastebasket-ball. If we weren't involved in a game, we were walking to or going home from a game. In bad weather, there were card games, chess games, pool.

Games offer structure and ritual. They allow release of emotions, the joy of victory and the agony of defeat, in situations that really do not merit strong feelings. Games promote pseudo-intimacy among boys.

Boys grow up in emotional isolation. They may be constantly surrounded by peers. They may be part of one or more teams. They may spend countless idle hours in one another's company, but they do not communicate, except perhaps in symbolic tales.

Watch the movie *Stand By Me*. Four preadolescent boys trek across the countryside in an adventurous search for a dead body. One tries to gross out the others with a story about a ridiculed fat boy who gets revenge by starting an epidemic of vomiting among the spectators at a pie-eating contest. One poses the provocative question: "Mickey's a mouse, Donald's a duck, Pluto's a dog—but what's Goofy?" Tempers sometimes flare and they nearly come to blows. They talk constantly, but it is only after interminable hours in forced company that the barriers are broken and true confidences are shared.

Much has been written about male bonding, the need men have to spend time with their peers and share emotional intimacy. Time together usually results in sharing little more than alcohol and recreation, free from the censure of women.

Just being accepted in the company of men confers a degree of validation. Inclusion means that the member meets the self-image of the others, that he will not embarrass them by behaving in a manner any more unworthy than they themselves would be guilty of.

Lapses into vulgarity or immaturity are tolerated. Weakness and vulnerability are less acceptable, for these flaws are those that the other men would least want to acknowledge.

Without being understood, one cannot be validated. Without self-revelation, there can be no understanding. If fellow males are incapable of providing validation, only females remain to supply it. And if no real women are available, the dream girl must fill in.

Hunting Games

Since the time of Cain and Abel, there has been rivalry among males, usually settled by one defeating or driving off the other.

Before they are taught manners (and even afterward), boys will seize one another's toys or push playmates to the ground in order to reach a destination more quickly. We can see countless examples of one man competing with another, from young lawyers trying to generate the most paperwork in the quest for a partnership to the exhausting one-on-one games of racquet ball in exclusive men's clubs and basketball in litter-strewn cement playgrounds.

But alongside this extremely natural proclivity for competition there seems to exist an equally strong, less easily met need to cooperate and to share. Freud called it the "herd instinct." It was the most controversial of his proposed instincts. The survival and reproductive instincts engendered some argument about whether we could speak of instincts to describe such complex human behavior, but no one would contest the idea that we all want to stay alive and that most of us want to engage in sex.

The herd instinct was less readily embraced as a concept, because togetherness does not seem essential for either the survival of the individual or the race. According to Desmond Morris, however, primitive men had a better chance of survival when they cooperated in bands than when they tried to be self-sufficient. When Homo sapiens, early in the course of evolution, turned to hunting animals as a major food source instead of gathering vegetable products, they adopted the strategy of the carnivores who hunt in packs. A four-legged beast might easily outrun a spear-chucking biped, but a band of men could surround their prey, one group driving the animal into the arms of their tribesmen.

When man became the prey of other men, a fraternal platoon stood a better chance against encroachers than one individual. The idea of strength in numbers did not require a human cerebrum to grasp it; baboons had set the example by fending off large carnivores long enough to allow child-toting females to clamber to safety.

Rivalry between males for mating rights to a female is one of the keystones of natural selection. Gorillas adhere to this code of aggression, with one male possessing a harem of females after defeating all rivals. Usually one or two of the leader's sons will be permitted to remain with the group, so that they may succeed the patriarch when he succumbs to death or infirmity. Without any knowledge of chromosomes, the father gorilla instinctively preserves as much of his genetic resources as he possibly can, using his sons as mobile sperm banks carrying half of his genes.

Chimpanzees have managed to abandon the winner-take-all imperative that characterizes the reproduction of gorillas, seals, horned animals, and lions. While male chimps will try to monopolize a female's attention or ward off other suitors, they live in packs consisting of equal numbers of males and females. Perhaps since they are blood relatives of one another, their skirmishes are rare and tame. What they have sacrificed in the insurance of passing on their genes, they have gained in their collective strength to insure the survival of the present generation.

Ontogeny Recapitulates Phylogeny

It is at this point that many people begin to raise objections. They protest any attempt to compare human behavior to that of animals. Such protesters are invariably women. Maybe men are so accustomed to being compared to animals, by such appellations as rat, ape, snake, weasel, wolf, and worm, that they have become insensitive to the intended slurs. More likely men find more to admire in the muscular, hairy, and aggressive gorilla than women do in the female of that anthropoid species, causing women to disclaim loudly any kinship.

My sixteen-year-old daughter, Laura, recently stumped me with the following brain-teaser, having warned me in advance that she did not fully understand the answer: An expedition of explorers makes an amazing find. They discover two perfectly preserved bodies, a man and a woman. And they know that these two people are Adam and Eve. How?

The man and the woman have no belly buttons. (The reason my daughter did not understand the answer was that she had the misconception, which I have often encountered among educated people, that mother and fetus are joined to one another at their respective navels.) Maybe *I* didn't figure out the answer because I think of Adam and Eve as having parents belonging to an apelike species one baby step removed from us.

I then posed to my daughter the most ancient of brain-teasers:

Which came first, the chicken or the egg?
and said there was no answer. I gave her m
always considered obvious and irrefutable.
reptiles, like the pterodactyl, evolved into f
birds, like archaeopteryx, and the chicken evo
first chicken resulted from a genetic mutation,
being similar to, but not quite, chickens. Thes
duced an egg from which the first true chicken   ne egg
preceded the chicken, unless you believe God zapped the chicken
into existence in the Garden of Eden.

The idea of evolution did not originate with Charles Darwin or
the geneticists. Every farmer understood the importance of
breeding only the sturdiest bulls or rams in order to produce the
largest, hardiest offspring. Dog breeders kept "the pick of the litter"
and destroyed runts with an eye toward the next generation.
Lamarck wasted his time cutting tails off mice to see if their offspring were born tailless; any unschooled stableman could have told
him that docking the tails of carriage horses did not result in foals
with docked tails.

It is curious that the most sophisticated and educated people,
who would proclaim themselves to be devout atheists or agnostics
and regard the Bible with as much reverence as they would show
Green Eggs and Ham, recoil with abhorrence at attempts to compare human behavior with that of animals and draw inferences that
a common biological impetus is in operation.

To them, I have three words to say: ontogeny recapitulates phylogeny. I doubt whether any scientific truth has ever been expressed
so thoroughly yet concisely. (I'll accept the merits of $E=mc^2$,
although I haven't applied it much to my personal belief system.)

So impressed was I with this scientific revelation that I have
adopted it as my automatic response to such annoying casual
inquiries as "What do you say?" or "What do you know?" Instead of
a flustered, "Oh, hi!" I furrow my brow, nod slowly, and intone,
"Ontogeny recapitulates phylogeny." No one has ever disputed me.

What does it really mean? Ontogeny is the biological development of the individual organism; the progression of a fertilized egg
to a ball of cells to an embryo to a fully formed creature ready for
life outside the uterus. Phylogeny is the development of a race or

it is usually applied not just to one species, but to the ...e animal kingdom, from water-dwelling invertebrates through bony fish, amphibians, reptiles, and mammals. The recapitulation means that a human embryo does not simply advance from a small humanoid to a large humanoid, but that its tiny body relives the entire march of evolution that took millions of years.

The early embryo has gill slits along its neck and it has a tail. If it is destined to become a fish, it will keep the gills; otherwise, the slits will close over as lung buds develop. The tail is kept by nearly all of the embryos, except for us ape-like types and a few other rebels. The spine starts as a cartilaginous rod; the shark stops there, but his bony brothers develop a more complex, harder backbone. The heart starts as a simple sac, much like the one a grasshopper uses, then subdivides into chambers, the mammals' going all the way to four.

At one point in their early development, the embryos of a swordfish, turtle, parrot, elephant, and human are, except for size, indistinguishable. They all start with the same C-shaped body, long tail, prominent eye bud, and row of clefts in the neck. Following an embryo to its predestined final form is a little like traveling on a turnpike. Until you reach the first exit, everyone follows the same initial stretch of road. The exit road for fish will ultimately lead to countless streets and lanes, each ending in a slightly different species. If you stay on the turnpike, you'll come to the exit for amphibians; if you stay on the main road, you will be riding with the lung-breathing reptiles.

By the end of the turnpike, the tail has become a bony coccyx, the limb bud features an opposable thumb, and the neural tube's anterior end has blossomed into a cerebral cortex. It's a nine-month journey, the start of which is shared with the lowly fishes.

Ontogeny proves that the life force does not start from scratch each time it invents a new species. Rather, it takes the initial blueprint as far as it can go and then makes the necessary modifications.

Brain Storms

My family always owned one or more cats. They spent most of their lives in a city apartment and, thanks to my mother's indulgence, developed very specific food preferences. One would eat nothing but fresh pork kidney. Another would eat only boiled codfish. Turned loose in the wild, one would have expected them to hunt for a supermarket.

Yet, when we took them to our rented summer home, their behavior was surprising. They would stalk and kill anything that moved: butterflies, slugs, caterpillars, and, rarely, a slow bird. It was not the slaying that was surprising, it was their devouring whatever they had killed. These pampered pets, who would have starved to death before eating canned cat food, were chewing on stuff that made Nine Lives cat food seem as appetizing as Sara Lee.

Instinct, of course. It was behavior that was contrary to their life experience from kittenhood and hardly gratifying from the gastronomic aspect. I never understood why Joy Adams had to teach Elsa, the lioness, to hunt, when my overweight, neutered felines would probably have pounced on any kangaroo rat, meerkat, or zebra that trespassed on our lawn.

Emasculated and sheltered as they had been, there was something in the genetic makeup of my cats that impelled them to hunt even when it made no sense to do so. Assuming that genes do not change as rapidly as society, it follows that men experience an inner imperative to hunt even in the absence of prey and hunting grounds.

Having already opened one can of worms with a foray into ontogeny, I have just released another abundance of annelids by implying that men's brains might be susceptible to influences that spare women; that male brains are different from female brains. This is an unpopular notion in a society that promotes the ideal of equality between the sexes.

Nature, unfortunately, is not a social libertarian. When she dealt out the chromosomes, males got short-changed. Oh, it is true that all normal humans (there are a few rare syndromes in which individuals have one extra or one fewer) have 46 chromosomes, comprising 23 pairs, but in the so-called sex chromosome pair, the female gets a nicely matched pair, while the male gets dealt one X chromosome and one stunted fragment called a Y.

I tend to envision chromosomes as "button candy," those cardboard strips studded with colored circles of sugar that break off.

The chromosome is the paper and the candy buttons are the genes. If you had a strip with a long row of button pairs and bisected it lengthwise, that would approximate a chromosome pair, with a gene at each corresponding location. You might have a yellow candy from your father and a green one from your mother, but the locations would match exactly.

A Y chromosome is cardboard with no candy. Every once in a while, some researcher will suspect he has found some type of gene on the Y chromosome, but it certainly is not the typical gene-laden chromosome. It is, however, more than a blank. It is the Y that gives the individual the appearance of being male. An individual with one X chromosome and no Y looks like a woman, with short stature, a broad shield-shaped chest with minimal breast development, and immature sexual organs with no menstrual periods or very irregular ones. Ovarian tissue, if present, is found in streaks, not well defined. A person born with two X chromosomes (the normal female comple- ment) plus a Y looks like a male, but with feminine breast develop- ment and fat distribution; the testes are small and he is sterile.

One important significance of this chromosomal imbalance is that about 4 percent of a man's genes will be unmodified by the influence of a mate. In the course of human development, there is a tendency to drift toward the norm. An unusually tall person will marry someone shorter, and their children, although perhaps slightly taller than average, will be shorter than the giant parent. The chil- dren, in turn, will wed mostly people of average height, with more dilution of the ancestral giant's genes. With rare exceptions, such as the gene for Huntington's chorea, a gene that would produce a dis- ease or defect is overruled by its normal mate.

In the case of the XY chromosome pair, one gene has all the say. Hemophilia and color-blindness are carried in this pair, with the result that only men are affected, except in the rare circumstances where *both* parents had the problem.

I present this well-known, undisputed information to show that men are definitely affected, in some ways, by genetic makeup dif- ferent from women. There are more men with exceptionally high IQs than women (sorry!) and more with mental retardation (sor- rier!). One explanation could be that, in the formation of certain aspects of intelligence, a gene pair, as females always possess, would modify tendencies toward the norm, while unopposed genes would produce marked deviations in either direction from the norm. In *Rain Man*, Dustin Hoffman portrayed an autistic individual, who despite childlike mentally retarded behavior, possessed phenomenal mathematical talents, such as instantaneous counting and selective accurate recall. In such well-documented idiots savants, it seems that some parts of the brain are overdeveloped in their capabilities, apparently at the expense of the total brain. I have never heard of a woman who was an idiot savant.

Any time one mentions differences in mental function and sex differences in the same paragraph or breath, controversy is bound to flare. Women are the objectors, and it is usually because they see themselves coming out worse in any comparison. Statements such as "Men have better mathematical ability, but women are better at discerning emotions" imply that men have talents that translate into dollars and power, while women should be consoled by their proclivity to serve others.

I refuse to believe that genetics can affect the eyes, the skeleton, and the blood but cannot affect the brain. The one difference is that the brain is so complex that it can improve and correct itself. A midget cannot work on growing taller. A color-blind man cannot improve his handicap by staring at a box of Crayolas. A hemophiliac must rely on others to supply his absent clotting factors. The brain, however, can be modified, within limitations, especially where proclivities are concerned.

Proclivities often affect our destinies more than abilities. I read somewhere that an elephant can run at approximately the same speed as a human sprinter. Given a race between the two, I would bet on the man, simply because I could not trust the elephant's motivation to run.

Women *can* become political leaders, astronauts, scientists, writers, and Nobel Prize winners. There are much fewer of these compared to men with similar achievements. They are obviously not incapable of doing what men do, but, like running elephants, would rather be doing something else.

Feminists claim that women choose to avoid high-achievement career pathways because society discourages them from such aspirations. This is certainly true in some areas.

A man carries an injured boy into a hospital emergency room and says, "This is my son. He's been badly hurt in an accident." The child is whisked into an examining room and the surgeon on call is summoned. The surgeon looks at the boy and says, "I can't operate on him; he's my son!"

Confronted with this apparent paradox, most people will fail to give the obvious solution: the surgeon is the boy's mother.

In the course of my own life span, I have seen medical school enrollment among females rise from 10 percent to 50 percent. I certainly cannot conclude that women evolved from a subspecies lacking medical ability into one with new genetic traits. But while more than half the doctors going into psychiatry and pediatrics are women, very few are surgeons.

Again, feminists will accuse the medical establishment of discouraging women from the more lucrative jobs. I disagree. I did not become a surgeon because I have bad eyesight and manual dexterity that is, at best, average. I became a psychiatrist because I *liked* relating to total individuals, not body parts, and had strong language skills and a good imagination. If women are intrinsically more empathetic and able to appreciate a patient's emotions, or if they are comfortable and happy with children, they will gravitate toward psychiatry and pediatrics. Most women doctors want to be wives and mothers, so it makes sense for them to choose a specialty that will allow them to have flexible working hours, with the option of reducing and increasing the time they spend practicing their profession.

I am making this lengthy digression into neuro-anatomy and genetics because in the rest of this book I will be making references to men's minds and how they work. If a woman is utterly opposed to the concept of any inherent differences between the sexes with regard to mental phenomena, she will automatically reject anything that I have to say.

It is my stance that our genes do influence our behavior, sometimes in the same way that similar genes direct lower animals and that genes and the brains they cause to be formed motivate the sexes differently. If you still disagree with this, you will, nevertheless, probably agree with me that men think differently even if that is solely the fault of their upbringing.

I do not, however, believe that we are slaves to heredity and anatomy. "Constella," who used to write the horoscope column for the New York *Daily News*, would always start with "The stars impel, they do not compel." I believe the same thing is true about biology; it impels us toward certain behavior, but the final choice we make might be something quite opposite. I call it the cortical override.

The Cortical Override

When I was a med student obligated to study anatomy and an aspiring psychiatrist, I always devoted any elective term papers to examining the biological basis of behavior. I wanted to know what made me tick. Honestly, I was most interested in the internal battles that went on between my intellect and my feelings toward the opposite sex. I was haunted by Don Juan's words: "My judgment was not to be corrupted: my brain still said no on every issue. And whilst I was in the act of framing my excuse to the lady, Life seized me and threw me into her arms as a sailor throws a scrap of fish into the mouth of a seabird."

I was no Don Juan. When I got giddy, irrational, intoxicated mental impressions in the presence of a woman, I moved a few paces back, just as I had learned when to switch from scotch and soda to ginger ale at cocktail parties. I was not contented with this degree of control. As a young teenager, I dealt easily with sudden genital stirrings, but this was affecting my *brain*, the organ that was a student's meal ticket.

I learned that emotional behavior originated in a group of primitive nuclei and circuits located in the brain stem and collectively called the limbic lobe. If you took a decorticate cat and cut the fiber tract called the fornix, you wound up with a very angry, irritable animal. The slightest touch or stimulus would provoke an intense, brief rage response: arched back, bristled fur, hissing and clawing, like the images that abound at Halloween. So you can conclude that the fornix mediates behavior that has to do with anger and fighting.

If you took a decorticate cat and destroyed its amygdala, a cluster of nuclei, you got a docile, hypersexual animal that licked everything, assumed sexual postures, and drooled. Clearly, the amygdala has a lot to do with affection and sexual behavior.

I just tried to slip something by you: the word *decorticate*. Before the experimenters began cutting specific tracts, they had scooped out most of the animal's cerebral cortex. The cortex is comprised of two convoluted hemispheres that make up about 90 percent of the brain's bulk, the thing mad scientists keep in jars and that you get when you order *cervelles de veaux*. The cat was left with the thalamus and points south, not much more than an enhanced spinal cord. Even a fish has more to work with.

It is remarkable that a cat without a cortex can do so much that a normal cat can do, reminiscent of the brainless Scarecrow in Oz. The point I want to make, however, is that normal cats do not show grossly aberrant behavior when their lower emotional centers are destroyed. The higher brain centers have come to control emotional behavior. I am sure that destruction of the lower tracts must have some subtle effect on the direction of a cat's behavior, but it is virtually negated by the cortex. Your average pet cat will hiss and spit if cornered and provoked, but it does not respond with such vehemence if you accidentally step on its paw; if you slap it, it will wisely run away, not take you on. The cat will respond with purring and rubbing if you pet it, but won't hound you like a horny sailor on shore leave.

This is what I call the cortical override. Our most basic impulses are always relayed to the higher centers for modification and judgment. Sometimes the lower centers have been rendered almost obsolete by evolution. Another name for the limbic lobe is the rhinencephalon, or "nose brain." The fornix, amygdala, and other emotional circuits receive their initial input from the olfactory lobe, the most primitive part of the cortex, the main higher center in the lowest animals. For most creatures, smell is a very important sense. It warns of the proximity of enemies long before they are in range of vision, so the threatened animal can prepare to fight or run.

Where sex is concerned, odors are necessary for attraction. Even among the apes, unless a female is in heat, she will not mate and males will not usually show any sexual interest. In humans, the role of smell is minimal. It is still probably more operative than we realize, since men who lose their sense of smell and taste through trauma to the olfactory fibers often lose their sex drive as well. Adolescent girls living in all-female dorms are said to menstruate earlier if there is casual exposure to males, such as workmen or staff on the premises, than if there is a total absence of men in their environment, and women who live together will notice that their menstrual cycles synchronize. There seems to be something in the air, possibly a pheromone, the odorific emission that governs animal attraction.

When the olfactory lobe with its interconnections to other brain centers was freed from most of its preoccupation with smell, it was able to assume other data-processing functions, including the deeper emotional experiences and associations that characterize human love and lust. What we lost in the process was sexual simplicity. Attraction became individualized and unpredictable. There was no longer the foolproof olfactory assurance that here was a fertile female, ready for sex, and, barring male rivals, there for the taking. A female impersonator in full drag might elicit a stronger arousal response in a thoroughly heterosexual male than a genuine woman who took less care with her makeup. A man could have cybersex with an Internet buddy who was an elderly male pretending to be a lascivious twenty-year-old woman. Our imaginations are forced to do the work our noses were initially intended to perform and they do a lousier job of it.

When it comes to sex, the cortical override has the final say. As a psychiatrist, I am very aware of it. I am in a position that involves women sharing their most intimate thoughts and feelings. While I am allowed to be empathetic, I am required to maintain a degree of emotional detachment and to admit none of the sexual or even personal feelings that might enter such a situation. Any time an attractive woman enters my office for the first time, I can realistically say, "That's another one I'll never have," knowing that the prohibition of therapist-patient sexual involvement is at least as strong as the incest taboo.

If that seems a terrible hardship and a difficult task, it isn't. Realistically, most men do not make inappropriate sexual advances to co-workers, relatives, baby-sitters, or strangers, nor do they feel a strong desire that they must overcome. Some men, of course, have never mastered or even used the cortical override and are perpetually leering, pawing, and harassing women. A larger number use the override just enough to discriminate when to trespass into an extramarital flirtation or affair and when to withdraw from a high-risk situation.

For me, the occupational hazard has its benefits. I have formed friendships with women far better than my bonds with men, free from feeling threatened by any potential sexual influx that might have dampened or destroyed them. I can rationalize my lack of "normal" male reaction by saying, "I'm married" or "I'm getting older," but marriage does not deter most men from temptation. I have encountered aged male patients who use their walkers to hobble after sixty-year-old "girls" and their Social Security checks to engage prostitutes, even when their genitals are as poorly operative as their cortical override. I can still deactivate my override when doing research on dream girls; it now takes more effort to switch it off than turn it on.

For some men, even professionals, the procedure is not effort-less. Once I was discussing a patient with a young resident I was supervising. He was one of the chief residents, nearly through his training, and highly regarded. He was telling me about an attractive, single young woman he had treated in the clinic, one of whose problems was a tendency to use drugs of various sorts to get high. After a session or two, circumstances led her to seek treatment else-where.

"I suppose it's just as well," the doctor sighed. "She could have manipulated me into anything. I probably would have wound up prescribing anything she wanted."

Before I responded, I had a flashback of an incident that hap-pened when I was a second-year medical student, doing a summer elective in a city hospital's gynecological service. My classmates had just learned to draw blood—on one another, not patients—but I was pretty experienced, having spent my first summer vacation on a research project that involved taking blood samples. Despite my rel-ative confidence, I said to the GYN resident supervising me, "If we have difficulty finding a vein, is there someone we can call for help?"

He sneered at me and said, "How can you be a doctor if you can't draw blood? Maybe you'd better dig coal instead!"

For a split second, I considered telling the young chief

resident, "If you can't handle counter-transference better than that, maybe you'd better dig coal." But I didn't. I commended him on his insight and told him he probably wasn't as susceptible as he thought. There are, after all, a few psychiatrists who do get sexually involved with their patients. (In one ludicrous case I read about, the psychiatrist terminated therapy and married the woman. She later sued him not only for divorce but for malpractice in encouraging personal intimacy.) Some psychiatrists maintain distance but gratify their egos by encouraging their patients to "explore the transference" by confessing feelings of sexual attraction and jealousy.

But the cortical override is there for anyone who wants to use it. Shaw's Devil says to Don Juan, "As to your Life Force, which you think irresistible, it is the most resistible thing in the world for a person of any character." For Don Juan, in his transition from hell to heaven, the goal is not to resist the life force, but to exert control and direct it in the most constructive and beneficial way. It is the aim of the brain, which Don Juan calls life's "darling object—an organ by which it can attain not only self-consciousness but self-understanding," to give foresight to blind drives.

So any time I say that men's sociobiological nature impels them to act in a certain way, feel free to say, "They don't have to!" and I will readily agree. DNA, the keystone of our genetic composition, may provide a good alibi in some murder cases, but it is not a good excuse for behavior that hurts others or oneself. The cortical override is powerful, but one cannot veto something without understanding what it is rejecting. Similarly, men and women should understand why Nature spurs men in certain directions before we can rein in harmful proclivities and override Nature.

The Ultimate Sex Organ

Male and female He created them.

—GENESIS 1:27

The Bible makes it clear that from the beginning there were two divine blueprints when humans were created. We are only beginning to decipher those blueprints. Any three-year-old can describe some of the differences between men and women, but other differences are still being disputed by our most highly educated adults, particularly those involving the brain.

The brain is often described by sex therapists as the most important erogenous zone. More than that, it is the most important sexual organ; not only does it direct us in our sexual acts, but it also dictates how we behave in all those activities and relationships that define us as men or women apart from reproduction and its preliminaries. In that role, the brain must require some distinct properties that differ in males and females.

Time magazine (January 20, 1992), in an article about gender differences and brain biology, quoted Jerre Levy, professor of psychology at the University of Chicago, as confessing, "When I was younger, I believed that 100 percent of sex differences were due to the environment." Then she recounted an experience with her fifteen-month-old daughter that shook her convictions. The child had just been dressed in a pretty nightgown and she walked into a room full of guests, "knowing full well that she looked adorable. She came in with this saucy little walk, cocking her head, blinking her eyes, especially at the men. You never saw such flirtation in your life." The brain researcher now concludes, after twenty years of investigation, "I'm sure there are biologically based differences in our behavior."

Objective differences have been detected in brains and on psychological testing. For the diehards, there is consolation that this evidence is not earthshaking in its implications. Men seem to be better at visualizing objects three-dimensionally; they can rotate a road map in their imagination more accurately than women. After the seventh grade, their math skills tend to exceed those of girls. Women, however, tend to be better at reading and at interpreting emotions from photographs of subjects. They have better vocabularies, as evidenced by being able to come up with twice as many synonyms for words. They have better memories for location and distribution of objects they have seen.

The chief gross anatomical difference between male and female brains is that women have a slightly thicker corpus callosum. This is the band of fibers that connects the two brain hemispheres and may signify more communication.

The implication that men rely more exclusively on their dominant hemisphere (the left one in right-handed people), while women use both, could explain why men seem more pragmatic and goal-directed, while women are more intuitive and emotionally attuned to their environment.

Women tend to localize their verbal skills in the frontal lobe, while men focus their language functions in the parietal. Since the frontal lobe is associated with intellect and the parietal with physical movement, the conclusion might be that men talk faster, but women talk smarter.

Women use both sides of the brain when spelling (but not during memory tests), while men use only their dominant hemisphere. The significance of this is probably small, but the evidence that the sexes are wired differently is strong.

Baby Talk

I had a close female friend in college, before women's liberation. She would periodically exclaim that life was not fair and that men, not women, should have uteruses and bear babies.

"But then they would be women," I would answer.

No, she would counter, they would still be men, only with uteruses. And I would insist that they would be women with hairy chests and no breasts and maybe even penises, but women, nonetheless, because the reproductive organs are what determine sex and the baby producers are female.

I was teasing her, but I wasn't that far off the mark. I later learned that it is the gonads (testes or ovaries) that officially determine sex. True hermaphrodites are extremely rare. They may look like men or women, or even have both a penis and vagina; what makes them hermaphrodites is the presence of both ovarian and testicular (often internal) tissue in their gonads.

More common are pseudo-hermaphrodites. They are usually female in appearance and, except for scanty pubic hair, tend to be sexually well developed. They fail to menstruate, which eventually brings them to medical attention. Biopsy of what should be an ovary shows testicular tissue; genetically, they are males. All embryos start out looking female, until their fetal hormones start changing the genitals to male form. For some reason, the turn-on switch was never activated, so they stayed female. Such individuals live normal lives as women, marry, and may adopt children.

In rare instances, hermaphrodites may have male appearance, including some that change from female to male at puberty, under the influence of a surge of testosterone from the testicular tissue. They may adapt well to their new sexual identity, but are always sterile.

We can better understand why Nature would design two different brains if we think in terms of function, not appearance, in defining a sex. Remember that Nature is economical, as we have seen in the embryo, not using a brand-new blueprint when parts of an old one are serviceable. Any modifications are bound to be the minimum necessary for Nature's goals. What are those goals? Most would agree they are survival of the individual and reproduction of the species. Of course, if you do not survive, you do not reproduce.

A woman is different in that she has babies and, as a mammal, provides nourishment for the infant. No matter how strong and swift and courageous she is, there are times of her life, such as late pregnancy, childbirth, and nursing, when she is going to be physically vulnerable. Nature likes to experiment and has included role-reversal in her repertoire: male seahorses accept embryos in a chest pouch and "give birth" to them, male jacana birds raise the chicks while the females seek new mates, and emperor penguin fathers stand in Antarctic snows for days incubating eggs held between their feet while maintaining erect posture worthy of a royal guardsman. This type of sex-switching parental option became impossible once uterus and mammary glands were assigned to one sex.

Humans are hunters. Vegetarians may like to think that Nature intended us to subsist on vegetable food rather than killing other creatures, but our eyes betray us. In grazing animals and other animals, such as rabbits, who serve as prey for meat-eaters and do not kill for food, the eyes are set on either side of the head, the better to scan the surroundings for danger. Wolves, foxes, and the cats have eyes set close together, in the center of the face, able to focus directly at the running prey they are pursuing. Where are your eyes?

If there was to be a division of labor between the human sexes, it would seem logical that men would take on the task of hunting for prey to feed himself and family, while the woman would be concerned with providing a safe shelter for children and limit her food-providing to gathering vegetable products. Among lions, and probably other carnivores, females hunt as well (lionesses almost exclusively), but a pregnant or nursing lioness has no enemies and the pack shares the kill. It would seem most advantageous to the survival of our species for the man to go out and hunt; not only is he bigger, he is more expendable in case the underdog prey scores an upset. So a male brain should be geared to linear pursuit, adept in sizing up terrain, and able to suppress emotions of fear or empathy toward fellow-creatures.

A woman's ability to perceive emotions would help her to relate to a preverbal child. A knack for remembering configurations could help her to return to areas where the bushes and trees had been particularly rewarding in their produce. Ability to communicate would be of value where a group of women, encumbered by children of various ages, must rely on one another if threatened, not confront an aggressor independently.

Man was designed to hunt, woman to parent.

We are still having children, but where did all the antelope go?

A Hunt for A Hunt

Hillbilly's Diary: *Jan. 12*—Snowing. Can't go hunting. *Jan. 13*—Still snowing. Can't go hunting. *Jan. 14*—Still snowing. Shot Grandma.

Usually the jokes I remember are the ones I have heard more than once. That one I read as a kid and it stuck with me, maybe because it is so understated and outrageous.

What do you do if you are a born hunter with no opportunity to hunt? With no game around, you might start killing people. This is not socially acceptable, except in the form of war, which had always been very popular until the weapons became so deadly that the risk became as great for the generals and the spectators as for the troops in the trenches. There are always wars going on somewhere in the world among people who must rely on killing at close proximity without the power of impersonal, long-range bombs and missiles.

War is not natural. Among mankind's fellow creatures, only five species of ants and two of termites are known to wage war against their own kind. You apparently do not need an advanced brain to wage war. Most creatures with advanced brains avoid it.

Sports and games are the most common substitute for the hunt. Desmond Morris points out that running and throwing are needed for primitive hunting; running gets you close to the prey and throwing (rocks, spears, boomerangs, bolas) fells it without hand-to-hoof combat. Teamwork also helps, both in trapping the prey and bringing it down.

Most sports involve running and/or aiming. When the major leagues held tryouts to find replacement players for the established stars who had been on strike, the hopefuls had to demonstrate their speed in sprinting and their ability to throw the ball from their fielding position. If they did poorly, they never got to bat. Maybe the new Babe Ruth was among those aspirants, a man who could have hit sixty home runs, but never had the chance to show his stuff. No matter. Running and throwing are the basic skills; you can learn to hit or pitch, but nobody can give you new legs or an arm.

Maybe sports are closer to war than to hunting. There are always winners and losers. The victory usually belongs to a side, not an individual; some score the runs or points, some make the outs or missed attempts, but the team shares the win or the loss equally. In high schools and colleges, tennis players and golfers, who tend to compete as individuals, are organized into teams.

In most sports, there is the threat of injury: the blind-side tackle in football, the beanball in baseball, the elbow beneath the backboard in basketball, the high stick in hockey. These blows, in turn, often result in fights, sometimes erupting in the two teams coming to support injured and assailants. It is true that these large-scale battles rarely result in serious injuries; among these athletes, intentional fighting is less harmful than hard play, but violence adds to the excitement.

Aggression and retaliation, although interdicted by the rules, are usually associated with desire to win. If two consecutive batters hit home runs off a pitcher, bet the person sitting next to you that the first pitch to the third batter will be close enough to force him to hit the dirt. Your bet will not be accepted, since batter, pitcher, and everyone in the park know what is coming.

During boyhood games of stickball, I had teammates become infuriated because, as a runner on first base, I was thrown out at second on a ball they hit to the outfield, depriving them of a hit. Remember, this was not an official league game. No records were being kept. The game would be forgotten as soon as it was over. Still, the desire for personal achievement exceeded all consideration of the team and the boundaries of reality.

Women will point out that girls also play sports. This is true, although the ones that have successful careers are usually those who excel in non-team sports, such as tennis or golf. Relay races in track or swimming are decided by cumulative effort, the summation of individual performances, not a concerted simultaneous effort by a group. Female basketball or volley ball teams may play hard and with skill, but I cannot recall ever seeing a fight break out among the competitors.

Sports remains a male province, where the best female never beats the best male. In tennis, Bobby Riggs, middle-aged and past his unimpressive prime, trounced Billy Jean King at her peak. In the annual New York City marathon, a dozen male runners invariably finish ahead of the women's champion.

Then there were the Colorado Silver Bullets, the first all-woman team to play its entire schedule against men. They were recruited from the entire country to play a forty-two-game schedule against minor league and semi-pro teams. Enchanted by the film *A League of Their Own*, I figured a team of excellent female players could make a decent showing against men far below major-league caliber.

The Bullets lost their opener against the semi-pro Northern League All-Stars by a score of 19 to 0. I was afraid some feminist group would sue the All-Stars for some sort of gender-related abuse. The Bullets ended their season with six wins and thirty-six losses. If this was sport, they may be clubbing baby seals on the infield next season. Worst of all, the women did not seem to be discouraged by their showing. Apparently, emerging alive and unmaimed was equivalent to a winning season.

Women engage in sports the way they engage in war. They may have the skills, they may perform adequately, but they never engage in one-to-one combat or killing at point-blank range, in the way of the hunter. Shaw's Devil said of man, "His heart is in his weapons." Hers is not.

Unfriendly Games

Oswald Jacoby, probably the world's most expert poker player, once said that there is no such thing as a friendly game of poker. If he is trying to take a man's money and a man is trying to take his, there is nothing friendly about that.

Women play cards perhaps more than men, but they do not play poker. When I was a youngster, two elderly female neighbors would invite my brother and me to play canasta, a wacky game played with two decks, including jokers, that included additional wild cards, bonuses for red threes, useless black threes, and the strategy of freezing the discard pack with a joker until it could be liberated. For a brief while, we augmented the idiocy by playing samba, a three-deck version of canasta. I was too young to know that men did not play canasta.

Women now have generally reverted to bridge, a game played by men at the professional level of competition, but rarely socially. Unlike poker, where collaboration invites a bullet, bridge is always played by cooperative teams. There are bidding conventions that allow partners to convey information about their hands to one another, but secret signals are considered cheating. If opponents are not familiar with a convention you are using, they have the right to ask for an explanation of what you have been telling one another. Scores are meticulously kept. If you play for money, you base it on points at the end of the session; it is not constantly changing hands during the game.

The chief difference between poker and bridge is the bluff. You bet on each hand depending on the strength of what you hold and your chances of improving. A bet usually means your hand is worthwhile. Raising someone else's bet means you feel your hand is better than his. Checking, instead of betting, means your hand is not very good. Dropping out is self-explanatory.

Good poker players often bluff. They bet on a hand as if they are holding something a lot better than it really is. The aim is to intimidate opponents into dropping out, rather than losing more money. It is nonverbal lying, and it is not only tolerated, it is expected.

Poker, then, can depend as much on psychological acumen as on luck and skill. A good player will try to discern what an opponent has by his expressions and manner, not by his actual bets. You may learn that a man habitually looks concerned, hesitates, then says, warily, "I'll raise you," when he has a terrific hand, but throws in his chips with a hearty, "I'll raise that!" when he's bluffing. Some guys *never* bluff; let them have the pot. Some start bluffing after they have lost a few big pots. If you pay attention only to the cards, you won't win.

There are ethics despite the sanctioned deceit. I always ask, "Any house rules?" (i.e., rules that are not in the standard books) and "What about sandbagging?" Sandbagging is the strategy of checking (no bet) with a good hand, then raising when someone else bets. This allows you to wager more than you could on an initial bet, which usually has a limit. It is a sound strategem, but some people regard it with as much abhorrence as concealed aces in your sleeve if you do it in the middle of a game. So, I ask first.

I have played poker with women in family games. They do enjoy it, but show little concern for the money. A good poker player has the same chance of drawing good hands as a bad one; what makes him a winner is not betting the good hands, but throwing in the bad ones. Oswald Jacoby was so rigid in his refusal to play losing hands in hope of improving them that one opponent said, "Gee, if everyone played the way you do, there would be no game." Jacoby conceded he was right. Jacoby would not sit in a game unless there were two "fish" present, bad poker players. He was interested in making money, not matching his skill against other good players.

The women would say that we were playing for stakes so small that it did not matter whether you won or lost. They wanted to play all the hands to the end. To me, the point was coming out ahead, even if the monetary amount was small. You had to play the same way whether there were pennies or dollars in the pot. Of course, I have encountered many men who played with the attitude that they were in the game for fun, not profit, like the "fish" Jacoby sought. But I have never met a woman who played the game conservatively.

There is one other difference between men and women that I learned at the card table, and I am sure many will dispute me, since I have never seen it written elsewhere. Women have very little interest in the laws of probability. I have tried, with absolutely no success, to persuade intelligent female relatives that it is folly to draw one card to fill an inside straight (e.g., you are holding a 3, 4, 6, 7, and need a 5). I explain that the odds are 11 to 1 against succeeding. The money you stand to win rarely justifies the investment to stay in and draw. An open-ended straight (e.g., 3, 4, 5, 6, needing either a 2 or 7) offers 5-to-1 odds and is worth it, unless most of the players have already dropped out. They listen politely, then draw to the inside straight the next time they get the chance.

Worse, when they are successful, they point out that I was wrong. It *was* a good play and their winning proves it. Women will even draw two cards in an attempt to fill out a three-card flush. In one circle of noted writers, three cards of the same suit became known as an "Esther flush" because Esther, the wife of one of the men, persisted in holding and drawing to such hands.

Are some women gambling addicts? Of course they are, but go into a casino and notice the difference between men and women. Women rarely play anything but slot machines. There is absolutely no strategy in playing slots; you press a button or pull a lever and wait to see if you won. A few may play roulette, which takes as much analysis as a wheel of chance at a charity bazaar. The simplest bets, such as red or black, odd or even, or one number, offer the best odds. Rarely do they play blackjack, and I am sure no woman has ever been barred from a casino for counting cards, a difficult mental skill that can let you beat the house.

I am not saying that women cannot master the concept of probability. Countless women have passed statistics courses and algebra courses, which require a sound knowledge of probability. Once they have learned it, they disregard it. In *Peggy Sue Got Married*, Kathleen Turner played a woman who went back in time to relive her adolescence. In one scene, she tells her algebra teacher that she knows, with certainty, that she will never use algebra in her life. That is the way most women feel.

Finally, I will let you in on a male secret that I call statistical addiction. You may have been amazed that a man who never opens a book or moves from the television set can spout batting averages, league champions from past years, and other trivial sports data with such accuracy. Some men join Rotisserie Baseball leagues, where they select fantasy teams by weighing one player's statistics against others and wager that their team will compile the best overall records as the real-life counterparts play out the actual season.

Then there is tabletop baseball. I am a controlled Strat-O-Matic addict; I am controlled because I limit the time I play the game and compile records to a few hours a week. I am an addict because I believe that I could literally play the game for days on end, in isolation, perfectly contented. There are boys and men who play out entire seasons and publish their statistics as proof. Because in real life fourteen pairs of teams can play simultaneously, but one man can recreate only a game at a time, the number of hours spent by these addicts is staggering.

One man said he could not wait to retire because he could spend all his time playing Strat-O-Matic. Another, when his fiancée left him, said, "Good! Now I have more time for Strat-O-Matic." Novelist Robert Coover wrote a brilliant book, *The Universal Baseball Association, Inc. J. Henry Waugh, Prop.*, about a lonely accountant who invents his own baseball game and populates it with fictitious players. The game expands into a universe of its own, with imagined off-field escapades, politics, ballads, and legends. When an outstanding young pitcher is "killed" by an exceptional series of dice rolls, the accountant progressively withdraws from reality, quits his job, and becomes totally immersed in the game. I know Coover must have played Strat-O-Matic or one of its precursors, such as APBA Baseball.

One January, on the day that the new set of Strat-O-Matic cards was released, about 150 men and boys lined up outside the factory in Glen Head, New York, to be the first to acquire the new cards. There was one woman among them. She was probably buying the cards for her son. I have never seen a published letter from a female Strat-O-Matic player.

A simple explanation is that women are not that interested in baseball. This is not universally true. There *are* female fans. Hilda Chester, who attended all the Dodger games in Ebbets Field, is probably the most famous fan in baseball history. The girl who shot Phillie first baseman Eddie Waitkus because she was in love with him was an avid fan. Susan McCarthy, the wife of baseball analyst-historian Bill James, not only is a devoted statistician, but she provided a service that James could not accomplish himself: She reviewed photos of players and selected the best-looking and ugliest men for each decade. There are women who love the game; they do not fall under the spell of the statistics, which have an existence and permanence far removed from grassy diamonds and sweaty humans.

Tabletop baseball can be and is played often by two opponents, each managing a team. It can also be played, as J. Henry Waugh played his game and I play mine, by one person who manages all the teams. It is played with individual cards recreating a player's performance during an actual season and dice that determine what happens during any one play. As manager, you select your lineups and pitchers and let the dice do most of the work; at times you must make decisions regarding strategy or substitutions. With a little expertise, you know, based on probability, what moves are correct. You cannot predict the outcome, but you play according to the odds. You keep full statistics and watch your season progress. The winning and losing streaks, the individual spurts and slumps, the injuries and the substitutions they necessitate form an unfolding story, which you help create but do not control. You are overseeing a small universe where all the happenings can be tabulated and preserved in perfect order.

For men, I believe that there is a profound reassurance in the laws of probability. They say that we cannot predict events with absolute certainty, but we can know what is likely to happen and make our decisions accordingly. At the card table, the craps table, or at your desk with Strat-O-Matic, you can say, "I made the right play, regardless of the outcome." Would that all of life were so simple.

I suspect that men have this unique fascination with games based on probability because they are risk-takers. They ask, "Do I try to hunt this animal or does it have a good chance of killing me? Do I fight this guy or back off? Is it dangerous to go into this area by myself? How dangerous?"

Perhaps it is women's commitment to their children that makes them far less interested in probability. My mother used to tell the story of a mouse in her living room that would not run from her but stared at her menacingly until she killed it with a broom. When she later pulled open the sofa bed, she found a nest with five baby mice. Females are less foolhardy than men, but they have imperatives that make analysis of odds irrelevant.

Mating Game

For a few years, there was a chess shop in Greenwich Village called The Queen's Pawn. The proprietor was a female chess champion. It was unique because chess-playing women, like poker-playing women, are a rarity.

Many years ago, *Psychology Today* ran an article offering a psychoanalytic explanation about why men played chess and women did not. It postulated that attacking and defeating the king recreated the Oedipal conflict. Since men had more unresolved conflicts with their fathers than women, only men played chess.

I do not think one has to invoke Freud for an explanation. Chess is a game designed to simulate war. The pawns are the infantry, the knights are cavalry, the bishops were originally ships, the rooks were elephants, the forerunners of tanks. The queen, in the Orient where the game originated, was a male chancellor of war, later feminized by the chivalrous English. The goal is to attack your opponent, decimate his troops, and vanquish the king. The word *checkmate* derives from *Shah mat*, the king is dead.

Women are quite adept at dealing with objects in two-dimensional configurations, which is how chess is played. They simply have a distaste for war, possibly inherent. Eve, in Shaw's *Back to Methuselah*, says to Cain, "If you, Cain, had had the trouble of making Abel, or had had to make another man to replace him when he was gone, you would not have killed him: you would have risked your own life to save his.... That is why there is enmity between Woman the creator and Man the destroyer."

Young men today do not play cards or chess as much as they used to. My generation could spend hours with 52 pieces of cardboard or 32 pieces of wood or plastic. Now, kids require $50 video game cartridges for their costly electronic systems.

What has not changed is that the video games are played

mostly by boys. Most of the games involve symbolic killing of a stream of opponents. Even the more childish ones involve zapping an opponent into oblivion or getting killed off yourself: the Mario Brothers must destroy a succession of running, flying, or swimming monsters, and even in the Disney World game by Nintendo, you must destroy spooks and pirates.

The other type of popular game replicates professional sports: football, basketball, soccer, baseball. Females do not go anywhere near these. Combat and sports, again: the substitutes for the hunt in which modern man can no longer participate.

I read one interesting article about homemakers who had become hooked on one of their children's video games, Nintendo's Tetris. This game involves no competition or combat, not even any human or animal figures. Groups of four squares descend from the top of the screen, arranged in different configurations: straight line, square, **L**-shape, etc. The goal is to rotate and move the groups as they fall to complete unbroken lines at the bottom. Each completed line is removed, making room for more falling blocks. The pace gets faster and the game ends when the screen is filled with unremoved blocks.

Tetris is a game of spatial relationships in two dimensions and putting things in order. There is no hint of aggression, no opponents to vanquish. One could predict it is a game that would appeal to women, if one was willing to assume that male and female brains are different in their proclivities.

I asked my older daughter, who spends a lot of time on the college campus, whether the girls today ever get together to play games. She confirmed what I expected. They get together and go shopping, to movies or restaurants. They talk. Guys, she said, play sports or video games and drink beer when they "talk." She doubts that they talk much, except about their games.

Where Have All the Dragons Gone?

In a section on games men play, in a book about fantasies, I have to mention Dungeons and Dragons, a blend of playacting and combat games that captivated large numbers of high school and college students in the eighties. Instruction books and figures are still being produced, but I doubt that there are anywhere near the number of players that participated at the height of the craze.

Each player assumed an identity. Usually his strengths and weaknesses were determined by throws of the dice, which influenced what type of character he would become. Warriors depended on physical strength, magicians on spells, thieves on guile. You could be a cleric, an assassin, a dwarf, or a bard, even if you were female. Your character, if he survived, would accrue points that increased his capabilities and enabled him to face progressively stronger opponents.

The success of the game depended on a devoted player who assumed the duties of dungeon master. He set up the scenario and ran the game. He plotted out the land, dungeons, caves, and castles that the band of players would visit, assembled an array of human adversaries and monsters to throw at them, and invented the rewards.

The players got to make choices in the course of play as to which routes to take and how to deal with the opponents they met. There was always combat, determined by dice throws that took into account the strengths and weaknesses of the combatants. A good dungeon master had enough knowledge of probability so that players did not get killed quickly and usually won or survived.

A psychologist who served as dungeon master for a group of college students recounted in *Psychology Today* how the girlfriend of one of the players came as an observer. The young man habitually assumed the persona of an alcoholic dwarf named Grogg, whose antics got the rest of the company into deeper trouble. During this particular session, the players were the guests of a king and queen. Grogg decided to stick his hand down the queen's bodice, which moved the group quickly from banquet hall to the dungeon.

"I suppose you've never seen Grogg before," the dungeon master said to the visiting girlfriend.

"On the contrary," she replied, "I've been in bed with him several times."

The game received considerable notoriety when the parents of a student who committed suicide blamed his death on his preoccupation with the fantasy world. Games were moved by some enthusiasts from the safety of a large table with cardboard diagrams to the mazes of tunnels and basements in the bowels of academic institutions. Rona Jaffee, in 1981, fictionalized some of these bizarre happenings in a best-selling novel, *Mazes and Monsters*.

Relatively few coeds played Dungeons and Dragons. I never heard of a dungeon mistress running things, although one or two might have tried it. One of the four students in the Jaffee novel is a girl, but she seems to be in the game because the boy she loves is involved.

Dungeons and Dragons, like most games, is a man's (or boy's) game. It involves the laborious construction of a fantasy universe, elements of warfare, a preoccupation with probability, and the keeping of statistics for each player.

It should be noted that fantasy worlds are always the creation of men: Tolkien's Middle Earth, Carroll's Wonderland, Baum's Oz, C. S. Lewis's Narnia, and Mallory's Camelot. Women sometimes create a small world of characters, as in the case of A. A. Milne's Pooh stories or Beatrix Potter's Peter Rabbit tales, but the environment lacks the scope and detail of the male fantasy worlds.

Scientific evidence tells us that women, in general, are more proficient in reading and have better verbal skills. Yet most writers are men and, in the world of fantasy, they are virtually unopposed as its fabricators. Women are too pragmatic to engage in such stuff. Or maybe the fantasy gene lies in the XY chromosome pair, so only men fall victim to its effects.

When Dungeons and Dragons players formed their characters, their degree of intelligence, physical strength, magical ability, etc., were determined by the roll of three dice, adding the totals for a score ranging between 3 and 18. The odds of rolling a 3 or an 18 are 1 in 216 for each, a probability of 0.5 percent, versus 27 different ways to roll a 9 or a 10 (12.5 percent probability). One of the traits a character possesses is charisma. With strong charisma, you can pet a roaring dragon, enslave an ogre, or persuade a warrior to hand you his sword.

If the dream girl exists in the realm of Dungeons and Dragons, she will be easy to identify. She's the one with eighteen points of charisma.

Ready to Fight

Once, when employed in a state hospital, I joined an assembly of staff members for a brief course in management of the violent patient.

The instructor called on me and told me to put a choke hold on him. Without any forethought, I placed my left arm behind his neck, grasped my right biceps, put my right forearm over his throat, and gripped my left biceps to complete the circle.

"Whoa! Hold on!" he shouted. I released the hold. "Just one arm," he said. He then proceeded to demonstrate how to break the hold.

Later, he approached me and said, "In all my years, I've never had a doc put a double-arm choke hold on me before."

I shrugged. "I had a book on American combat judo when I was a kid," I explained.

"So did I," he said, "but I don't remember it."

"I ride the subways every day," I said. "I suppose I'm always mentally rehearsing these things, just in case."

Violence is part of the male universe. It differentiates men from women. Boys grow up fighting other boys or learning how to avoid fights without loss of honor.

I am not saying that the average man is a good fighter or willing to fight. He may be terrified by a situation in which he is confronted by an aggressor. Still, it is equally disturbing, probably more so, to back down or flee.

Every male is a potential adversary. In the playground, an accidental shove during a game or a particularly stinging taunt could cause a physical confrontation, even among friends. It didn't matter how well you fought, but whether you were willing to fight that determined where you stood in the pecking order. The boys who never fought were endlessly tormented by the others. It was worth taking a few punches to avoid that fate.

Recently I was in my office with a 280-pound man whom I have been treating for fifteen years. He needed a prescription for a controlled drug, and I had to open a fresh pad, which I had received in the mail. I took out my pocket knife from my jacket and opened its five-inch blade to cut the tape on the package.

"You carry *that*?" he asked.

"Have to open prescription boxes, don't I?" I said blandly.

"We *all* carry something," he said. He lived in a bad neighborhood in the Bronx. "Sure you know how to use it?"

"I went to medical school, remember? I took anatomy."

I do use the knife to open prescription boxes, not hearts, but I have carried one for twenty-five years, ever since I was held up in an elevator by two guys who had a knife when I didn't. I was making home visits alone, a very dumb thing to do. When the tall teenager pulled the knife, I took out my wallet, handed him the eight dollars in it and returned the wallet to my pocket. I was afraid he was going to order me out of the elevator and go to the roof or staircase where he could rob or stab me at leisure, so I grabbed for the knife, which resulted only in cutting my hand. I then threw myself on the floor of the car, yelling, figuring that if he stabbed me, he would hit a lung or kidney, a wound I could survive.

Maybe it was a dumb strategem, but it worked. The muggers grabbed the manila folder of forms I was carrying, probably thinking there were checks in it, and ran off the elevator and down the stairs.

I gave notice at that job, and for the remaining weeks, never went out to homes alone. I left my wallet, rings, and watch in the office, wore a trench coat buttoned at the neck, wore dark glasses that looked tougher than my regular lenses, kept a thick notebook over my heart, and carried a pepper-spray canister in one pocket and a knife in the other. It seemed that the inhabitants of the run-down neighborhoods my team serviced would look at me with an expression that was almost fearful.

If you asked me if I had any further dangerous encounters, I would be tempted to say no, but then I would be disregarding the times I have been approached on the street by aggressive strangers, who may have been merely panhandling. "Back off!" I have said. "I don't know you!" Take two steps back, look straight at him, one hand on the knife with its blade now open, the other on the pepper spray, uncapped. The intruder usually protests, berating me for my paranoia, but he backs off.

I was jostled and pushed on the street one day by a teenager coming out of a bar, obviously stoned. I warned him off and asked a shopkeeper to call the police. The guy, with two friends, was still in the vicinity. The cops searched him and I pondered the irony that *I* had the weapon, not him. He told the police that I had run into him with my open umbrella, which I may have, and his friends told the police he had been mentally unbalanced since his mother's death. The police refused to take him to a hospital for psychiatric evaluation and let him go, with a warning not to "bother old guys."

I am not a great physical specimen and I have not been in a fight since high school, but I follow the same rules that I did as a youngster. Look your adversary in the eye, set limits, and be prepared for anything. In the psychiatric emergency room, a doctor frequently encounters "bad dudes," people with no psychosis, but who are under the influence of drugs or trying to manipulate you into giving them a bed or a handout. There's an art to setting limits without provoking an attack. I have known doctors who were seriously injured by patients and it was almost always because they tried to be authoritarian and never considered the possibility of the attack.

Few women are ready to fight or resist. I had a female relative who held a black belt in karate. Three times she was robbed in her lobby or on the street and never used her martial arts skills. Maybe she was sensible and maybe she would have acted if the robber had physically assaulted her, but a male with similar training would probably have felt obligated to use it.

My daughter told me a story about a coed who was approached in the lobby of her dorm by a young man. He stuck a firm object in her back and said it was a gun. He directed her to take him to her room, where she got her money and credit cards. Then, he went into a series of stores with her, directing her to purchase items for him. Finally, he told her to accompany him to a deserted park. There he warned her not to follow him and left.

"Well, what could she have done?" my daughter said.

"I'll tell you what," I fumed. "When she went into one of the stores, she moans and falls to the ground, faking a faint or a seizure. Even if the guy had a gun, which I doubt, he was not going to shoot her in front of a bunch of witnesses, especially if he didn't know whether she was really ill or not. That was certainly safer than going to a deserted park, where he could have killed her with impunity."

This is not a book of advice on how to behave in dangerous situations. Police usually advise people to offer no resistance on the grounds that the assailant's intent is *probably* not to kill but to rob or rape. Yet men do kill victims, particularly women, especially if they are safe from detection.

The point I do want to make is that men would feel a profound sense of shame at being passive victims. A doctor I knew was robbed in his apartment building by men with a knife who followed him into the elevator. He experienced rage afterward and says he ran into the street hoping to find them. After my elevator trauma, I felt a curious sense of exhilaration. I no longer had to wonder whether I would resist or punk out in such a situation; I may have acted stupidly, but now that I knew what I was going to do, I would be more ready next time.

The women I work with will wait for me at night to walk them to the subway. I know that it's my obligation to protect them in any way that I can and I accept that, just as I instinctively put my body between a belligerent male patient and a female resident doctor. I remind myself that Tupac Shakur took seven bullets, including two in his head, at close range and survived. There are worse things than getting shot or stabbed.

The streets are rougher than they were when I was a kid. We lived with the threat of fistfights; today, high school students in the inner city pack guns and I have treated patients whose young sons have been killed for talking to a girl or "dissing" (making a disrespectful remark) a classmate. These cases do not even make the New York City newspapers because they are so common.

Men are potential enemies. Every proper banker or mild-mannered accountant has to face frequent confrontations: the driver who cuts you off and curses at you, the guy who wants the same parking space that you do, the salesman who insults you, the vagrant who hassles you, the passenger who pushes you on the subway to get to a seat. Most times, you let it go, but it takes its toll on your psyche.

As with the gorillas, most hostile encounters between human males consist of posturing and threats, with no physical harm done. One or both parties back down in a way that preserves the dignity of both.

Competition with other males is an inevitable part of being a man. Women may consider it immature, vain, and stupid, but it is not likely to change. Men depend on women for their emotional security because they cannot trust other men.

As Pogo said, "We have met the enemy and they is us."

~ CHAPTER 11 ~

Dream Girls and Other Psychosexual Nightmares

*T*he dream girl: good or evil?

She's probably like the girl with the curl in the middle of her forehead. When she is good, she is very, very good, and when she is bad, she is horrid.

At her best, the dream girl comforts boys during their periods of greatest emotional isolation, alleviates loneliness, and helps them rehearse for their first real romance.

At her worst, she fosters unrealistic expectations in men and destroys potentially good relationships by encouraging men to regress to an unhealthy fantasy.

She is a fantasy, unique for each man, but common enough that all men know who she is and virtually all have experienced her in one form or another. Like the prostitute and the madonna archetypes, she has a place in the male collective unconscious.

Bad Girls

Because of the dream girl, we tend to think of female fantasy figures as beautiful and benevolent creatures, but classical mythology and folklore abound with fascinating but destructive women who lure men and then destroy them.

Lilith is the grandmother of the bad girls. According to Hebrew mythology, she was the first wife of Adam, before Eve. In paleo-feminist fashion, she refused to be subservient to Adam and bolted into the cosmic void, where she gave birth to all manner of demons.

The Greeks gave us the sirens, who tempted sailors to approach by singing to them until the ships foundered on the rocks where the temptresses were perched. They gave us the Furies, who pursued and tormented relentlessly those guilty of crimes; the hybrids, such as the lion-bodied Sphinx who met her match in the ill-fated Oedipus; and the Harpies, who had birdlike wings and talons.

The Bible begat Delilah, Salome, and Jezebel, whose names live in infamy.

Medieval tradition celebrated the succubus, a female demon who engaged sleepless men in acts of nocturnal intercourse, a not unpleasant practice that drained them of their vitality.

America had its witches, the minions of Satan who flew on broomsticks to participate in profane ceremonies and uninhibited revels.

Young boys today who have abandoned the classics might not have been exposed to this plethora of deadly women, but thanks to the home video collection of Disney classics, they have access to their own harem of hellions: Snow White's Wicked Queen, Maleficent the evil fairy, Wonderland's Queen of Hearts, Camelot's Mad Madam Mim, Cruella de Ville, Madam Medusa, and Ursula the sea witch. Even Tinker Bell, in a fit of jealousy, tried to exhort the Lost Boys into shooting Wendy down while in flight.

Under Threat

A close look at male myths about women reveals a recurring theme, that of the female, often beautiful, who will destroy the men whom she can seduce. She usually has magic powers, which render the man's free will inoperable.

Men are powerfully attracted to women, a situation that may result in considerable satisfaction, but more often will lead to frustration. Men have the unenviable role of initiating courtship; they may not build elaborate twig structures like the bower bird, fan their tails like a peacock, or wave a stick like a chimpanzee, but they do have to attract the woman's attention and sell her on their desirability.

They know they are in competition with other men, even if none are in the immediate vicinity. Women are selective and will be putting the new arrival through a mental screening process, comparing him against her preconceived standards and any males she has recently met. This is not a situation analogous to the dream-girl syndrome, where a fantasy woman interferes with a real-life relationship. This is a situation in which the woman is playing for keeps with real men. The man may not have to bang heads with his rivals, as the deer and sheep do, or bite an opponent into submission like a lion or wolf, but in the arena he may face elimination without even a chance.

So, here is woman, whom he desires intensely, but who can reject and exile him for no reason other than his failure to measure up to the competition. It's enough to drive a man to inflatable dolls.

The other problem men face is the erratic course of their own libido. At the peak of their arousal, every muscle fiber is tensed, their blood pressure and heart rate are increased, their adrenaline is flowing, and, of course, their penises are erect. Immediately after orgasm, everything shuts down abruptly, as though the air had suddenly been let out of a balloon. The proud organ, tall and stiff as a unicorn's horn, has become like a flaccid turkey wattle. The preceding experience makes it more than worthwhile, yet there is the nagging wish that men could remain permanently in that potent, exhilarated state.

One can easily see how the myth of the succubus was generated. First perceived during a vivid wet dream accompanying nocturnal emission, she is transformed by male guilt and frustration into a demon who robs him of his vitality and virility by her demands.

But if the men fortunate enough to have a sexual partner feel sometimes frustrated, their discontent is minor compared with the misery of those doomed to celibacy by their failure to meet society's standards of achievement. I am particularly aware of this because I treat large numbers of schizophrenic men. Most of them live celibate lives, reluctantly, because, despite average-to-handsome looks and average intelligence, they live on the fringes of society. Most subsist on disability checks. Those who find employment are usually messengers or fast-food handlers. Their social skills are marginal. When they try to sell themselves to a prospective partner, there is not much in the display case. They sometimes engage prostitutes, but even this can be difficult if they live in supervised residences.

Mentally ill women have no trouble finding partners; many, in fact, are exploited by men for sexual purposes. It is not unusual for them to find caring, devoted husbands, who often show an incredible tolerance for living with insanity.

I have a patient in her mid-thirties who, despite antipsychotic medication, believes she is Frank Sinatra (and her eyes aren't even blue). She frequently claims to be George Michael or Bruce Springsteen. This might be possible to live with if she didn't get so angry over her lack of recognition, which she attempts to remedy by calling the police or knocking on neighbors' doors in the middle of the night to complain.

She recently married a man she met when they were both hospitalized (he had a depression). She went on to a state hospital and he went home, but continued to visit her and volunteered to take her home with him; this struck her therapists as an excellent discharge plan and they implemented it immediately. He rationalizes her delusions as the result of her having had a good voice that never resulted in a successful singing career.

Maybe Sinatra's husband has a rescue fantasy. Maybe she makes his own mental condition seem trifling by comparison. Maybe he didn't have to worry about being rejected.

I think of the sideshow attraction billed as the Mule-Faced Woman. Advertised to be the ugliest woman on earth, she nevertheless received many proposals of marriage. She married the carnival owner (who may have had some financial motivation) and bore him children. I think of the story, hopefully apocryphal, of the Russian prince who was presented with a captured female yeti, an abominable snowwoman. Soon afterward, he fathered a tall, powerful, hirsute son.

And, ruefully, I think of Billy Crystal's pronouncement in *When Harry Met Sally* that men could not be friends with women because sexual desire was always there. When Meg Ryan asked if it were okay if the women were ugly, Crystal confessed, "No, you want to nail them, too."

It is the old story, repeated throughout Nature's kingdom. Males want to engage as many females as possible, and females, faced with long periods of pregnancy and infant care, want to select carefully the partner with whom they will merge genes. Powerful attraction and the probability of rejection are invested in females.

Thus arises the archetype of the evil female magic-user, sometime witch, or sorceress, or demon, or monster. These are the nightmarish counterparts to the dream girl, who always says "Yes."

With Restraint

In a recent issue of *Elle*, there was an unusual perfume ad. There was a photo, black and white, of the rear of a woman's torso. Her hands were clasped behind her, partially covering her buttocks. A perfume bottle, in a pale yellow color, seemed to be wrapped around her wrists, like handcuffs, even though using a bottle for handcuffs made as much sense as using a pencil sharpener for the purpose.

The ad attracted my eye, of course, and after I said, "What the hell?" I surmised this must be part of the new mainstreaming of sadomasochism I keep reading about.

The November 28, 1994, issue of *New York* proclaimed on its cover, illustrated by a spiked metal collar, "In 1974, It Was Free Sex. In 1984, It Was Safe Sex. In 1994, It's Mean Sex." The article inside justified its claim not only by detailing the whippings, clampings, and hot-waxings inside the easily accessible S&M clubs, but by pointing out fashion's increasing emphasis on leather, Madonna's kinky videos, and the craze for piercing intimate body areas.

I find it strange that there is so much emphasis on the emergence of S&M into general public consciousness, when it seems I have always been surrounded by it. By "it," I mean stories or pictures that involved restraint, whipping, torture, and terrorizing of victims, usually unclad or partially clad, that were sexually stimulating. To a heterosexual male, "victims" translates into "women." The comics were the primary source of such material and the bondage was scarcely incidental to the plot because it happened so often. Wonder Woman, who was so nearly invincible that she could only be bound by her own golden lasso, always kept the treacherous rope attached to her belt, which facilitated things for the bad guys. The jungle girls wore leopardskin bikinis, the superheroines were stripped for action, and the more conventional ladies seemed to have discovered the miniskirt several years ahead of the garment district.

I was too young for the *Perils of Pauline* and *Nyoka, the Jungle Girl* serials (Frances Gifford managed to get tied up six times in the course of the episodes), but there were plenty of memorable bondage scenes, from Peggy Castle's dragging herself across the floor in the movie *I, the Jury* to Deborah Kerr's near martyrdom, as she stood diaphanously clad and bound to a stake in *Quo Vadis*.

I couldn't even open an art book without encountering *naked* bound women, such as the pale-skinned redhead bound to a tree in Sir John Millais's *The Knight Errant* or Hiram Power's statue of the shackled *Greek Slave*.

And there is the ubiquitous Andromeda, with her bare manacled arms extended above her bare torso, awaiting death or rescue. I have concluded that the three most depicted women in world art are the Blessed Virgin Mary, by virtue of religious worship; Venus, by virtue of men's fondness for nude women; and Andromeda, by virtue of men's fondness for bound nude women. Really, what was this girl's claim to fame? She wasn't a goddess, she wasn't a heroine, she wasn't even guilty of an offense; she was chained naked to a rock because her mother offended some sea nymphs and probably because her mother didn't have the body to be chained naked to a rock.

So, Venus winds up with a planet named after her and Andromeda rates not only a constellation but an entire spiral nebula, consisting of billions of stars. Venus had the body, but not the chains.

Maybe the mainstreaming of S&M will relieve men of some of their guilt, although their fascination with submission was never much of a secret. In *Casino Royale*, a James Bond spoof, one of the bad guys petulantly observes that whenever there are women to be tied up, everybody shows up. Less amusing was Terence Stamp's statement to his captive, Samantha Eggar, in *The Collector* that if more people had the money and time for it, there would be a lot more of what he was doing going on.

In the world of S&M, the boot is often on the other foot. The dominatrix, leather-clad and whip-wielding, is queen of the realm, humiliating men and never permitting them to have sex with her. In the world of prostitution, there are far more men paying to be dominated than to play the master. Men are on the thin end of the lash far more often than women.

What does it all mean? French philosopher Michel Foucault maintained that all social relations, institutional and personal, were about discipline and punishment. Some have claimed that the rituals are a way of confronting death and surviving for a while. Feminists claim that all heterosexual relationships exploit women and that all pornography is sadomasochistic.

As a pursuer of the dream girl, I have little interest in trying to ascribe cosmic philosophical significance to these activities. From a purely sexual point of view, I find that males are forced into a quest for dominance, which is really an illusion as long as it is the female who actually does the choosing and rejecting. The males who assume the masochistic role are calling a spade a dirty shovel and casting off all pretensions of being in charge. It is no coincidence that most patrons of the dominatrix are wealthy men in positions of power who long for a respite.

The man who is mesmerized by the bound woman resolves his conflict by rendering the woman helpless. Most of the time, he does not fantasize about hurting her; traditionally, he is the rescuer. The victim is, in the tradition of Marquis de Sade, innocent and virtuous. In the S&M fantasy, the captor may have his way with the reluctant maid, but she invariably finds profound ecstasy through his sexual expertise and becomes an emotional slave as well. In the rescue fantasy, the woman is eternally grateful to her hero, more bound to him than she could have been if her bonds had not been cut.

In formal psychiatric terms, sadism and masochism must involve sexual excitement through actual, not simulated, acts of pain infliction, bondage, or humiliation. It seems that with all this new-fangled nipple-piercing, rubber-wearing, and perfume-bottle-bondage, there's a heck of a lot of pseudo-sadomasochism going on and soon it will be hard to get back to basics—like a rock, a chain, and a maiden.

My daughter, Rita, noted that the only time I ever laughed aloud during a movie was in *9 to 5*. Jane Fonda had joined her co-workers in kidnapping their boss, whom they had restrained in a very elaborate system of shackles, straitjacket, and hoists. Her boyfriend intruded, misconstrued the situation and accused her of getting into S&M. Ms. Fonda, the former leather-clad Barbarella, ran after him, protesting she could do anything she pleased, including "getting into M&Ms."

I suppose it struck me funny because as people stray further from the norms in sexual behavior their behavior gets less and less sexual. I have warned overadventurous patients, "If you keep going this way, you'll wind up one day waking up with a banana in your ear. And you'll say, 'Hey, this isn't sexy, it's stupid!'" At least with M&Ms, there's no chocolate mess.

They say that the masochist, who subtly sets the limits, is the one who has control. The dream girl, submissive and supportive, is bound eternally to one man, who directs the fantasies in which she gives undying love and admiration. And, boy, it's often impossible to escape from her!

~ CHAPTER 12 ~

The Changing Dream Girl

" 'Dream girls' changed over the years, as they continue to. No single 'dream girl' has prevailed. Therefore, hard to answer these [questions] with precision."

Ralph, a divorced magazine writer in his forties, wrote the above on a questionnaire that I had distributed to males at Columbia University. His comment made me aware of something I had failed to address in my pursuit of the dream girl—she often changed over the course of time or was replaced by other dream girls. In fact, successful resolution of the dream-girl dilemma often depends not on abandoning her, but on coming to terms with her limitations as an imaginary being and ceasing to regard her on the same plane with real women.

Ralph kindly agreed to let me interview him. His questionnaire said that he first had fantasies about his "dream girl" when he was "very young—under five." This, it turned out, was a real person, but later in childhood he had a genuine, completely imaginary dream girl with a name, one of the classic, secret type.

Ralph defined "dream girl" as the woman you're fantasizing about when you're thinking about women.

His first dream girl was the little girl who lived upstairs. He was about four and she was slightly younger. They would play house together and talk as if they were going to be married someday. Ralph remembered their "playing doctor" once, which a parent quickly stopped.

183

The true dream girl came into Ralph's life when he was seven and went away to camp. It was an all-male environment, campers and staff, and Ralph believes his dream girl was a defense against his longing for a supportive female. Her name was Mary and she was his age, although he could easily imagine how she would look as his grown-up bride. "She looked like Mary Todd Lincoln, only prettier," Ralph said. She had long dark hair, parted in the center, in the nineteenth-century fashion.

Ralph did not know where her name came from. "I never knew anyone named Mary—except the Virgin Mary," he said. Ralph is Jewish, but he said his mother used to "drag me to a lot of churches in those days," because she was interested in religious art.

Ralph would think about Mary, particularly at night. It was a very private fantasy. "I didn't tell anyone—it would be embarrassing," he said. Mary loved him and she belonged to him alone.

I asked him if Mary stayed in his thoughts after he returned home. He said he did not think so. She became a forgotten daydream soon afterward.

There were other daydreams. Around the fifth grade, he had what he calls "altruistic crushes" on various girls in his class. What he meant by this was that he would have fantasies about rescuing them from various perils, at great risk to himself, and earning their admiration and undying gratitude. Many of the fantasies were about defeating Nazi and Japanese soldiers. I pointed out that he was born after World War II, but he said that his parents talked often about the war and, until the Russians qualified as the archenemy, many movies and television shows employed the wartime villains.

During elementary school, Ralph had a great admiration for Dale Evans, whom he regarded as supermom. At the time, Roy Rogers and Dale Evans had a weekly television show. They had no children, but there was considerable domesticity around the ranch. They had a Jeep, as well as Trigger and Buttermilk. There were bad guys, just as there were bad guys on *Lassie*, but the plot was not the impersonal "ride-'em-down-shoot-'em-up" format of the classic western movies. While Dale was the ideal mom (although childless in her TV role) to Ralph, he conceded that he wanted to be like Roy and marry someone like her.

He said he is "capable of creating the most incredible crushes" on women he works with. The attraction is not immediate, but "spikes up" as he gets to know them better. The closeness and emotional exchanges around work-related projects take on a personal significance and he builds a little into a lot within a short period. Ralph is not the kind to worship a woman from afar. "I need something back," he explained, which means he has to know a woman better before he gets emotionally involved, even on a fantasy level.

Ralph met his wife on the job and got disillusioned even before their marriage, which lasted more than ten years. He has a girlfriend and stops himself before fantasies about the women at work get out of hand.

He admitted to one "crush" on a celebrity as an adult. He mentioned a local television news anchor, whom he had actually met through his boss during the course of work. I expressed some surprise because, while she is an attractive person, this newscaster is not the Diane Sawyer type, the glamorous blonde, exuding sophistication and class.

Ralph said he was turned on by his dreamcaster's coquettishness and playful bantering. "Heck, that's her trademark," he said. "She's not a journalist, she's an entertainer." The fact that he had actually met her raised the exciting, although remote, possibility that something could happen between the two of them.

I asked Ralph if he ever worried that, by picking one woman, he was closing the door on the possible later appearance of a dream girl. No, he said. It was not a question of "what's out there." He felt there was no danger of his "compromising on something like this." When he married again, he would not settle for someone short of dream-girl standards.

Ralph had been burned before, but he was not soured on love. "When it's great, it's really great."

My brief interview with Ralph brought no surprises to me, but it reinforced several points for which people have little regard, if they even have any awareness of them.

The first is that very young children think about romance and marriage, quite independent of any sexual curiosity.

The second is that the dream girl usually appears before

puberty and is a fantasized love object that fills a void, such as Ralph experienced in the all-male camp.

The third is the need for approval and validation from females, even at an early age. Ralph's heroic-rescue fantasies exemplify this. He called them "altruistic" because the reward, as in the old Lone Ranger stories, was not physical gratification or commitment from a girl, but simply admiration and gratitude. That's a lot!

The fourth is the blend of maternal and romantic elements in the early dream girl. Dale Evans was his beautiful fantasy mother (with no television siblings to share her affections), but she was also the woman he would someday marry. She was the pretty, asexual madonna, present mother and future virtuous wife, the Oedipal mother without the children, including pseudo-son Ralph, to bear testimony as to her past sexual experience.

Finally, there is the need for validation ("getting something back"). Ralph talked of the "spikes" of excitement he would feel just from sharing the adventure of a challenging assignment with female co-workers. Attractive appearance and physical proximity posed no threats, but having a sidekick to share your achievements, bringing some maternal help and feminine spice to the work, was a powerful aphrodisiac. Ralph has enough insight to separate the fantasy elements from the real, but many a man in his situation would think he had found his dream girl, when he actually had glimpsed only a fragment of a dream in a very different woman.

Twenty Questionnaires

I have co-authored two books based on nationwide surveys, so I am familiar with surveys. I never had any intention of conducting a survey for this book and I am not pretending that I did one.

The problem with surveys is that you try to take a large sample and make that representative of *everyone*. Subject matter is important. Knowing that 65 percent of the population likes to buy its detergent in blue boxes, with red the second preference at 25 percent, would influence me to manufacture detergent in blue boxes. But telling me that 65 percent of the population has sex at least twice a week and 25 percent at least once a week is less helpful. Does it mean nine out of ten people have good sex lives? That one in ten has a lousy sex life? How many of the lowest percentile are older than sixty-five? How many are single or widowed?

My sample for *Beyond the Male Myth* was four thousand men, considered valid in terms of size. Ten percent of the men surveyed were black, in accordance with the general population. But are four hundred men representative of blacks? We broke down the sample by age brackets and income levels. Again, any sub-sample was bound to be far smaller than the total.

Surveys have value because they give *some* information. They tell you about norms, but not much about exceptions to the norm.

Sampling methods and subject matter are very important. A recent large-scale survey concluded that only about one-quarter of men cheated on their wives, an estimate considerably lower than earlier studies. The researchers, in this case, had conducted face-to-face interviews with their subjects. Even though Kinsey did it that way, I am convinced that most unfaithful men in that situation, especially if they did not expect the question, would lie.

Why? Because they have nothing to gain by telling the truth and, although the possibility of revelation is small, why risk it? My feeling is that if you give a man an anonymous questionnaire, let him fill it out in total privacy, then seal it in an unmarked envelope, he will probably be truthful because there is no chance of detection.

Anyway, this is not a survey-based book and I will not belabor the reasons that it is not. Just to give myself a ballpark estimate of whether young men today are as susceptible to the dream girl as they were in my generation, I devised a questionnaire about her. My twenty-three-year-old daughter, Rita, distributed some to undergraduate males at Columbia University and my wife, Joy, distributed some to male university employees under the age of fifty.

The key question of the eighteen was: "Did you ever fantasize about the women or type of woman ('dream girl') you would someday marry or live with?" If nearly everyone had answered no, I would have had serious questions about doing this book, but that did not happen.

I am reproducing the questionnaire here because I think it would be good for women to know their husbands', boyfriends', or male friends' responses. It can give you some insight into the past and present role of the dream girl in their lives. You might get the man in your life to fill out a copy of the questionnaire or just elicit some of the answers a bit at a time.

Finally, I will give you the answers I received on the first twenty questionnaires that were returned. No, that is not a statistically significant number. Neither would two hundred or even two thousand be. The population is not a balanced one. But all I want to convey is that men do have dream girls and do think about them. If I asked twenty people if they ever saw a ghost and five said yes, I would consider believing in ghosts.

Eighteen Questions

Age (Optional) _____

1. How well do women understand men? (a) Very well (b) Fairly well (c) Minimally (d) Not at all _____

2. How well do you understand women? (a) Very well (b) Fairly well (c) Minimally (d) Not at all _____

3. Would you be more likely to confide in a male or female friend? (a) Male (b) Female (c) Either (d) Neither _____

4. With what female would you feel most comfortable sharing confidences or talking about yourself? (a) Mother (b) Sister (c) Other female relative (d) Romantic partner (e) Platonic friend _____

5. Would you share personal problems or feelings of insecurity with male friends? (a) Yes (b) Only with closest friends (c) No _____

6. Which parent understands you better? (a) Father (b) Mother (c) Equally well (d) Neither very well _____

7. Do you ever worry about settling for the wrong person instead of waiting to meet your ideal partner? Yes _____ No _____

8. Did you ever have an imaginary playmate as a child? Yes _____ No _____

9. If you could have a romance or an affair with *anyone*, whom would you choose (other than your real-life partner)? _____

10. What quality would you consider most important in selecting a wife? (a) Beauty (b) Sexiness (c) Intelligence (d) Emotional compatibility (e) Loyalty (f) Kindness (g) Mothering ability (h) Other (specify) _____

11. Did you ever fantasize about the woman or type of woman ("dream girl") you would someday marry or live with? Yes _____ No _____

IF YOU ANSWERED "NO" TO QUESTION 11,
YOU MAY OMIT THE REMAINING QUESTIONS.

12. How old were you when you first had fantasies about your "dream girl"? _____

13. Was your "dream girl" based on (a) A movie star or celebrity (b) A fictitious character from a book, comic strip, movie, or TV program (c) Someone you knew very well (d) Someone you had seen but didn't know well (e) No one you ever encountered? _____

14. Did your "dream girl" have a name? Yes _____ No _____

15. What was the most important quality of your "dream girl"? (a) Beauty (b) Sexiness (c) Intelligence (d) Emotional compatibility (e) Loyalty (f) Kindness (g) Other (specify)
_____

16. When you first started thinking about her, was your "dream girl" (a) Older (b) Same age (c) Younger than you? _____

17. Do you still think about your "dream girl?" (a) Often (b) Occasionally (c) Rarely (c) Never _____

18. How do real women compare with your "dream girl"? (a) Superior (b) Equal (c) Inferior _____

A cover sheet explained that the questionnaire was being used in preparing a new book, with its title, author and publisher. It was explained that the questionnaire was anonymous. Participants were encouraged to return the questionnaire even if they answered no to question 11, because, although the book is about dream girls, the answers of those who have never had one are as important as those of the others.

Dreamers and Non-Dreamers

With no further preamble or apology, here are the answers received on the first twenty questionnaires received. Of the eighteen who gave their ages, two were eighteen, three nineteen, five twenty, three twenty-one, and one twenty-two. The other four ranged from twenty-seven to forty-four.

1. *How well do women understand men?*

    Fourteen said fairly well; six said minimally. Nobody thought women understand men very well.

2. *How well do you understand women?*

    Fourteen said fairly well; five said minimally. One said not at all; he didn't give his age.

3. *Would you be more likely to confide in a male or female friend?*

    Nine said either; eight said female; and only three said male.

4. *With what female would you feel most comfortable sharing confidences or talking about yourself?*

    Nine said platonic friend; eight said romantic partner; and one chose both these answers. Two said their mother, the twenty-two-year-old and the fellow who didn't understand women at all.

5. *Would you share personal problems or feelings of insecurity with male friends?*

    Ten said only with closest friends; seven said yes; and only three said no. Men are not opposed to sharing emotional problems with one another, they simply don't know how to go about it. As my daughter Rita has observed, they say they are going to talk, but they wind up drinking beer and playing games.

6. *Which parent understands you better?*

    There was a wide scatter here, indicating that it really depends on what kind of family you come from. Seven said mother; five said father; four said neither very well; three said equally well; and one gave no answer.

7. *Do you ever worry about settling for the wrong person instead of waiting to meet your ideal partner?*

    Half of them said yes; half said no. (All were single at present.) That's a lot of worrying.

8. *Did you ever have an imaginary playmate as a child?*

    Only three said yes and one said he was not sure. This is unreliable, since most imaginary playmates occur well before the age of five and are gone within a year. I don't remember mine, a boy named Roger, and only know about him because my mother told me.

9. *If you could have a romance or an affair with anyone, whom would you choose (other than your real-life partner)?*

    Six left this one blank and one said "wouldn't." Six named celebrities (Meg Ryan, Teri Hatcher, Halle Berry, Winona Ryder, Vanessa Williams, and Princess Diana). One said, non-specifically, "*Playboy* model." Another said, "My former dance partner."

    One mentioned a name we cannot identify, so we assume she is a real person he knows or has encountered. Two wanted to get involved with my daughter Rita, who distributed the questionnaires (she declined). The final respondent said, "Many."

10. *What quality would you consider most important in selecting a wife?*

    Because many gave multiple answers to this question, the responses total more than twenty. Thirteen selected emotional compatibility. A distant second were the five who chose kindness. Four picked intelligence; there were two mentions each for beauty, sexiness and mothering ability; and one said loyalty. There were two write-ins: "How attached I am to her" and "Badassness."

I had to ask Rita what the last term meant. She said it connoted a certain street-wise sophistication, almost a toughness. Was it a compliment? Apparently it described a woman who had plenty of self-confidence and knew how good she was.

11. *Did you ever fantasize about the woman or type of woman ("dream girl") you would someday marry or live with?*

This is the question I was most interested in. Seventeen said yes, only three said no. I think that's significant even in a sample this small.

People might argue that *everybody*, even men, must give *some* thought to eventual marriage, but the use of "fantasize" and "dream girl" should imply more than a fleeting thought. Subsequent questions, of course, elaborate on the nature of the "dream girl."

12. *How old were you when you first had fantasies about your "dream girl"?*

Remember that at this point, the three who said they never had a dream girl dropped out, so the sample size is seventeen from now on.

Fifteen gave an answer, one leaving it blank and one writing "?". Here are the ages they gave, in chronological order: four (twice); "very young—under five"; seven; seven–eight; "elementary school"; ten; eleven (twice); twelve; thirteen; thirteen–fourteen; fourteen and eighteen (twice).

With the exception of the two who said eighteen, these ages fit the expected pattern of early adolescence, at an age when a real love object would not yet be realistically available.

13. *Was your "dream girl" based on (a) A movie star or celebrity (b) A fictitious character from a book, comic strip, movie, or TV program (c) Someone you knew well (d) Someone you had seen but didn't know well (e) No one you ever encountered?*

They had drawn on all sources. Six said someone they had seen but didn't know well (the Dante Alighieri syndrome); three each said a celebrity, someone they knew well, and someone completely original, with two reporting a fictitious character. The above answers include a subject who said his dream girl was based on both someone he knew well and someone he had seen but didn't know well. The seventeenth respondent was Ralph, the fellow who had a history of multiple dream girls.

14. *Did your dream girl have a name?*

Eight said yes; nine said no. (Actually, Ralph wrote "sometimes," but he had told me about "Mary.")

It was interesting that two of the men who said their dream girl was based on someone they knew well said she did not have a name. People whose dream girls were based on celebrities or fictitious characters also said no. This assured me that the dream girl was, indeed, merely based on the models, a true fantasy creation, not just a wish that the actual person, star, or character could be a lover.

Of those who did have names, three were based on celebrities; three (including "Mary") were original creations; one was based on a fictional character; and one on someone who had been seen but was not well known to the man.

15. *What was the most important quality of your "dream girl"?*

Including the responses of two who gave multiple answers, six selected beauty; four emotional compatibility; four sexiness; three intelligence; and two kindness. Two wrote in "a certain, all-encompassing bad-ass-ness" and just plain "badass-ness." (See comment for question 10.)

Here you can get some indication of the roots of the dream-girl dilemma. While emotional compatibility was by far the quality considered most important in selecting a wife, it carried only moderate weight here. Beauty and sexiness were much more prominently sought in the dream girl.

Since a man has carte blanche in constructing a dream girl, he might as well give her as much beauty and sexiness as he wants, in addition to less physical qualities. But when he becomes disenchanted with his real-life partner, she will be up against an unrealistic but formidable rival.

Of the three men who never had a dream girl, two had made multiple selections for the qualities they considered most important in a wife. Perhaps they had a dream girl in mind and did not know it.

16. *When you first started thinking about her, was your "dream girl" (a) Older (b) Same Age (c) Younger than you?*

Ten of the subjects said she was older. Six said she was the same age, and only one, who was eighteen when he first thought of her, said she was younger.

Of the men who said their dream girl was the same age as themselves, one was thirteen and one eighteen at the time the dream girl entered their lives. Three were younger at the time, one in "elementary school," one only four, and Ralph, who was enamored of the girl upstairs when he was less than five. One did not give his age at the time of first encounter.

In most cases, as expected, a fantasized older woman had been invoked to supply the confidence a boy lacks in the area of love.

17. *Do you still think about your "dream girl"?*

There was a little bell curve here. Three said often; five said occasionally; five said rarely; and four said never.

For most men, the dream girl has not been forgotten.

18. *How do real women compare with your "dream girl"?*

I didn't ask for write-ins on this one, but I got five written comments, three from subjects who did not pick an answer, and two from those who said inferior.

Seven said real women were inferior to their dream girls; four rated them equal; and two said that real women were superior.

One of those who said real women were inferior added the cogent observation, "They do exist, though." Another who gave the edge to his dream girl said, "I don't know of anyone who's perfect, but I found someone who comes close."

The three who abstained from choosing an answer wrote in their own:

"All of these."

"Different, but not necessarily better or worse."

"In some qualities real women are superior, in others equal or inferior."

Can dream girls coexist in harmony with real women? That's what the rest of this book is about.

~ CHAPTER 13 ~

Detective Story

Dracula? Frankenstein's monster? The Wolf Man? The Mummy? In the pantheon of Hollywood's horror stars, who would rate the place of honor? Which one is the scariest, the one you would least want stalking you, the one you would have to hunt down and destroy?

I would vote for the Invisible Man. He was human, vulnerable, and possessed only average strength, with no supernatural powers. Yet, while it is terrifying to have a hideous enemy confronting you, it is infinitely more frightening when the enemy *may* be right beside you without your knowledge. You can flee from the monster you cannot possibly beat, but you cannot run away from something that may not even be there.

The dream girl is an invisible woman. She is just as invisible to the man who created her, although he may be fully aware of her presence. Often, however, he has come to ignore her or forget about her; then, when she makes a comeback, he may notice her effects on himself and others, but not realize the cause behind those effects. Like Victor Frankenstein, he has probably lost control of his creation—or, worse, he has become too fond of it to dispose of it.

Mistresses, extramarital girlfriends, and women with designs are common and dangerous enough, but once their existence is known, they cannot hide easily. Real-life rivals threaten and destroy marriages and relationships; their devastation is more immediate and total than that caused by the dream girl, who, like most ghosts, can disturb things but not wreak much physical damage.

Dream girls resurrected in a man's adulthood can lead a man into affairs and liaisons with actual women. For the child and adolescent, a sexual body is still only a fantasy, something no more directly experienced than the vaporous dream girl. Once the man has abandoned a real mate for his old dream girl, the phantom is likely to become a body snatcher. The man will try to fit the dream girl image into the form of a warm, three-dimensional female, so that what started as an esoteric quest becomes a garden-variety affair. If the man is truly in the grip of the dream girl, routing the mistress will be an incomplete victory. In a matter of time, the dream girl, like a displaced hermit crab, will find another attractive shell to inhabit.

A woman can give her man an ultimatum to rid himself of ties to human rivals, but how can you be sure he has given up his fantasy? ("Did you get rid of that dream girl like I told you?" "Yes, dear. You don't see her around, do you?") It's worse than trying to get rid of mice.

Mortal Syndromes

> Last night I met upon the stair
> A little man who wasn't there.
> He wasn't there again today.
> Oh, how I wish he'd go away!

Just because you cannot see something, it does not mean it isn't there. Air, gases, X-rays, and sound waves are part of our daily lives. Thoughts, dreams, emotions, virtue, and vice are invisible. Nobody ever saw Captain Ahab, and Herman Melville has not been seen for more than a century, but they continue to entertain and affect people.

Doctors are accustomed to dealing with invisible foes. I have never seen a hepatitis virus, but I know how to detect it and how to deal with it.

The dream girl can never be seen, but she can be detected. Dealing with her involves three phases: detection, confrontation, and resolution. A detective needs evidence before he can arrest a culprit. The first discovery is that something is amiss. It may be a vanished item or a bloody corpse, but something has to be going wrong before the detective abandons his cozy office to conduct an investigation.

It usually takes more than one clue to solve a case. The more clues you discover, the more convinced you become of your convictions.

Doctors are like detectives in that they can often diagnose an illness by discerning a cluster of symptoms (complaints by the patient) and signs (things that can be verified by sight and sound, such as fever, high blood pressure, and congested lungs) that in combination are typical of a particular condition. We often speak of such groups as a syndrome.

Premenstrual syndrome is defined as swelling and tenderness of the breasts, pain in the abdomen and lower back, headache, thirst, and emotional irritability, occurring about three days prior to a menstrual period. Any one symptom, such as headache or pain, would not strongly suggest the diagnosis, and one or more symptoms, such as thirst, could be lacking in a genuine case.

Cough, fever, night sweats, weakness, and weight loss suggests tuberculosis. Frequent urination, excessive thirst, weakness, and mental confusion suggests diabetes. You will need a blood test, culture, or X-ray to confirm the diagnosis, but a good doctor would be willing to bet the office rent on the basis of his clinical observations.

The dream-girl syndrome is a group of occurrences and observations about the behavior of a man that indicates problems with his love relationship and the strong danger of his resurrecting the dream girl to help him cope. The more his current attitudes and actions differ from what they have been in the past, the more significant the symptom. If a patient tells me he has been urinating at least every two hours, I would be more likely to suspect diabetes if he used to urinate twice a day than if he used to urinate every three hours. I am more concerned about a patient who weighs 105 pounds if she weighed 140 six months ago than if she weighed 112 six months ago.

Throughout the rest of this book I will be addressing at least three different types of relationships that are threatened by the dream girl. One is marriage, where the couple has established a firm, permanent commitment and may have children as well as property to share. The second is a committed relationship that has developed to the point that the couple plans to marry or, at least, reserve their love exclusively for each other. The third relationship is one that has not yet reached the stage of commitment, but has been mutually satisfying and seems to be on course toward engagement and marriage. Strategies for dealing with the dream girl will vary depending on the type of the relationship, but the syndrome tends to be consistent, regardless of the degree of prior commitment.

He Thinks, Therefore She Is

Women may raise the objection that the man might never have had a dream girl in the past. Assume that he did. Even if he didn't, he could fabricate one for the first time, even as an experienced adult.

If the man has the dream-girl syndrome and no dream girl, following the guidelines is bound to improve your relationship anyway and cement your commitment to each other. So, don't be like the child who discovers early in December that his parents have already bought and wrapped his presents and is angry that he has been good when he didn't have to be.

All men have dream girls because all men dream. They come to need love when they have outgrown the limitations of parental care and affection and before they are ready to find a mature woman. *South Pacific*'s Bloody Mary wisely observed that you've got to have a dream before a dream can come true. He has to imagine what an adult love partner will be like before he can hope to find her.

The boy is not likely to expect the dream girl to find him. His genes have made him a hunter, of love as well as of food. A girl may be content to warble, "Someday my prince will come" and nap for a few months or years in a glass casket or thorn-covered tower awaiting his arrival, but boys are not raised to be passive. In time, the girl, like a cub grown to lionesshood, may grow impatient and set out to hunt one of the hunters; by then, she craves something more substantial in her claws than fantasy.

The boy, who has been trying to establish his manhood in schoolyards and playing fields, expects to have to prove himself once more, but the dream girl spares him much anxiety. She has the wisdom and maturity to recognize his merit and take him in her arms, while ignoring the rivals who would desire her with the same intensity. Not only does she provide perfect love, she supplies it at very little expense.

Real love can be nearly perfect, but it is rarely without effort. Since love involves two people, with different minds and goals, it requires cooperation, which means work. Thus, a man may find love with a real woman close enough to meet his long-held fantasy, but he will never be able to sustain it without effort.

Great Expectations

The New York *Daily News* runs a feature each Sunday in which readers are invited to share past experiences related to a particular theme. One woman, in response to a request for childhood disappointments about unmet expectations, told of how her aunt promised to take her to Radio City for her birthday. The little girl thought she would see a city constructed of all types of radios and was unimpressed with the majestic Music Hall theater. She kept thinking, "Where are all the radios, and who are these dancing ladies?"

As a child, I was disappointed when I turned on the TV to watch New York's Easter Parade and failed to see any floats or balloons like in the Thanksgiving Day Parade. When I first heard of London's Piccadilly Circus, I imagined it to be filled with clowns and elephants. I remember reading a letter to the editor in a children's magazine in which a little girl confessed that she used to think the *Red Skelton Show* was a scary program about a bloody skeleton.

Remember Principle Two: Satisfaction depends not on what you get, but what you expected.

A recent news story was about two workers who stumbled across $85 million in traveler's checks that had been packed in the wrong cartons and misdirected. The bank gave them each a $2,500 reward and the finders made no secret of their disappointment.

Even though they could not have converted the traveler's checks to cash, they felt they were entitled to much more, based on the face value. One explained to a newsperson that one percent of $85 million is $850,000. He didn't expect *that* much, but, gee, only $2,500?

How could a person be disappointed about getting $2,500 he had never expected the week before, with no appreciable effort or achievement? Because when he found the checks, he *expected* to get more than that and it made the difference.

Do *all* men have unrealistic expectations about love and marriage? Probably not. Some do not have any expectations at all, except for the assumption that it will be much like the marriage of their parents, which may or may not be a good thing. Even men who have had dream girls might not be susceptible to the dream-girl syndrome, if their fantasy, like earlier imaginary playmates, stayed just long enough to support them through a rough transitional period and then disappeared.

Dissatisfaction may be better than complacency, since it may help to improve a bad situation. It may even improve a good situation.

The dream-girl syndrome is most malignant when it leads a couple to give up a relationship that is salvageable or causes moderately severe conflicts to deteriorate into very serious ones.

Warning Signs

The dream-girl syndrome usually involves changes. Typically, a relationship or a marriage starts out very promising. On a scale of 10, you would have rated it at least a 9. Suddenly, your score has slipped to a 6, and it continues to drop. What's so frustrating is that you cannot put your finger on precisely what went wrong. Sure, he could have stood some improving; who couldn't, yourself included? But you loved and accepted him for what he was and he seemed to feel the same way about you. Even now, he can't tell you what's wrong.

Was he a lemon from the start? Is he an incorrigible womanizer? Have you been making his life miserable?

If you have answered no to all of the above, consider the presence of these symptoms of the dream-girl syndrome:

1. He has stopped talking to you. This doesn't mean you are both so furious that you refuse to speak to one another. He will ask you to pass the potatoes, tell you he will be late coming home, or remind you to pay the electric bill. He will answer your questions with brief precision. But he talks only when he must. He has stopped sharing details of what's happening at his job and no longer asks you how your day went. There is no sharing of newspaper items, no comments about television shows, or conversation about weekend plans. If you talk, you cannot be sure whether he is really listening and he volunteers no feedback.

2. He is irritable. If you ask him whether he remembered to mail the letters you gave him, he will respond that he is not an idiot. If you suggest seeing a certain movie, he will tell you what bad reviews it received or that the leading man is a no-talent jerk. If you ask him whether he has taken out the trash, he will launch into a listing of all the more important concerns he has on his mind. You soon reach the point where you avoid saying anything to him for fear it will trigger an excessively angry or critical response.

3. He is not affectionate. Maybe he was never that demonstrative to begin with, but there is a decline from his previous level. Now he leaves the house without even a perfunctory peck. He no longer puts his arm around your waist as he peers over your shoulder to see what's cooking or pats you playfully as he squeezes past you. He doesn't use affectionate terms, such as "darling" or "baby," when he addresses you. Sex is conducted like a transaction with a hooker: few preliminaries and quick detachment when it's over—except you don't get paid.

4. He is preoccupied. He sits in front of the television set, watching programs he usually doesn't watch and that he still doesn't seem to be watching. He stares at the newspaper and rarely turns the pages. He often doesn't hear you when you talk to him. He misplaces things, like his keys. He seems to be lost in thought, but if you ask him what he is thinking about, he says, "Nothing."

5. He wants time alone. He may "take a drive" or go out for a

bottle of soda at eleven P.M. He may simply seclude himself in the den or bedroom, saying he has "things to do." If he goes out, he isn't gone long enough to be spending a romantic evening with another woman, just too long to be doing the simple errands he claims.

6.   He wants time with his friends. He never was much of a buddy-bonder before, but suddenly he wants to go bowling or play tennis or watch a football game with male neighbors or co-workers. You get the uncomfortable feeling that he would enlist in a war just to spend time away from you.

7.   He starts paying attention to women. He may not make a pass at the lady next door or take his secretary to dinner six months after National Secretaries' Day, but he is suddenly looking at the lingerie ads in your *Vogue* and watching late-night TV movies like *Bikini Body Shop* or *Cybersluts On-Line*. He knows who Christy Turlington is, even though he has never read a fashion magazine (except for the lingerie ads).

8.   He gets nostalgic. He mourns "the good old days" that happened five years ago. He looks at his college yearbook. He plays his old albums. He watches late-night syndicated reruns, usually something he watched in college, ranging from Mary Tyler Moore to *Quantum Leap*, depending on his age. He is returning to the pleasures of a time before your time together.

9.   He feels unappreciated. It's difficult to get him to say anything, but when he does he interprets anything you've done as disapproval or criticism. When you finally get him to confide something, he comes out fighting.

10.   He says nothing's wrong. He denies what he can and minimizes whatever he can't deny. He says he doesn't want you to change anything, nor does he want to change anything. He says everything is fine, when it obviously isn't.

11.   You have the uncanny conviction that he's involved in an affair with another woman, even though you know it's not possible. Affairs take time and money. He comes home at night, stays home on weekends. You keep track of every dollar he makes. There's no lipstick on his collar, no perfume on his lapel, no

hang-ups when the phone rings and you answer. And you're right. There is no other woman—except *her*.

Differential Diagnosis

They told a story when I was in medical school about a student at a conference who went from the height of admiration to the depths of scorn in a matter of seconds. The professor had just presented a perplexing case of a man with pain in the left side of the abdomen, just below the rib cage, with no other significant abnormalities on physical examination or laboratory tests. He challenged the class to venture a diagnosis.

Only one hand shot up. When called upon, the medical student said, confidently, "Subcapsular hemorrhage of the spleen."

The astonished professor, as impressed as the student's classmates, exclaimed, "Why, yes! How did you come to the correct diagnosis?"

The student shrugged and said modestly, "Well, what *else* could cause left upper quadrant pain?"

As you can imagine, there are many things that can produce that symptom and the student showed his ignorance by inadvertently admitting he knew only one.

A good doctor not only ventures a plausible diagnosis but includes other possibilities, with his reasons for ruling them out. This is called a differential diagnosis.

A differential diagnosis for the dream-girl syndrome should include Don Juanism, commitment phobia, depression, and infidelity.

Dashing Suitors

This possibility should be considered only in men you have recently met. If your man suffered from Don Juanism, he would not have been around long enough to be married or even engaged.

If he has only been with you a few months, he may be a slow-moving Don Juan, who does not flee as quickly as most. Men became hunters of game so that they could eat well, and they became hunters of women so that they could have families and pass on their genetic attributes to offspring.

There are riflemen who love to go hunting but wouldn't consider eating anything they kill. They donate venison and pheasants to their neighbors and head for McDonald's. The activity of hunting has, for them, lost all connection with its original purpose.

Similarly, there are men who delight more in the pursuit of women than in women themselves. They want the reassurance that they are considered masculine and desirable and they become very adept at the courting ritual by which men persuade women to give their love and bodies.

The reassurance of one woman is not enough, for the Don Juan has no confidence in his own worth and, therefore, cannot trust the judgment of a woman who knows him less well than he knows himself. So, in compulsive fashion, he moves on until he encounters another woman and repeats the courtship, triumph, and flight.

Don Juans are not mere libertines looking for sex. Libertines want intercourse and seduce women by pretending they want love and a committed relationship. The trick does not last for long, but if the sex is good and the woman attractive, they may stay with her until she catches on to the deceit.

Don Juans are looking for validation. Once the woman says yes, they would be just as happy to leave then, since sex was not what they were seeking, any more than they were seeking love.

Don Juans do not usually have dream girls. A dream girl provides an illusion, and they do not stay with a partner long enough to get disillusioned. If they took the effort to construct a dream girl, they would have to ask themselves, "What am I looking for in a woman?" and they would come to realize that they are really looking for something in themselves, the confidence and strength they know they lack. Theirs is a quest for self-love, and they are perpetually looking for love in all the wrong places.

Fear of Trying

One step above the Don Juan is the commitment phobic, whom I will henceforth call simply the phobic. While the Don Juan will probably have been out of your life before you have completed your analysis and course of action, the phobic may stay around a while, often far beyond the point when continuing the relationship made any sense.

He may show many of the symptoms of the dream-girl syndrome, and it is important to recognize him for what he is, because the chance of getting him to try to make a relationship healthy and permanent are about as great as getting someone with a fear of flying to obtain a pilot's license.

The phobic does not put distance between himself and his partner because she is not meeting his psychological needs or because he envisions a dream girl who would make him happier. It is permanence and obligations that he fears, so, paradoxically, the better a relationship gets, the more panicky he becomes.

Very few phobics are married, although a few may have gone through the ceremony when the partner gave a marry-or-forget-me ultimatum. People with fear of flying, heights, or leaving the house often seek therapy because they do not want to be afraid. Unlike the lothario who has no interest in commitment and the Don Juan who has more pressing goals, the phobic may want the security of marriage but cannot cope with his anxiety. It is this ambivalence that keeps him, like Nathan Detroit, in long-term relationships with "fiancées," such as Miss Adelaide of *Guys and Dolls*, always on the verge but forever short of the merge.

The phobic tends to have a pattern similar to the Don Juan, in that he tends to excess in the courtship. He showers the woman with attention, wanting to see her as often as possible and making frequent telephone calls when not in her presence, even during working hours. He tells her how special she is and may quickly proclaim his love and his desire to spend his life with her. He is skillful at this, because he has had a *lot* of practice.

When I first learned how to play chess as a kid, I fancied myself to be a damned good player, since I invariably trounced my limited sphere of opponents. But when I encountered better players, I realized I was half a player. I was good at the openings and pretty good at the middle game, but I didn't know how to manage an end game. All my experience had been in games where I captured several major pieces and then coasted to a checkmate with a queen and two rooks. Against real players, we wound up with a knight or bishop and a couple of pawns each and I had to learn how to maneuver carefully when I had no advantage over the opponent.

Phobics never get to an end game. Their relationships are a repetitious series of beginnings. They like to play, but not to finish.

If the phobic has a dream girl, it will probably be an idealized version of the first love or an early love in his life. This is a rationalization, of course. The relationship did not work then; why is she so perfect in retrospect? If the present relationship has to be scrapped, he could conceivably find a dream girl in the future, but while the future lies ahead, unknown for everyone, nobody can return to a known past.

Identifying the phobic and distinguishing him from a curable case of dream-girl syndrome is important. As in winning at poker, you have to discard bad hands as soon as possible. Luck will doom all players to a number of poor holdings at the start of each hand, but the bad players cling to fantasies about improving the hand through subsequent cards to protect the small amount of money they have anted. Improving the hand usually makes things worse, because players who had you beat going in will also improve; you bet because you've improved and lose more than you would have if your hand stayed as bad as it was originally.

The phobic often makes just enough of a concession to keep you in the game, perhaps to the point of moving in with you, giving you a ring, or setting a wedding date. In dealing with the dream-girl syndrome, you're usually trying to recapture a previous level of satisfaction. With the phobic, you are usually trying to get somewhere that you have never been.

If a man has a fear of commitment in relationships, that same phobia will probably extend to other areas of his life. Not only will he have had a long series of evanescent girlfriends, but he also will have followed a similar pattern in his work history and lifestyle. He probably attended several different schools and switched his majors. He is likely to have moved from city to city. He never stays in one job for long. He probably does not have a pet.

Even when your relationship is in the honeymoon stage, when he is heaping praise and gifts on you, he starts setting limits. He does not want you to meet his friends. He does not introduce you to his parents. There are aspects of his life that he refuses to discuss. While you are mentally constructing extensions on a cottage for two, he is carving out a back door for escape purposes.

"I need more space" and "I need more time" are his refrains. He makes vague allusions to having to "find" himself. He stops seeking sex, forcing you to make the advances; this is a losing proposition, because if he declines or fails, he becomes more unhappy, and if you do seduce him, your cutting down the distance he has been building between you may cause him to stampede away.

The phobic takes refuge in work, despite his previous lack of enthusiasm for his job. He may turn to alcohol or drugs, because he *is* experiencing true anxiety and wants to be numbed. He may get involved with another woman, the surest way to end any illusion of commitment to you.

Finally, he does everything in his power to provoke arguments and fights, giving him the excuse he needs to back out of the relationship.

When a man has the dream-girl syndrome, sincere efforts on your part to improve your relationship are soon appreciated and bear fruit. In all probability, your contribution to the relationship has been decreasing, and as you get emotionally closer, his self-esteem and happiness will increase proportionately.

The phobic does not *want* to get closer. The more you reduce the distance between you, the more desperately he moves away.

If you are convinced that you've been involved with a phobic, is there anything you can do besides getting rid of him? (And *that* is not always easy.) Occasionally, in poker games where the antes have accumulated to an impressive size because no one was able to open for several hands, you should stay in and try to improve a poor hand. So much has already been invested that a few chips more can be risked on a long-shot chance of winning a huge pot. A poorer reason for pursuing it is the reason given by a gambling addict who was warned by a friend that he was playing in a crooked game: "I *know* that, but it's the only game in town!"

If you want to cure a phobic, a task much better left to trained and impartial psychotherapists, the key is to refrain from closing the gap between you. To get friendly with a nervous cat or timid deer, you have to make them approach you, not try to approach them. The behavioral therapists call it desensitization: expose the phobic to just as much stress as he can endure and, after his anxiety subsides, take it one step further.

If your man genuinely wants commitment, but seems to have doubts about whether you are the woman with whom he wants to spend his life, then it's you against the dream girl. That's a hand worth playing.

Moody Blues

Unhappiness, decreased interest in sex, impaired concentration, and isolation may by now be familiar to you as symptoms of the dream-girl syndrome, but they are more widely recognized as symptoms of psychological depression. How do you know that the man in your life is not suffering from a depression, which can cause radical change in behavior?

Depression is usually pervasive. Men with the dream-girl syndrome do not run out of energy; they rechannel it. They may spend more time at the office. They may spend hours in the company of male friends. They may stoke the fires of their imagination by renting movies or perusing magazines. Even when they seclude themselves, they are active, although the chief activity may be fantasizing.

They are angry and irritable rather than glum. If they fail to talk, it is not because their thought process has slowed, as in the case of depression, but because they do not want to share their discontent.

Men with depression need professional attention. Men with the dream-girl syndrome need your attention.

Know When to Fold 'Em

Kenny Rogers summed up the formula for successful poker playing and romantic relationships in one line: You've got to know when to hold 'em, fold 'em, walk away, or run.

Men with a true dream-girl syndrome are worth holding in nearly all cases. Then there are men who seem to have the dream-girl syndrome, but who actually have much deeper problems. As in the case of a three-card "flush," the time to hold on and invest in these men is never. You fold 'em, throw them in, and walk away. If they follow, you run.

The worst of the lot is the narcissist. His world does not merely center on himself, it *is* himself. The sociopath will consciously manipulate you to get what he wants. The man with an impulse control problem may become periodically violent and make hasty decisions with bad consequences. The substance abuser will lose his judgment when under the influence of alcohol or illegal drugs. None of them are promising mates, but they all have their rational moments and will make concessions to keep you involved in the relationship.

The narcissist cannot even give you a few good moments. His vision is limited to his own perspective. No amount of training can teach a dog, who is color blind, to select red or blue objects on command.

The diagnostic criteria set forth by the American Psychiatric Association for identifying a narcissistic personality disorder are the presence of at least five of the following:

1. Reacts to criticism with feelings of rage, shame, or humiliation (even if not expressed)

2. Is interpersonally exploitative: takes advantage of others to achieve his or her own ends

3. Has a grandiose sense of self-importance; e.g., exaggerates achievements and talents, expects to be noticed as "special" without appropriate achievement

4. Believes that his or her problems are unique and can be understood only by other special people

5. Is preoccupied with fantasies of unlimited success, power, brilliance, beauty, or ideal love

6. Has a sense of entitlement: unreasonable expectation of especially favorable treatment; e.g., assumes that he or she does not have to wait in line when others must do so

7. Requires constant attention and admiration; e.g., keeps fishing for compliments

8. Lack of empathy: inability to recognize and experience how others feel; e.g., annoyance and surprise when a friend who is seriously ill cancels a date

9. Is preoccupied with feelings of envy

Of all those criteria, I feel the most important is number eight. Many people, including very nice ones, may find themselves in circumstances where they have to put their priorities ahead of others and say, "I understand what you want, but I cannot concern myself with that. I have to take care of myself here." The narcissist does *not* understand that others could want something other than what he wants. It would be like a goldfish appreciating someone's need for air.

In the early seventies, I watched a TV interview with Nguyen Van Thieu, then president of South Vietnam. The United States had been withdrawing troops from Vietnam and nobody thought any longer in terms of winning a military victory. The problem was extricating the United States with as few catastrophic consequences and as little loss of honor as possible.

The interviewer asked Thieu if he would ever consider resigning as president if it was in the best interests of his country.

Thieu looked at the interviewer with an expression of puzzlement and replied, "I am doing fine."

Thinking that perhaps the question had not been really understood, the interviewer repeated it in more detail, stressing the existence of hypothetical circumstances where Thieu's resignation would avoid more bloodshed and effect a peaceful transition to a new government, perhaps a coalition that would protect the interests of both the North and South.

Thieu stared impassively and repeated, without emotion, "I am doing fine."

Thieu's behavior struck me as the epitome of narcissism. I do not believe that his reply was a calculated ploy to insure that the United States, which had supported him for years, would not throw him to the wolves and would provide him with a safe haven and financial security. His motivation throughout his life had apparently been to gain personal power and wealth, and he had no other frame of reference. Talking to him about the welfare of the Vietnamese people was like lecturing a leopard on the conservation of impala herds.

In dealing with narcissistic patients, I have to remain aware of their blind spots and inability to grasp concepts such as the feelings of others. If they are engaging in actions that cause distress to others, you can only get them to modify their behavior if you can convince them that the injured person's reaction may result in a loss of the services and concern that they have come to expect.

Nearly everyone seeks admiration, hates criticism, wants to receive recognition for his achievement and wants the most perfect love he can find. Nearly everyone understands that these goals must be earned, that if you want admiration you must be admirable and that love is a reciprocal process. The narcissist has an irrational sense of entitlement, as though he somewhere along the line received a free pass that provides unlimited services from everyone he meets.

While most men will try to attract a woman's interest by making her feel as if she is special, the narcissist invariably relies on impressing her with how unique, accomplished, and generally desirable he is. She usually succumbs because he seems too convincing to be insincere. The reason he is so convincing is that he believes all the wonderful things that he says about himself. A delusional person will give a normal polygraph test not because he is telling the truth, but because he believes he is.

The narcissist does not have a dream girl because he cannot imagine anyone who would deserve him. If he had one, it would be a genie of the lamp who would be available to provide him instantly with everything he thinks he deserves.

Even Barbara Eden would have dumped a man like this.

Mama's Boy

Many years ago, when I was director of a community mental health clinic that served an underprivileged neighborhood, one of my co-workers, who lived in the community, invited my wife and me to dinner. Other guests included her daughter, who was in her early twenties, and the daughter's fiancé and his mother.

After dinner, the young man lay on the rug with his head in his mother's lap, while his mother continuously stroked his hair and kissed him frequently on the face, as his fiancée and future mother-in-law looked on.

When we left, I said to my wife, "I give the marriage eight months." I was wrong. It lasted four.

When the man's dream girl is his mother, you don't want to take her on, you want to move on. The book on American combat judo that I ingested as a kid told how to incapacitate an assailant and how to disarm someone with a club or knife. It very reluctantly advised how to take on someone with a gun. In the brief section on handling *two* assailants, the part about why you don't want to do this was longer than the oh-well-if-you-must advice on how to proceed. There was nothing on handling three or more attackers. I liked that book because it was honest about the odds in a world where film heroes routinely defeated enemy squads with their fists and feet. Like Kenny Rogers, it said you had to know when to run.

I would hope your man loves his mother. A man who does not probably will hate women in general or has been so scarred by maternal deprivation or abuse that he will not be able to return the love he so desperately craves. The love that a normal man shows for his mother will change with time, not in its depth, but in its quality. There is a natural progression from total dependence to ambivalent attempts at independence, to independence with respect, to taking care of *her* needs. The mother gets all of the child's love. As he gets older, he shares his love, but there is more to share because his capacity to love, in new adult ways, changes.

The mama's boy never achieves independence because his mother does not let him. Since she knows that his emerging sexual drive will motivate him to cultivate relationships with other women, the mother becomes seductive, to degrees ranging from subtle to what psychiatrists charitably term grossly inappropriate. I had a boyhood friend whose father, divorced from his mother, took him to a whorehouse in Puerto Rico on his thirteenth birthday. His mother in New York had a different approach. She stripped and invited him to inspect her naked body, because she did not want him to turn to other women to satisfy his curiosity. It took him a very long time to settle into a committed marriage.

Do not confuse the mama's boy with a man who has a possessive mother. A clinging mother will try to interfere with her son's love relationships and will not usually be successful at disguising her hostility toward perceived rivals. Many men are able to escape the parental clutches by setting firm limits or, if that is impossible, keeping contact with mother to a minimum. If your man seems cool to his mother, you may have an insensitive boor, but more likely the guy is making a praiseworthy attempt to preserve his special ties to you.

Just as the narcissist wants his own way, with little compunction or conflict, the mama's boy wants his mother's way. He telephones her often and spends a long time on each call. He consults with her on decisions and feels obligated to keep her informed of *every* development in his life. He wants you to spend every holiday with her and probably much of every weekend. He frets about her health, which is characterized by a multitude of symptoms without a diagnosis, and her age, which is around that of Joan Collins, who seems to be her role model.

If you have not married this guy yet, don't. If you have, don't waste your time searching for dream girls to battle. The game here is not poker, it's partnership hearts and the strategy is to discard the black queen. If it's too late to walk away, you can still put as much distance as possible between you and your mother-in-law, keeping your man beside you every step of the way.

Too High to Reach

A social worker intern at the clinic confided to me, "I kind of like working with addicts. They're interesting."

I scowled. "It's good that you feel that way, since we are involved in treating them, but watch yourself. The problem with people who are still using is that the drug is *always* the main consideration. They'll keep appointments and may genuinely like you and appreciate your help, but when they need a fix, they'll steal from your purse or take anything you have. They will lie about everything from their drug use to why they missed appointments. And, if it stood between them and a fix, they wouldn't hesitate to harm or even kill you.

"Look at their histories and you'll see that they have stolen from their mothers and other family members, and beaten their wives and girlfriends if they tried to withhold money. Why should they treat you differently?"

That may seem harsh coming from a compassionate physician, but it is realistic. A lion tamer does not hate or abuse the animals that he works with, but he never lets himself regard them as harmless pets. Not all addicts (and I include those hooked on alcohol, as well as other drugs) are violent. Some, such as many alcoholics and abusers of prescription drugs, never break a law, but it is nearly impossible to find a substance abuser who has not brought distress to someone other than himself, either family members, employers, or lovers. Those hooked on illegal drugs who do not resort to theft or prostitution support their habit by dealing drugs, or dragging others into the slavery of addiction.

Drug abusers do not always fit the usual image of a seedy, unkempt, unemployed derelict, whom women would shun without hesitation. I have detoxed many addicts who held high-paying positions as executives, musicians, lawyers, and doctors. They often have wives and girlfriends, and sometimes it is only when the supportive woman leaves or throws them out that they seek treatment. Relapses among those that do not comply with aftercare are frequent.

I include these men in the fold-'em category because they are poor risks, certainly so while they are hooked. Because they may be intelligent, wealthy, and affectionate, women may regard their substance abuse as a flaw that can be corrected. The woman may rationalize that she herself has gotten drunk on occasion, smoked pot, tried cocaine once or twice. Take your cue from the experts. Recovering addicts in residential programs, even those who limit their rehabilitation therapy to meetings of Narcotics Anonymous or Alcoholics Anonymous, are prohibited from getting emotionally involved with the opposite sex until they have maintained abstinence from drugs for a long period, usually a year.

It's a tough rule to enforce. Therapeutic communities tend to be coed. A.A. sponsors cannot follow their charges around all day. So there are slips into sexual indulgence, just as there are slips into drug use, but the counsel is sound. Recovering addicts are vulnerable emotionally, and a supportive woman can seem like a natural, healthy "high." Judgment in these areas, however, is not much better than it had been when under the influence.

If your partner is on drugs (and that includes alcohol, the perfectly legal one), insist that he get off them, preferably with professional help. The real dangers of withdrawal may make a brief hospitalization for detoxification necessary. Staying off is usually harder than getting off, so make sure he follows through with the recommended rehab therapy. Freedom from withdrawal symptoms does not eliminate cravings, especially when the recovering addict feels stressed or unhappy. The twelve-step programs (A.A. and N.A.) offer not only regular meetings but dedicated people who have been through the same hell themselves and will offer a trained ear at any hour. Don't you try to be the one to supply around-the-clock access.

If someone is in recovery, wait and see. Friendship is fine, but hold off on anything deeper. If he sticks with the program and turns his life around, there will be plenty of good years ahead, ones worth waiting for. If he relapses, you'll be a complication, not a source of support, if you've committed yourself prematurely.

Substance abusers do not have dream girls. Their habit is far more important than any woman, real or otherwise. It is interesting that while enthusiasts such as boaters, drivers, pilots, and musicians may refer to their vehicles as "her" and even designate them with female names, drug addicts do not romanticize their passion for chemicals. Marijuana is sometimes called "Mary Jane," but most users call it "reefer," "grass," or "pot." I have heard of heroin being called "lady," but this is not a common term. Even though cocaine is reputed to enhance sexual enjoyment, the real users soon "burn out" and, as the neurotransmitter chemicals in their brain get depleted, turn to the drug just to feel an average degree of contentment and alertness.

Liquors bearing names or images of people are designated as male: Johnny Walker, John Begg, Jack Daniels, Beefeater. Except for the Bloody Mary, reportedly named after a woman who spilled one of the first ones on her white gown, and the Margarita, cocktails (Rob Roy, Harvey Wallbanger, Jack Rose) are not named after females, unless it's a cocktail such as a Pink Lady or Shirley Temple that no man would dare order. Among beers produced on a large scale, I can only think of St. Pauli Girl, despite the abundance of seductive women, including the Swedish Bikini Team, in beer commercials.

Don't look for a dream girl to confront here. You'll feel foolish trying to compete with a Blue Nun.

CHAPTER 14

Face to Pretty Face

*I*n *Who Framed Roger Rabbit*, when Joanna Cassidy, playing Dolores, found Bob Hoskins, playing boyfriend Eddie Valiant, in the arms of a tall, extremely bosomy, ravishing redhead named Jessica Rabbit, Ms. Cassidy, confronting the ultimate dream girl, delivered her scathing lines while glaring into the face of Betsy Brantley.

Betsy Brantley was the performance model (a fancy term for stand-in) for Jessica. Outside of their sex, there was little resemblance between the petite, pretty, but unimposing brunette actress and the formidable, voluptuous, flame-haired hellion who was unnerving the hapless detective. But Ms. Brantley, despite her human limitations, was as necessary as the rubber rabbit and weasels that were used to help the actors visualize the title character and his enemies. Without the comely performance model, Ms. Cassidy would have had to imagine herself in a showdown with the most alluring, charismatic female conceivable while she was looking at and talking to thin air.

Unfortunately, a woman confronting the dream girl winds up doing just that. Having detected the signs of the dream-girl syndrome, she must proceed to the next step of confronting her rival, just as a detective who knows that a criminal has committed a heinous act must find the perpetrator. The investigator usually doesn't know who the criminal is, only what sort of a person he is. When he finds the blaggard, there will probably be some sort of fierce struggle, which is all part of the job, but that takes relatively little time compared to the tracking stage. The face-to-face meeting is inevitable and is the guaranteed payoff for good detective work.

In confronting the dream girl, there is no such satisfaction. Her face is certainly beautiful, but you will never see it; even your man has only a vague impression of it, unless he has invested her with the unmodified visage of a celebrity or a woman he once knew. You are in conflict with a phantom, an imaginary creature that your man may even deny the existence of, and worst of all, you're *losing*.

One consolation is that a detective can often reach a satisfactory solution without capturing and removing the villain. If the sleuth recovers the stolen jewels, if he defuses the bomb in time, if he rescues the hostage from her secret prison, that may be good enough. In fact, this was usually the preferred pattern in the struggles between the old superheroes and their most challenging adversaries. Lex Luthor, Superman's arch-enemy, either never got to prison or escaped soon afterward, so he could hatch another fiendish plot. Batman's comic-book foes, like the Penguin and the Joker, always lived to fight another day, even though they never won a fight.

So, let me assure you that most battles against the dream girl are not resolved by the man's confessing her existence, providing a full description and history, and renouncing all further fantasizing. It is not because of guilt or embarrassment or possessiveness that men guard their secret women, but simply because most of them have repressed the details of her identity. They remember vividly the sense of security she brought them in their loneliest hours, the contentment that accrues to the conviction that there is a woman who will be exclusively theirs in the near future; they do not remember as sharply the girl behind those feelings and, if they do, they will underestimate her as a childish fantasy they discarded in favor of real women.

The search for the dream girl in the hidden recesses of a particular man's memory and imagination is worthwhile because the more he is able to remember and recount about her, the better he is able to understand his own attitudes, needs, and desires and put the dream girl into perspective as a mere fantasy.

You cannot understand his dream girl until *he* understands her. The quest is similar to psychotherapy, which is not a therapist learning about a patient, but a patient learning about himself. The therapist helps the process by leading the patient down pathways of experience that the patient has neglected or forgotten, often because where they lead makes him uneasy.

In a common false analogy, the therapist has been likened to a guide, leading the patient into self-awareness and insights. Actually, the therapist is more like a hunter who presses the patient into service as a guide. The therapist knows what he hopes to discover, but only the patient knows the territory and the way to get to the goal. A guide takes you to a place that he knows how to reach, which he would not have gone to except for your wishes. He knows the way and you don't; you want to get there and he does not care, but you both arrive at the same time.

The dream girl is a discovery for you and a rediscovery for him, but you will both be seeing her with fresh vision.

Mad About the Girl

Would you accept an invitation to a witch hunt?

Probably not. Either you don't believe in witches and know you would be wasting your time or you do believe in them and, from your conception of them, have no wish to encounter any. Besides, what would you do with one when you came face-to-warty face? While you were reading her the Salem version of the Miranda rights, she might be turning you into a frog. Why stir up something unpleasant that you might not be able to get rid of?

Dream girls are much better looking than witches and can cast a meaner spell. They don't have to transform an earthly rival into a frog; in their presence, a woman feels like something only Kermit would leap at—and then she would lose him to Miss Piggy anyway.

A dream girl in adult life is the result of discontent with what a real relationship has to offer—a relationship with *you*. Whatever her attributes are, the dream girl's are different from yours, since you are being rejected and she is being idolized. You do not like this creature and you are liking progressively less the man who dreamed her up.

You are angry: first, because you *know* you have been one fine partner, probably a lot better than he deserves, and yet he is dissatisfied. He is not only an ingrate, but his judgment is impaired. Second, he is setting impossible standards, which neither you nor any real woman could meet; he is setting you up for failure. Third, like Alice in Wonderland, you become periodically aware that this irritation and abuse stems from sheer nonsense; this dream girl has less substance than a cardboard Queen of Hearts or a wooden Red Queen, yet you, a logical and sensible person, are expected to take her seriously.

Finally, the implication is that, since the dream girl does not really exist and you do not want your man to look for her among the competitive general population, you will have to change to become more like her. Any woman is willing to shed a few pounds or experiment with cosmetics, but changing one's identity strikes at the core. If your man had his way, you surmise, he'd want his dream girl to move into your body (perhaps a few pounds lighter), as in *The Invasion of the Body Snatchers.* Whatever you changed into would not be *you.*

Supply the Demand

The dream-girl syndrome develops when a need is not being met. It is not a search for a woman but for satisfaction.

If I want a hamburger, I don't need Ronald McDonald to cook and serve it. The person who meets my need could be male or female, young or old, attractive or homely. A smile and a courteous manner make the experience more pleasant, but the hamburger is what I really want.

A man does not want his dream girl to materialize. He wants a woman who will supply for him in reality what the dream girl promised and, to some extent, supplied in fantasy. She made him feel good, feel important, and feel secure. Most important, she made him feel like a *man.* In a word, she gave him *validation.* Later, I will discuss in detail what validation entails. While it has many components, none are rare or difficult to employ. Virtually all women make a man feel validated at the start of a relationship; without that encouragement, relationships would never advance beyond the encounter and flirtation stage. The woman invites the man into the relationship and would not do so if she failed to see anything desirable or promising in him.

What causes a bright situation to look dimmer? Think of a situation involving electrical power. When the lights dim, one of two things has happened: the power source is delivering less energy or there has been an increased demand for energy from the source. If you can cut back on the demand, by shutting off a few appliances, fine, but in either case a step-up in power output will remedy the problem. Whether a man needs more validation because circumstances have shaken his self-esteem or because the woman in his life has become too busy with her own concerns or a bit disenchanted with the man, a woman can easily supply what he needs—if she wants to.

Let us not assume that every woman will readily agree to do whatever it takes to fill the role of the dream girl—and, since she cannot *become* the dream girl, she can only play the part. What the woman does is not pretending, however; she is taking a fantasy and making it real. Like an actress skimming a prospective script for scenes that call for nudity, the prudent woman will want to know what the role entails before she accepts it. In this case, the role is a continuous one, to be played all your life, like the role of a mother. What does it demand?

Does the man want you to be someone else? No. If a casting director is hiring actresses, he doesn't begin with a rigid set of standards in mind. He wants someone who can fill the role and do a good job while bringing her own personality and interpretation to it. Several actresses in different productions of the same work can turn in excellent performances, although they are far from identical. Ethel Merman, Rosalind Russell, Tyne Daly, and Bette Midler have all received acclaim for playing Mama Rose in stage, film, and TV productions of *Gypsy*; they spoke the same lines and sang the same notes, yet Midler's Rose was different from Merman's and no one criticized her for that. Maybe the dream girl had a face, a name, a shape different from yours, but she never owned the role. Like an understudy in rehearsals, she never gets to go on before a live audience. The star role is yours, if you want it.

Does he want you to be a sex object? No, because the dream

girl was not invented to supply sexual gratification. Men are visually oriented when it comes to sexual arousal, as evidenced by the proliferation of erotic videos, magazines, and look-not-touch table dancers. An invisible woman is the last type of female a man would choose as a sex object. Having an attractive and enthusiastic sex partner will obviously add to a man's self-esteem, but it is usually not the place to start. Unhappy men have little interest in sex, unless they throw themselves into an affair; even that is a bid for validation, not sex.

Is he looking for a mother? Definitely not. Mothers do supply a great deal of unconditional love and excel at caregiving, but what they have difficulty doing is regarding their sons as adults. When a male is still on the threshold of adolescence, the dream girl may be sometimes imagined as an older woman (usually not old enough to be his mother) who has the sophistication to enable him to make a difficult transition. He may not imagine her as ever aging, but he knows that he is getting older. Men may seek mothering from wives, secretaries, and, of course, mothers, but not usually from dream girls.

Does he want you to be a cheerleader, centering your life on his projects and goals, while giving up any ambitions and potential achievements of your own? No again, because dream girls are strong women who have been able to transmit some of their confidence to men at the phase in their lives when they feel least secure. The more capable and independent a woman is, the more her respect is worth to the male who receives it. Men may seem gullible at times, but few are too simple to be able to recognize empty flattery when it is offered. Occasionally, the fantasy script calls for the man to rescue his dream girl, but more often she is the one pulling him out of scrapes and doldrums. When, in *Pretty Woman*, Richard Gere "rescued" Julia Roberts and asked what happens after the woman gets rescued, the happy hooker answered, "She rescues him right back."

So, don't be angry. Once you get to know the typical dream girl, you will find that she is probably very much like yourself, a woman willing to put up with a few male faults but able to discern and encourage the best qualities; someone who is a star in her own right and who has no desire to become a supporting cast of one.

But how do you get to know the dream girl when the only man with access to her has lost track of her?

On the Trail

Every once in a while, a detective lucks out. He walks into the drawing room where suspects are assembled on a dark and stormy night and says, "All right, the murder could only have been committed by one of you, someone who was present in this house before midnight."

And Colonel Mustard says, "Oh, I might as well own up, since you won't give us a moment's peace until you find out who did it. I clobbered the blighter with a candlestick in the billiard room, then planted the lead pipe under the lid of Miss Scarlet's piano in the conservatory to throw you off."

Sometimes you can simply ask, as I have been doing lately, "Have you ever had a dream girl?" By now you know the definition in case he asks what you mean by the term. Of course, if he needs a definition, you are in danger of being victimized by the "no" reflex, which plagues takers of sex surveys who ask about infidelity. Most men will automatically answer "no" on the grounds that no possible good can come of answering "yes" and no possible harm can come out of a "no."

Is it not true that many men have forgotten about their dream girls? Yes, but if you ever had an Easy Bake oven, a Shrinky-Dink set, a Koosa Bear from the Cabbage Patch, or a Growing-Up Skipper whose breasts expanded when you rotated her arm, you probably had forgotten about them until I just mentioned them. Besides, a man in the throes of the dream girl syndrome is likely to have better-than-average recall when it comes to fantasy women.

You can even show him a copy of this book and say, "This distinguished expert says that most men have had a dream girl at some time in their lives. I never knew that. Is there something to what he says? Did you ever have a dream girl?"

If he says yes, you're home free and he will tell you anything you want to know. This will serve to stop you from reading the rest of the book, in case you already haven't. He's afraid that any author who would spill *that* secret has probably included a lot of worse stuff better left unread.

If he says that he is no expert himself but has never had a dream girl, forget about an effortless confession and proceed with different strategems.

If he says that I'm nuts and it sounds like a lot of bovine ordure, he is being ultra-defensive and definitely has a dream girl he will try to hide.

Overcoming Listlessness

The things men like to talk about the most are probably sports, money, and women, not necessarily in that order.

This may explain why communication is so poor between men and women. Women do not usually know or care much about sports. Women are often interested in money, which is precisely why men avoid the subject, fearing women will find a way to part them from their holdings. Men do not talk about women to other members of the female sex probably because they do not want to risk arousing feelings of jealousy, which will lead to bad temper, which will be vented on those who had the poor judgment to broach the topic.

It is a shame that men do not talk more about women to women. They would not hesitate to discuss baseball with a baseball player or money with an investment banker; they would be delighted at the opportunity. Women have more expertise, not to mention direct experience, with regard to men's opposite sex and could probably improve intersexual relations by providing a degree of education.

If a discussion of real women might threaten a man, he could be much more comfortable talking about women he has never met, which, fortuitously, covers most dream girls. As the Devil said of Don Juan, and might have said of most men, "Now that we have got on to the subject of Woman, he will talk more than ever. However, I confess it is for me [the Devil being male] the one supremely interesting subject."

Men, being competitors by nature, are great makers of lists. They can spend hours ranking sports players in order of their overall skills. This proclivity probably begins in the playground, where every game involving teams requires choosing sides; the captains (invariably the best and second-best players or, at least, the strongest) take turns selecting teammates. Their choices are usually based on ability, with the worst or smallest boy chosen last. The craze for Rotisserie Baseball, a form of gambling as well as intellectual stimulation, is based on the choosing process.

Nearly every male fan plays the game of lists to some degree. The most common challenge is to select the greatest players of all time at each position. Modifications might include limiting selections to American League or National League players; to players from one team, such as the Yankees; or to men who have played within the past decade. More whimsical variations have included an all-Italian or all-Polish team. *The Baseball Book of Lists* includes dream teams consisting entirely of players born on Christmas Day, players with short names (May, Cey, Ott, Lee) and long names (Raffensberger, Grabarkewitz, Yastrzemski, and Schreckengost).

What do dream teams have to do with dream women? The game can easily be adapted to a highly revealing exploration of men's ideals and preferences when it comes to women. In *Bull Durham*, Susan Sarandon noted that men will put up with just about anything if you tell them it's foreplay. Similarly, a woman can get men to cooperate with almost anything if, like Mary Poppins's method of getting the nursery tidied up, she makes a game out of it, particularly a game they have already played.

Some evening when you are ostensibly perusing an issue of *People*, ask him casually who he thinks are the three most interesting women in entertainment today. He will probably answer your question with a question, maybe on the order of "What's it to you?" or, more likely, try to set some limits. Do you mean the prettiest? The most talented? The most controversial? Does it include singers or newscasters, as well as actresses?

Make it as open-ended as possible. Let him throw in non-entertainers, such as Princess Diana or Hillary Clinton, if he likes. You could have asked simply for the three most interesting women, but if one of his co-workers or one of your neighbors came to mind, even briefly, he might have panicked and dismissed the whole project.

If he comes up readily with three choices, expand the list to ten or more. Or, ask him to pick the prettiest, the sexiest, the most talented or the best wife material.

If he's an avid reader, ask him to list the most fascinating women in fiction. If he reads the comic section, ask him who his favorite female character is. Who is the most attractive female athlete? The most intriguing political figure?

Do not castigate his choices, but don't hesitate to question how he arrived at them. Your goal in this seemingly innocent game is to learn how he thinks about women, particularly in terms of what constitutes the ideal.

There was a memorable beer commercial in which three young men are shooting pool and playing a nostalgic rating game. "Ginger or Mary Ann?" one says, without preamble.

One of the two young women observing them murmurs to the other, "Ginger was a bimbo."

The man being questioned hesitates, then says, "Mary Ann."

"Mary Ann or Jeannie?" persists the questioner.

There is not much hesitation and general approbation as he answers, "Jeannie!"

My question is, what about Ginger or Mary Ann? Are we talking about one night together, steady girlfriend, who you would marry, or who you would want to be stranded with on Gilligan's island? Is the choice between Tina Louise and Dawn Wells or between a fictitious bimbo and a wholesome girl who looks great in shorts?

If we are talking strictly in terms of a remote island, anyone would choose Jeannie; she could fold her arms, blink her eyes, and zap you into central Los Angeles. Or, are we talking about a fair fight between Mary Ann in her shorts and Jeannie in her harem outfit without any magic powers to add a Mercedes convertible and a condo in Aruba to her personal delights?

In such games, men usually do not obsess about such technicalities. Each man's imagination sets its own limits, which generally encompass a wide space. There is room enough for Tina and Ginger, Barbara and Jeannie, Dawn and Mary Ann. Despite this latitude, men are always prepared to name one of dreamland's denizens to the top-ranked spot. That is how dream girls come to be.

You may wonder, if many men base their dream girls on someone they actually have met or whom they have never seen, what the point is in exploring the realm of real or fictitious women who are well known. The goal in such pastimes is not necessarily to capture the personal dream girl, although you might stumble upon her in romping through his imagination, but to understand what a particular man admires and values in women. By using well-known females and characters, you have mutual reference points for comparisons.

If you say, "Ginger or Mary Ann?" and he says, "Can I pick Mrs. Howell?" you know that you are with a man whose tastes do not run to the conventional.

Be prepared to play the game yourself. He might ask, "Dylan or Brandon?" or which performer on MTV's top ten videos this week you would choose to be shipwrecked with. Chances are he won't try to turn the tables, though. Your fantasies do not threaten him, since he has been living with fantasy creatures long enough to appreciate their incapability to get physically involved with you, which is usually men's main concern.

Be wary about posing questions that do threaten him and bring any game to an abrupt halt. My younger daughter, Laura, once stunned me by suddenly asking, "Which of Mommy's friends do you think is the prettiest?"

I could honestly respond that I had never thought of any of them in that particular frame of reference and I did answer her more or less that way. If she had asked which of my female co-workers … well, she didn't, so let's not pursue that one. I am certainly not going to state in print that none of my wife's friends could be considered pretty; neither am I ever going to designate one as the prettiest, even though I suppose I could select the prettiest alligator in the Bronx Zoo's reptile house if I were asked to, such standards being relative.

Fortunately, my wife does not consort with women who make their living at being pretty. I might then have had to say to my daughter, "Well, I suppose I would have to say most people would consider Aunt Madonna the prettiest."

The next question would have been, "Who do you think is prettier, Aunt Madonna or Mommy?"

Easy answer, but you can appreciate how I would prefer questions such as "How is adenosine triphosphate involved in glycolysis?" or "Where do babies come from?"

Anyway, avoid questions such as which of your cousins is cuter or which member of your feminist issues group has the best figure, since your question and his answer might unnerve both of you.

And do not ask, "Ginger or Mary Ann or me?"

Smooth Talking

They want us, but they don't want to want us. They need us, but they don't want to need us. They need to want us, but they don't want to need to want us!

—CATHY

While many females inhabit the comic pages of daily newspapers and a few, such as Brenda Starr and Mary Jane Parker, still qualify as such stuff as dream girls are made from, Cathy is unusual because she is the star of her own strip, which is funny (unlike Ms. Starr's) and which is not shared by a husband (unlike Blondie's). Her humor is not based on wacky fantasy friends and environs, as in the strips of Broom Hilda or Mother Goose.

Cathy is a modern, single career woman, trying in vain to lose weight, get out from under a pile of accumulated work assignments, and communicate with the men in her life who manage to keep her single. She craves and fears verbal interchanges with the males who frustrate her and has come to dread the phrase, "We need to talk," which always bodes deep trouble if not sudden death for a relationship.

Talking between a couple undoubtedly helps either to resolve differences or, at least, clarify the conflicts that are impeding a peaceful solution. Even when the problem is mired so deeply in one partner's personal traumas that it has little bearing on the relationship, talking may help him unearth the difficulty, shed some light on it, and perhaps enlist some help from the partner. As a practitioner of "talk therapy," I have often remained silent throughout an entire session while the patient talked without interruption, unraveling knots as he unwound the skein of his tale and coming to a better understanding of how to deal with a problem more effectively. My greatest contribution to the session was not interrupting his train of thought.

Talking to a man who has the dream-girl syndrome is especially difficult. He is vulnerable and has no wish to let that be detected. He feels he is unappreciated and wishes he had a woman in his life like the one he used to fantasize about; he is angry at you for not being that woman. He is even angrier at himself, because he, naturally, suspects that if he accomplished more or satisfied you more, you would have met his need for approval and admiration. Communication reveals the self, and he is no more eager to do that in his present state than you would be to reveal your midriff after a twenty-pound winter weight gain.

You can, nevertheless, communicate with a reluctant partner if you do it in a way that makes him feel comforted and hopeful, instead of attacked and put down. People come to therapists primarily because they are unhappy or anxious. Therapy itself can elicit fears and tears, but the patient is willing to undergo anything if it will break the existing pattern that has caused so much distress.

While I am sharing a therapist's secrets, I am not asking you to become his therapist. A therapist has a sacred duty to keep his own emotions in check and not to make any demands on the patient other than keeping appointments and paying for them. His job is not to pass judgment or to make over the patient according to his own ideals. While you should respect a partner's individuality, you also have the right to decide what you will or will not tolerate in *your* relationship. A therapist shares an occasional hour or less with a man; you have to live with him or work toward the day when you will. Yet you will need to achieve effective communication as much as a therapist does and what works in a therapeutic setting will also work for you.

The first requisites are privacy and time. An appointment specifies a place and a time, preferably a stopping time as well as a starting time. Do not try to catch his attention or sneak a point across while teams are changing sides between innings or when he is switching sections of the newspaper. If you have noted that he is approachable while unwinding with a six P.M. cocktail, while browsing through a magazine in bed before turning off the lights, or while sipping a cup of coffee after dinner, you may be able to avoid making an appointment.

Otherwise, give him a specific invitation. Do not say, "We *need* to talk." Try, "Can we talk about a few things?" or "I'd really like to discuss a few things with you and get some input." He may sabotage any attempt to pinpoint an appointment; he's too tired at night, too hurried in the morning, too interested in his television programs in the evening, and at other times—"When am I supposed to relax?"

Don't let him deter you. Tell him you will talk about talking about it at a certain time and he will soon decide that talking about talking is as bad as talking, or even worse, since there is no hope of a finish.

Remember, you are not talking about dream girls (which you have probably tried, without success) but the dream girl syndrome. Let him know how you feel and stress that it is how *you* feel. If you say, "You've become moody and withdrawn," he can reply, "I have not." If you say, "I feel that you've become—," he cannot deny your feelings, even if he says your perception is off.

If you say you feel something is wrong and he says there is nothing wrong, you can counter that a wrong feeling is something wrong. Once he realizes that this discussion is not going to result in a barrage of criticism and that you sincerely want to make things better, he will stop retreating and evading, allowing some interaction.

Businessmen who habitually make presentations in order to sell a product or an idea often advise: Tell them what you're going to tell them, tell them, then tell them what you told them. This is not a presentation, so don't take that advice. Saying it once is communication. Saying it more than once is nagging.

Be as unemotional and logical as you can, but do not sound patronizing. It may be more constructive to come across as the distressed partner that you are than as a mother or, worse, a psychiatrist.

I frequently warn the residents whom I supervise, "There will come a time in your marriage when you will try to bring your professional expertise to a quarrel with your spouse. You will strive to remain calm and objective, confronting anger and vituperation with reason and equanimity. It is at such a time that your spouse will say, 'Don't pull that psychiatry crap on me!'"

You can and should, however, do what a psychiatrist does best:

listen. When we were first married, my wife would often complain after a social event, "You hardly said a word all night."

I would reply, "Did you hear any silences? If there had been any, I would have filled them. People love to talk about themselves. If they really want to know about you, they will ask. There are a lot of talkers in this world, but few good listeners, of which I happen to be one."

When I am in a therapy session, I don't usually fill silences. While people in social situations talk freely because they can choose only pleasant subjects, people with emotional distress find self-disclosure painful, even more painful than silence. Silence makes therapists uncomfortable as well, and many novices impetuously intrude on a silence to relieve the tension. If the patient is convinced that the therapist will not be the first one to speak, he will talk; he can, after all, bring up some nonthreatening material if he chooses to defer the more disturbing confidences. I can recall many times when I almost spoke just for the sake of speaking, resisted the impulse, and, seconds later, the patient made a startling disclosure that I had almost blocked.

"A sympathetic ear" is almost synonymous with "a good friend." The act of listening is in itself a way of validating someone. We attend lectures and speeches because we respect the speakers, because they have reached a level of expertise and achievement where their words will be a valuable aid to us in sharing their knowledge or emulating their accomplishments.

But a person does not have to be successful to merit careful listening. The emotionally crippled patient, down on his luck, feeling scorned by society, often reports an increased sense of self-esteem and well-being simply because someone paid careful attention to him and felt he was worth the time.

Once a man starts to talk, do not interrupt him. You don't have to feel obligated to respond to every statement he makes, even if you support him. On the other hand, you don't have to be impassive, either. A response can be anything from a direct look into his eyes to a nod or even some thoughts of your own when a pause calls for it.

Make sure there are no distractions. If the telephone rings, ignore it. If you have children, make sure they are tucked in for the night or otherwise not around. Turn the television and radio off. You wouldn't want such distractions during a psychotherapy session, a lecture, or a movie, so give your intimate conversations the same consideration.

Suppose he just doesn't want to talk or doesn't seem capable of it. Then, let him listen to you. Invite comments or rebuttals. Don't tell him what he does that upsets you without offering specific suggestions about what you would like him to do instead. Grievances without remedies are just complaints. Concentrate on what he does and don't criticize what he is. Pejorative comments, such as "You're selfish," "You're a slob," or "You're insensitive," will only make him withdraw or counterattack.

If you ask him to do specific things, such as telephoning you when he is going to come home late or spending Saturday with you at the mall instead of playing softball, invite him to tell you how you could make him happier.

Don't use sarcasm. You may think it's better than a direct slam, but it usually provokes more anger than an insult. Sarcasm is intended to draw laughs or amusement at the expense of the target and most people would rather be upbraided than mocked.

If you feel yourself losing control, call a time-out and compose yourself. Tears may melt the resolve of many men during a fight, but your discussions are supposed to strengthen a man, not throw him into emotional turmoil. Keep your voice soft and your eyes dry.

Do not dredge up the past. Do not anticipate the future. Concentrate on specific present problems and prospective solutions. Don't clutter the field with the debris of past disputes.

If he expresses some feelings or conflicts for the first time, do not be too quick to give advice. Many men keep things from their partners because they are afraid of being told what to do. This is a no-win situation, since if they take a woman's advice, they feel they have lost control over their own affairs, even though they might have chosen the same course of action without her input; if they ignore the advice, they risk a woman's anger or her feeling ignored.

If he truly wants your advice, he will find ways of obtaining it. In *The King and I*, the king of Siam fears that a visiting English delegation will consider him a barbarian and use this misperception to justify seizing his tiny country as one more colony for the Crown. Instead of asking Anna, the English schoolteacher, for advice, he urges her to guess how he is going to handle the situation. Thoroughly aware of his motives, Anna supplies the answers and lets him take the credit. Not all men think of themselves as monarchs who must exercise absolute rule, but most want to feel in charge of their situations.

Try to see the world through the man's eyes. Understand his frame of reference. Years of practicing psychiatry have convinced me that even the most illogical statements and behavior make a lot more sense when you are aware of situations that have put a patient in a certain mind-set. One young man, living in a residence for the emotionally disturbed, suddenly seemed to become paranoid, insisting that he needed a hospital because if he stayed in the residence he would be killed. A few days after that he confessed a strong attraction to a female resident and his annoyance at a streetwise fellow who kept intruding and making bolder advances than the patient would have dared. I was willing to bet that the tough rival had warned the patient to stay away from the attractive woman, implying dire consequences if he persisted. Overwhelmed not only by the threat of violence but also by his humiliation at abandoning his courtship, the patient could not bear to remain at the residence. He was miserable, but not delusional. I learned that I was right.

A patient with a much looser grip on reality once asked me to prescribe Cogentin so that he could become more sociable. Cogentin is a medication used to reverse certain side effects, such as muscle spasms and stiffness, caused by antipsychotic drugs. I did not understand why my patient, who was intelligent and well-read despite his illness, thought that Cogentin could affect social interaction. Then he explained that "co-" was a prefix indicating "with" something and "gens" was the Latin word for people. He had concluded that Cogentin was a medicine that would help you to be with people. He still had a psychiatric illness, but his thought production was not as disordered as his medication request had first led me to believe.

Always remember what I call Principle Three: If things don't add up, you're probably missing one or more pieces of information. If you don't understand why a man acts the way he does, there are probably things going on in his head that he hasn't yet shared with you. Life is like a jigsaw puzzle; you don't need all the pieces to distinguish the picture it forms, but you need most of them to make any sense out of it.

What does all this communicating have to do with discovering the dream girl? You might have come to a better understanding of one another's desires and needs, maybe even become better at meeting them, but he probably still does not or cannot produce the dream girl who had contributed so much to the discontent in your relationship.

You may not have met the dream girl, but you have been thoroughly invading her territory. Since a man carries her around in his imagination for many years, he feels she understands him completely and provides a source of support.

This is really just a wish. The man is not psychotic and, therefore, does not really believe in the dream girl's existence. Only he can know his own mind. Since he cannot fully trust his own dreams and values, he longs for the day when a woman will share his every thought and give him the support that he needs.

You, of course, have been getting to know, through your improved communication, more about him than anyone ever has in the past and, it is hoped, ever will know. By understanding what he is, by listening without censure, by sharing his goals, you have taken on the function of the dream girl. And function is really all that matters, since she never had a material presence to begin with.

Scoreboard

The Mills Brothers, about fifty years ago, used to sing a song about a man who was going to get a paper doll to call his own, because he could no longer tolerate his unfaithful girlfriend. He made it clear that he would rather have exclusive possession of a paper doll than be involved with a fickle-hearted, real, live woman.

Choosing a dream girl over any real woman is not exactly the same as selecting an imaginary object. It is more like a stance of non-engagement or detachment. The man elects not to get involved with anyone at the present time. He knows what he wants and the dream girl approximates it. Like the paper doll, the satisfactions she can give are limited, but she does not make the man feel hurt and frustrated.

I recently found among my clutter a twenty-year-old skin magazine that had a couple of advertisements for inflatable life-size "love dolls." One ad made reference to "personal attractions that I'll reveal to you as soon as I arrive"; I am sure that's a reference to penetrable vinyl orifices.

The thing that shocked me a little was an ad for a doll three times the price of the "personal attraction" beauty; there was a sentence that said she was "made just for love," but that was not the chief selling point. The ad described how a satisfied customer had danced with "Judy," practicing all sorts of new steps, which she followed all the way. "I really felt I had a new friend," he reported. He liked "Judy" so much that he sent for "Susan," a companion doll of darker complexion and "The three of us began to play. I danced with one, then the other, then both together!" The ad urges you to "Ride around town with Judy by your side and impress your friends."

Okay, I could understand an ad that offered a new masturbatory aid sent in a plain brown wrapper that can be deflated and hidden when not in use so that nobody will discover what a pitiful loser you are. But "impress your friends"? "At cocktail parties, they're conversation pieces"? ("Should we call an ambulance for Melvin now, or try to lock him and that balloon in the spare bedroom until the party is over?")

This ad was not in *Psychotics Monthly*. The magazine was, ironically, titled *Stud*. Apparently, horny but sane men were supposed to believe they would "never be bored or alone again!" by buying Judy, who had allegedly fully satisfied more than 100,000 users.

Anyway, I am using this bizarre digression to illustrate that men have needs that go beyond sexual release and will go to considerable lengths to supply in fantasy what they are incapable of finding in a real woman.

The dream girl even has distinct advantages over her earthy opponents:

She is perfect. Whatever attributes or qualities a man wants, she can have. There are no building code restrictions or zoning laws in the business of fantasy construction.

She thinks the man is perfect. This is even better than her perfection. The man, being rational except for his involvement with the dream girl, does not believe that he is perfect. Naturally, he doesn't expect to find a woman who does, either. The dream girl, however, likes him just the way he is. She bolsters his ego against the erosion caused by his own realistic self-doubts.

She knows everything about him. She lives in his head, so she is thoroughly familiar with its contents. She has been there for years, so she is aware of each new thought that comes in and of every rearrangement of goals and ideals that he periodically makes. He could never transfer his entire brain contents to a real woman, and there isn't space enough inside his skull for her to access it herself.

She never disagrees with him. When he feels insecure or uncertain, he has a built-in supporter to second every motion he makes. There is never any debate and no amendments are proposed. He may fail in the end, but he has the illusion of not going down to defeat alone.

You, as an actual woman, have some advantages of your own:

You have a body. People of both sexes and all ages usually crave physical contact with another human. Children deprived of it in infancy become chronically depressed, fail to thrive, and may even die, despite receiving adequate nourishment and shelter. Adults can survive without it, but are much happier with it. The absence of hugs and being held during the preadolescent years for most boys may be a strong influence in their love of physical contact sports; a hug may be better than a tackle, but you take what you can get.

The fetishist may prefer leather or rubber, but most men prefer the warmth and softness of flesh. Pygmalion never complained about losing the piece of cold marble he had so laboriously carved when Venus transformed the first love doll into a woman. Having a body, regardless of its dimensions or its imperfections, is enough of an advantage over your insubstantial opponent to assure you of victory if your nonphysical components are not totally incompatible with his.

You are vulnerable. That may sound like a disadvantage, but having a perfect woman without any weaknesses or flaws can eventually discourage a man, even if he was the one who endowed her with spiritual perfection. Sometimes a man's need to feel superior, even in one or two areas, outweighs his need to be supported by someone who is practically invincible. Aristotle once said that true friendship can exist only between equals. Since men, being human, are vulnerable, they need someone who shares that quality for a true unselfish and loving relationship.

You are objective. I once saw one of those talking boxes in a novelty store, the kind that has a button that activates the sound of several different phrases. Some of those boxes laugh, some emit the sounds of gunfire and explosions, and some insult you, but this one emulated a corporate yes-man, saying things such as "Right you are" and "You're terrific." That's the kind of support you get from a dream girl. It's automatic and brainless. Any support from you may be less effusive, but it is more trustworthy, because a critical brain appraised the situation before evaluating it. Maybe you won't endorse every idea or decision of his, but the ones you support will have a seal of approval that is worth something.

You can help. Two heads are often better than one in analyzing a situation and finding a solution. If a dream girl has a head, it's inside him, so it's the same one. The mind you have to offer is as valuable as your body. Most men don't want to be told what to do, but suggesting different options gives him a wider scope of power for the decisions he ultimately makes.

You can be shared. This doesn't mean he will want you to spend an evening with one of his friends, but he can have you beside him in the company of friends, with justifiable pride. Dream girls are kept hidden and, because of their invisibility, would be difficult to share even if this were desired.

Finally, *you are real.* Humans are so incredibly complex that any fantastic facsimile, no matter how carefully constructed, is bound to fall disappointingly short of the intended result. Our literature abounds with manmade creations that do not measure up to human expectations. The Tin Man lacks a heart. Tik-Tok, the mechanical man of Oz, needs constant rewinding, even depending on a separate spring for thought processing. R2D2 has a definite communications problem. And Frankenstein's creature—well, where shall we begin!

The dream girl begins as a wish for a real woman. In time, like Pinocchio, she takes on a life of her own, although she cannot be real. Confronting the dream girl is merely saying to a man, "Tell me what you're looking for."

We all hope he will say, "Someone like you."

That's a job description you should be able to fill.

CHAPTER 15

The Dream Is You

Why are there dream girls? What do men really want from them and can a real woman meet that need?

The answer is not difficult. Validation. It is something that any real woman can supply, although not without effort.

Validation is central to existence. It is one thing we cannot provide for ourselves and for which we must rely on others. A man can turn to other men for validation of himself as a person, but needs a woman to validate him as a man.

If a tree fell in a forest and no living creature was within earshot, would it make a sound? The solution to this old paradox depends on your definition of sound. Many actions, including the concussion of heavy objects, generate waves of a specific frequency that we call sound waves. When the sound wave strikes an eardrum or similar receptive organ and a nerve transmits the impulse to the auditory cortex of a brain, sound is perceived. Oscillometers and recording devices can detect, measure, and reproduce sound.

With regard to the tree in the deserted forest, I would say there was no sound, because the final receptor in the process was missing. If I failed to turn on my television set during the telecast of *Saturday Night Live*, there was obviously a show nonetheless. But if, due to a transmission catastrophe, the TV signal never left the studio or if the United States president took over the network to address the nation, then there was no episode that night. A television show that no one could watch is nothing more than a dress rehearsal before an audience. If the performance were taped and telecast later, it would become a TV episode only at that point.

What does this have to do with validation? A woman, to have the power to validate, must be the receptor instrument. A man may think he is a success in terms of achievement, as a desirable lover, as a basic human being, but how can he be sure? Paychecks, school grades, certificates, and awards are all instruments of validation, but they say more about what one did than what one is. Many patients suffering from mania or paranoia have high opinions of themselves—grandiose, as a matter of fact—that are not based in reality. We need to be evaluated objectively by an outside person, because we can never trust our own biased self-evaluations.

In addition to our sense of a human identity, we also have a gender-based identity that involves perception of ourselves as a man or a woman. Despite attempts during the past few decades to get society to adopt an androgynous attitude whereby sexual differences are minimized, most men want to feel masculine or manly and most women want to feel feminine.

Validation, not sexual gratification or aimless fantasy, was the raison d'être for the dream girl. The boy believes that no real man lacks a real woman to affirm his manhood—and perhaps the boy is right.

If your man has fallen into the dream-girl syndrome, validation is what is probably lacking. For sex or adventure, men turn to real women. They sometimes turn to real women for validation as well, but that is not easy to achieve quickly. Validation requires knowledge of what you are validating and that takes time. If a man holds a position of power, has attained a degree of fame or can throw a few dollars around, some of his strong points will be immediately apparent to any woman in the vicinity, while his weaknesses will take time to be detected. This is an ideal situation for instant validation, so it is not surprising that the rich and famous have problems with fidelity.

The average man, however, upon perceiving a lack of validation, will find a readier supplier in the dream girl, just as he will find more convenient and less complicated sexual gratification in fantasy. He is vulnerable, of course, to involvement with other women because they are possible sources of what he seeks. Your relationship is in jeopardy because, while he does not know where to find validation, he thinks he now knows where he cannot find it.

Embarking on the Seven C's

Women are no strangers to the concept of validation. Many bestselling books, such as *The Cinderella Complex, Why Do I Think I'm Nothing Without a Man?*, and *Men Who Hate Women and the Women Who Love Them*, are about the problems that result from women depending too much on male approval and support, at the sacrifice of their own autonomy and achievement. People generally say that women dress and apply cosmetics in order to please men, even if they are already in a secure relationship. One major problem in our society is that validation as *women* seems to be based on youth, beauty, and sexiness, not personality or achievement.

Men need validation as much as women and their needs are more complex, but the importance of feedback is minimized because men are loathe to admit their vulnerability. Whereas a woman will often complain to her partner that "You never say you love me!" or "You never compliment me or notice how I look!", such protestations coming from a man would be likely deemed unmanly and justify his lack of validation.

Your man obviously felt validated at the start of your relationship or he wouldn't have gotten into it as deeply as he has. Somewhere along the line, there was a decrease in your output. Maybe he deserved it or maybe he has suffered some reverses in fortune that have increased his need, but the lack is there.

We can assume that you do care about the man and genuinely like him. There are enough strengths in him to make you stay in a monogamous relationship. You probably have a higher opinion of him than he has of himself, but he has lost sight of that.

Validation may sound easy enough. The dictionary defines the word as "corroboration or support on a sound basis or authority." The word has its etymological roots in the Latin term, *validus*, for "strong." Validation, therefore, is a process of strengthening through external assistance or internal inspiration.

Strength cannot be gained quickly or sustained without effort.

Physical strength of better-than-average degree must be increased through faithful exercise; once it is attained, it must be maintained through continued effort or muscle will atrophy and be replaced by fat.

Likewise, emotional validation cannot be achieved by giving an occasional pat on the back or encouraging word. Validation has many components, all of which must be employed on a regular basis.

I have analyzed seven different components inherent in the art of validation. I call them the seven C's, which seems a fitting term, suggestive of a sea voyage that is bound to be rough at times, pleasant and refreshing at others, and that can lead to a variety of adventures for a crew of two, both of them mates. You might come up with a few more components, but I feel that if you master these, you will have smooth sailing without taking aboard extra gear.

Here they are:

> Confirm
>
> Condone
>
> Compromise
>
> Compliment
>
> Confide
>
> Co-operate
>
> Commit

You need to do all of them. They are not too difficult, but if you do not think about them, you will neglect one or more of them and, like an engine with missing parts, you will not be able to accomplish your purpose.

Confirming without Reservations

I don't expect you to memorize and be able to enumerate the seven C's of validation, any more than I expect you to name the seven bodies of water you studied in the fourth grade. But do remember this one: Confirm.

Confirmation is an affirmation, a stamp of approval. It is your way of saying, "I know this man and he is an okay guy." By confirming someone, you also have an effect on him, making him firmer or more settled in his situation.

In the Christian rite of Confirmation, similar to the Jewish bar mitzvah, a child who is deemed old enough to make a mature decision formally accepts the belief system under which he was raised. He is not adopting a new set of values, but he is taking a stance of following the past practices that he engaged in under the direction and influence of elders now as a matter of personal choice. Confirmation takes study and preparation, since it is an act of will, not faith or obedience. It requires the participation of elders, because they must agree that the child possesses sufficient wisdom to know what he is doing and that he is now to be accepted as an equal among responsible adults.

The United States president has the power to appoint certain people to positions of power, such as Supreme Court justice or surgeon general, while Congress has the duty of *confirming* his nomination. The ratification process is one of informed consent. The appointee's past record is scrutinized and he is questioned. By the time he takes office, he and the American people have the security of knowing that his record showed evidence of sufficient merit and absence of malfeasance to make him a logical candidate who should do a creditable job in office.

Confirming a man means that you approve of him, but your responsibility goes beyond rote reassurance. You have the obligation to know as much about him as you can. Learn what his work entails. Visit his workplace if possible. If you can type a report for him, prepare a chart or deliver something, do it, not just so you can provide a service to him, but to help you understand his world better.

If he belongs to a bowling team, go to the alley and watch occasionally. If he participates in a weekly card game, volunteer to be hostess one night, so you can get to know his friends in the course of serving sandwiches or clearing glasses from the table.

If he is enjoying a certain book, read it yourself. If he builds things with power tools, don't let his workshop become off-limits to you.

Confirmation in the worlds of politics and religion is a one-time ceremony. For couples in personal relationships, it must be taken care of on a daily basis. This does not mean you have to make a formal declaration of approval each day, but you have to say in your attitude and actions, "You are the man I have chosen because I want you more than anyone else and I value you for what you are. Believe me, I know."

You should know him like a book, preferably a favorite one that you reread periodically. Talk to him, not just about his activities, but about his likes and dislikes.

I once had a female patient who came close to having an extra-marital affair with a co-worker. Her husband was a hardworking, good-hearted tradesman, but they had little in common intellectually. Her co-worker shared her profession and she delighted in their daily lunchtime conversations, during which they shared confidences. He seemed so much more attuned to her, mentally and emotionally, than her husband, to whom she had been married for more than ten years.

"We even have the same favorite movie!" she said wistfully. I asked her what her husband's favorite movie was. She had never asked.

One of G. B. Shaw's characters, around the turn of the century, said that a husband is like a man who owns a phonograph with a half-dozen records. He expects you to listen to the same familiar music over and over again whenever company comes to visit. Today, most men own several dozen tapes and CDs and their ideas and experiences in our fast-paced society also expand at a faster rate than they can convey them. If you make it a point to share the day's happenings with your partner and ask for his opinions, you are not likely to hear the same record twice, unless he is evading you with a prerecorded "Same as ever," or "Oh, I don't know."

You may need to remind yourself occasionally about all the things you like about him. Make a list of what endeared him to you and keeps you with him. Then, throw it away, so that you will have to think about it anew the next time you make the list.

Pay attention. It's easy to get absorbed in a TV show, some needlework, or even a personal daydream when you think he has launched into an account you have heard before. If he thinks something is important, then it should be important to you, if only for that reason.

The small gestures of affection and caring can have a large impact, simply because they are unexpected and special. Perusing the TV listings and finding a sports event he may not have known about, separating out the business section from the newspaper and handing it to him, mixing him a drink, or ensuring that the good-bye kiss—and, especially, the hello one—are not perfunctory pecks can go just as far in confirming your love as a formal declaration.

Declarations, such as "You're a good man and I'm glad you're mine," are never unwelcome, by the way.

Absolute Absolution

Confirmation depends on never losing sight of your partner's virtues. Condoning depends on overlooking his faults.

Men fall in love with a woman and expect her to stay the same forever. Maybe it is their early association with ageless dream girls that makes them that way. They are always a little disappointed when the sexy girl they married spends less time painting her face, wears her skirts longer and her blouses looser, and gains a few pounds. They are more disappointed when the demands of a rising career or a growing family gives her less time to spend attending to the man in her life.

Women, on the other hand, are born renovators. They rarely look at a man and think that he is just perfect. Just as a jeweler is not content to market a rough, unpolished stone, a woman accepts the rough-edged suitor with definite plans to make the modifications that will raise him from second-rate to prime marriage material. She no more doubts her ability to do this than a dressmaker would hesitate to shorten a hem or let out a waistband.

Since women do not bother to tell men about the impending modifications, men are unpleasantly surprised when the process gets under way. They assumed the woman was perfectly happy with them originally and that something has changed in the relationship now that she is finding fault with them.

Some things are easier to change than others and some call for change more than others. If he drinks too often or bathes too seldom, some intervention is warranted. If he strews his discarded clothes on the hallway, bathroom, or bedroom floor, you don't have to doom yourself to a lifetime of picking them up as you would for a three-year-old. If he comes home late without telephoning, tell him what you expect of him.

How you go about trying to effect change can make a big difference, not only in the success rate but in the quality of your relationship. Women may tend to repeat the same request without variation until the man becomes progressively angrier and vows never to change, just so he doesn't feel henpecked. Repeated criticism of behavior is nagging. It is easy for the nagging partner to progress to attacks on the man, not his disturbing behavior patterns, by calling him a slob, a baby, or a selfish pig. This does not raise his self-esteem, although it may elevate his blood pressure.

Don't talk down to him as though he were a child. As Eric Berne pointed out many years ago in his books on transactional analysis, if one person communicates as parent to child, the other is compelled to respond on the same wave-length as child to parent. A calm, mature reply to a parental harangue just doesn't fit; even a childish tantrum makes more sense in the context of the interaction. The choice is either to communicate in a heated fashion or break off communication, unless the one under attack can redirect the complainer into an adult–adult interaction.

Tell him how *you* feel and what *you* would like him to do, but don't become a nagging mother. Men may love their mothers, but not in the bedroom. And you will probably want to retain your sexual relationship regardless of how other aspects are going.

Alcoholics Anonymous employs the Serenity Prayer, which asks God to grant the power to change what we can change, the serenity to accept what we cannot change, and the wisdom to know the difference.

Some changes that the bride envisions are predictably doomed from the start. Do not expect a man who has been an avid baseball fan all his life to find more rewarding ways to spend his weekends and forgo the World Series to view autumn foliage with you. Do not expect a man addicted to barbecued ribs and grilled steaks to adopt a vegetarian diet because it is better for his health. Do not expect to have a man become enthusiastic over a season subscription to the ballet if his concept of dance is the Radio City Music Hall Rockettes. You might get your cat to nibble on a french fry, but that won't make him a herbivore.

Try to find out what a man is willing to change and how far he will go. Let him know why you want him to change and ask what you can do to help.

If the problem is an unacceptable one, such as infidelity or alcoholism, let him know it is unacceptable, then delegate the work to a professional therapist. You can participate in the therapy, but don't try to be the therapist.

Most "problems," fortunately, are not of that magnitude. While you are asking him about change, ask yourself if you can condone the behavior. "Condone" not only means to forgive or pardon an offense, it means the *allowance of its continuation*.

When a priest gives absolution to a believer, it is a wonderful thing, for it allows the penitent to leave with a clean slate, not a sense of guilt; however, the confessional process starts with an admission of having sinned and ends with an admonition and resolution not to do it again.

In condoning, the aim should be accepting, not tolerating. You would like him to lose some weight, to spend less time watching sports, to make love more frequently, but you are willing to keep the status quo because, on overall balance, the relationship is a good one.

Sometimes, when the nagging stops, the man miraculously makes the change that he knew was desired but which he refused to effect under duress.

In the *Peanuts* comic strip, Lucy once handed Charlie Brown a long strip of paper and informed him that she had made a list of all his faults. Charlie scanned it and protested, "These aren't faults! They're character traits."

Maybe without some of those irritating traits, your man wouldn't be the great character that he is.

Compromising Positions

Women upset everything. ...The woman wants to live her own life; and the man wants to live his; and each tries to drag the other on to the wrong track. One wants to go north and the other south; and the result is that both have to go east, though they both hate the east wind.

—GEORGE BERNARD SHAW, *PYGMALION*

In the preceding diatribe, Professor Henry Higgins explains why he is a confirmed old bachelor and likely to remain so.

Higgins does remain a bachelor, while Eliza Doolittle goes on to marry Freddy Eynsford Hill, the meek, adoring aristocrat whose temperament is more compatible with her strong-willed ambition. Shaw was careful to explain this in a brief epilogue, although my wife, after exposure to the more romantic musical version, *My Fair Lady*, declared flatly, "Shaw was wrong!"

Just the one quote above should be sufficient to indicate that Higgins was not marriage material, since he has a faulty concept of what compromise entails. (He also isn't very good at the physics law of vectors, since opposing forces pulling north and south will either send you in one or the other of those directions or leave you right where you started if equal. But then, he was a professor of language, not science.) Compromise is essential to any two-person relationship and most compromises result in getting what you want part of the time, not in neither getting what they want all of the time.

The dream girl never had to be consulted when the man wanted to go somewhere. She was like an intracranial Siamese twin, joined to him at the imagination. Whither he went, she followed.

Women cannot realistically expect to find a man who shares all their preferences and aversions. The sex difference alone is bound to have exposed them to different pastimes during their formative years. If you have an all-consuming passion, such as opera or mountain climbing, then you should find a partner who can share your enthusiasm in that area, but that still leaves a lot of other territory to share.

During the years when a wife is devoting most of her time to raising children at home, she may be eager to go out to dinner or otherwise get out of the house at the end of the day, just when her homebound husband is longing for the peace and idleness of an evening by the hearth. In a situation such as this, it does not take much communication to discern who wants to do what, but the more complicated part is to determine how much each partner wants his or her way, how much the other partner would object to ceding on this particular night, and the terms of a future payback when the next inevitable difference arises.

The important thing is that you always let your partner know how you feel. Many women quickly let the man have his way, but resent it so deeply that they spoil his enjoyment and then subject him to lingering hostility. Others may express reservations in such an unequivocal way that the man quickly abandons a cherished plan that the woman could have easily lived with.

If one partner wants to go to California and the other to New York you don't compromise by going to Missouri, a compromise may involve a satisfactory second choice rather than either of the original preferences. When he wants Mexican food and you want Italian, both of you may be amenable to Chinese. When he wants to go to an action-adventure movie and you want a romantic epic, you might both be content with a comedy.

I usually encourage my patients to consider all options in all situations, even those they and I can predict will not be employed. Think about divorce and even murder. Contemplating and discarding such options will make you feel more secure about your eventual choice. No option, even for a single person, is perfect. When you choose one path, you must forgo another. Each option has advantages and disadvantages.

Even when a particular compromise results in letting your man have his way, there is an advantage to that option. You have shown that you love and understand him, better than any dream girl, who wouldn't have had any choice in giving him his way.

Compliments of the Spouse

In Shaw's *Getting Married*, the ambivalent bride-to-be says indignantly, "Does anybody want me to flatter and be untruthful?"

One of the proper male guests says, "Well, since you ask me, I do. Surely it's the very first qualification for tolerable social intercourse."

Flattery and deceit is not recommended as a means of validating a man. Complimenting him is.

Flattery is either praising someone for an attribute he doesn't have, such as musical talent or good looks, or giving him far more credit than is warranted by whatever merits he does possess, such as leadership or intelligence, so that you might as well be lying.

Compliments are essential to validation because they verify the good points he may think he has, but of which he cannot be an objective judge. There is no purpose in flattery, simply because most men are realistic enough to know their limitations. They may not appreciate how good they are, but they can tell what they lack.

Men take pride in the qualities that are typically considered masculine, such as physical strength and courage, even if their major strengths lie in the areas of intelligence and sensitivity. Of course, they will not be unhappy if they are complimented on their strongest assets.

Men are not very good at receiving compliments. Little girls are told constantly from an early age how pretty, sweet, and adorable they are, and it tends to continue into adulthood. After age four, the only compliments most boys get are "Nice catch!" or "Way to go!" So if your man seems to scowl or furrow his brow in response to a compliment, don't assume he isn't pleased; he just doesn't know what to make of it.

It's okay to ask him to use his strength to open a jar of spaghetti sauce or his height to reach a can on the top shelf, provided you haven't been opening the same type of jar or taking things from the same shelf for years.

But usually you won't have to fish for things on which to compliment. You can even draw on the things you like about him and attracted you to him. He might have eyes that are a nice shade of blue or skin that is exceptionally smooth and unblemished. These may not be the sort of things that get Sylvester Stallone his multi-million-dollar roles, but your man isn't up for a part in *Rocky XIV* anyway. As long as you like it and it's uniquely his, he wouldn't trade it for Schwarzenegger's deltoids or van Damme's rectus abdominis.

If you have the opportunity to praise him in front of others, take it. Even if he is not within earshot, such things have a way of getting back. Conversely, never criticize him in front of others. You can take back your cutting remarks later, but the others won't hear the retraction.

Finally, one of the nicest compliments you can pay him is to keep yourself dressed and groomed so that you attract them yourself. Other people will look at you and think, "He must be something special to rate a woman like that." Maybe you don't want to be judged strictly by your appearance, but people can always get to know the real you *and* him better in the future. You can't judge a book by its cover, but publishers still employ artists and jacket designers to lure readers into taking it from the bookstore shelf.

Men will nearly always describe their dream girls as beautiful. It's simpler than trying to say that she would have the charms that only the best men could hope to win and that he wants to be among the best.

Strictest Confidence

Sometimes when I close a letter to someone special, where "love" would sound too intimate and "sincerely" too aloof, I fall back on the Latin phrase from which "sincerely" was derived, *sine cera.*

It means "without wax" and connotes a sense of special trust, even though the sentiment was directed not to the recipient of the letter but the bearer. In ancient times, letters were sealed with wax and imprinted with the seal of the writer. There was no postal service, so the writer had to rely on a friend or servant to deliver it. If the letter was sent without being sealed with wax, it meant the writer trusted the messenger implicitly and would not feel threatened by the possibility of his reading the letter. It obviously let the recipient know that he, too, could place unwavering trust in the messenger.

Confiding in someone is another method of validating them. Today, we usually think of it as telling something to a person that you would not want generally known, but "confide" also means to entrust or place in charge of. The Latin root words, *con fide,* mean "with trust."

Confidences are not particularly flattering to the one who reveals them. They are not necessarily about events that the person is ashamed of or regrets, but they usually involve human conflicts and emotions that reveal vulnerability. Women are better at confiding than men.

For several years, I have worked on weekends as a supervisor of psychiatrists in training who cover the emergency room. It has been rewarding to share my knowledge and experience with these younger doctors, who are commendably enthusiastic about twenty-four-hour shifts during which they receive no additional pay.

After many hours together, our conversations tend to shift from discussing patients and treatment to more personal matters. I have found it striking how the women so often begin talking about intimate aspects of their lives. One spoke about the strong feelings she had toward her supervisor and wondered whether he might not have similar feelings toward her that circumstances prohibited him from showing. When she completed her residency at the end of the year, how would her chances be of having a romance with him? (This was not as confidential as I first thought; I later realized that all her colleagues and most of the attendings were aware of the feelings she openly displayed.) One woman, juggling motherhood and career training, talked of how her current pregnancy had intervened just when her youngest child had reached the age when she and her husband had more time for each other. Another, in her late twenties, confided that she would not engage in premarital sex despite considerable grumbling from her boyfriend.

Male residents tend to be much more reserved. Occasionally, one may question whether he chose the right specialty, or ask my advice about the psychiatric job market for new graduates, but that's as personal as it gets. The only exception was an overweight doctor who told me how hard it was to find sexual partners and who shared a Spanish-English dictionary that emphasized vulgarisms not taught at Berlitz.

A confidence is a compliment. It means that the confider considers you to be special, whether by virtue of experience, professional expertise, age, or her intuitive trust in your integrity and kindness. While it is not a direct request for help, the revelation of a confidence gives you the opportunity to offer feedback, whether in the form of advice or your observations in past similar situations. While listening to confidential material from women is a daily part of my job, when I am approached by someone outside the doctor-patient relationship, I feel particularly honored.

Confide in your man. The dream girl knew his secrets, but had none of her own to share. It might make you feel a little vulnerable, but that emphasizes that you are human—a quality denied to the dream girl.

Pulling Together

Co-operate with your partner, since it is one of the most active forms of validation.

I have spelled the word with a hyphen because I wanted to emphasize the verb *operate*. It implies activity and I am talking about joint efforts that require pulling together, like a team in harness. Cooperation does not have to be a physical thing. You can cooperate by talking things over and even cooperate by refraining from some action you want to take, if it would interfere with a plan of your partner's.

Partners may support one another emotionally, yet tend to keep out of the way when one has a battle to fight. It seems that couples who have become adept at knowing one another's fighting styles from inevitable spats rarely get to join forces against a mutual adversary.

I always enjoy "double-teaming" someone with my wife. Say that she is dissatisfied with an appliance she purchased. She requests a refund, but the salesman doesn't want to give it to her. He may claim that too much time has elapsed or that store policy permits only exchanges or that she has to take the appliance to its factory of origin. I then support her, using the tone of an objective observer rather than a husband. He turns to argue with me and she resumes her attack on his flank. Any argument she offers, I enthusiastically support, offering additional reasons, which she supports. Sometimes we engage in cross-conversation about the salesman's incompetence, ignorance, or duplicity, in the impassive tone of clinicians examining a psychopath. If my wife drives him to loss of composure and he raises his voice, I assume the male-defending-his-mate role. We discuss courses of action, ranging from talking to the manager to calling the police. We get the refund.

I remember one ludicrous but retrospectively enjoyable altercation years ago at Disney World, hardly the appropriate setting for a potential brawl. Laura, our youngest daughter, was about seven, although by the end of a fatiguing day her level of frustration tolerance had regressed to that of a four-year-old. We were at Epcot Center in an area where a man-size robot was surrounded by a circle of kids who could operate him through telephonic controls.

Laura desperately wanted to operate him, but definitely did not want to wait in line.

Rita, her fourteen-year-old sister, stood in line for her, but when Rita finally was at the controls, Laura was peevishly sitting on a bench. A little boy behind Rita lunged for the controls.

At this point, my wife tried to fend off the kid so Laura could have a chance. This prompted an intrusion by the boy's father and an escalating dialogue between my wife and him. He finally hurled an invective at her that he later claimed was "Flake off!" but which my wife and I had perceived otherwise.

Well, that was my cue to do the masculine thing and come to my wife's defense; I castigated him for using profanity in the presence of so many innocent children while attacking a defenseless woman. I also did something provocative, a throwback from my adolescent street-fighting days—I took off my glasses. It wasn't exactly a Clark Kent-to-Superman transformation, but it did send the message that I was ready to get physical.

The man, a stocky, short redhead with a redder neck, began to mutter that he would mop up the floor with me, "big as you are" (which was sort of flattering, since I'm 5'9"). "Call security," I said to no one in particular. A guard, who should have been keeping the impatient kids on line in order, pointed to a phone and within a minute I was surrounded by a small phalanx of men in natty blazers.

My wife, meanwhile, was commiserating with the redneck's wife, who lamented, "That's the way men always are!"

I introduced myself to the security platoon as a New York City psychiatrist who had been dealing with a potentially murderous disturbed man. Nothing much came of it. My adversary sputtered some defensive remarks and we dispersed.

I was amused to learn from Rita that while she was watching my heated confrontation with the redneck, a woman beside her had asked, "Is that your father?"

"Yes," my usually decorous daughter replied. "Want to make something out of it?" The woman apparently did not.

We could have sold TV rights to the Fox network, except they already have the Bundys on *Married with Children*.

In the staid, sober world of a psychiatrist, it is shamefully enjoyable to bolster your marital alliance with an occasional fight that involves people other than yourselves.

You don't have to join your man in military maneuvers. Help him pull together an updated resumé and look through the want ads, just in case a spectacular career opportunity looms suddenly. Make a major purchase together after careful comparison shopping. Adopt a cause and write protest letters, or join a demonstration.

They say that coyotes roam and hunt in pairs, a male and a female. I would surmise that coyotes are among the best-validated males in the animal kingdom. Even a roadrunner would have no chance against a pair like that.

Voluntary Commitment

In the world of psychiatry, we use the term "involuntary commitment" when a patient, deemed potentially dangerous to self or others, is placed against his will in a psychiatric hospital. Voluntary commitment is oxymoronic; a voluntary admission is the opposite of a commitment.

According to the dictionary, however, "commit" can refer both to voluntary and involuntary actions. It can mean to obligate or bind someone to take some position or action, which could be imposed without consent, or to pledge to some particular course of action. A pledge is a voluntary promise to abide by a conviction.

When you commit yourself to a relationship, you provide the ultimate validation. It is the easiest of the steps toward validation to take and perhaps the hardest to sustain.

When you commit yourself to something, whether it is a person, a goal, or course of action, you are making a pledge to stand by the object of that commitment, regardless of circumstances. If a soldier commits himself to the defense of his country, he doesn't qualify his oath with "unless the odds are against my survival." If an adoptive parent commits himself to the care of a child, there is no escape clause if the child gets sick or has behavior problems. Commitment to a marriage means what the ceremony says: "For better, for worse," etc.

Here's how to commit: Each day, think about your man and reaffirm your determination to love and support him and to cherish your relationship. A commitment can be made for a lifetime, but renewing it daily will remind you that this is something you still believe in and want to do, not because you were trapped into it.

You don't have to announce your commitment to him daily, but if you remember it, your actions will be all the reassurance he needs.

Dream girls are immortal and their influence can be permanent. Mortals are not immortal, but commitment can keep their influence strong for decades—not forever, but close enough for human purposes.

~ CHAPTER 16 ~

Waking to a Dream

I hope that this book does not lead to the wholesale destruction of a slew of dream girls, because I kind of like the critters. Those few that have survived a man's adolescence have outlived their usefulness and may be seriously interfering with current relationships, but they did serve an important psychological function once. Also, the dream girl is a part of a man's imagination, and any time you destroy a part of the imagination, you may be doing serious harm to the creative process.

While I have written this book to help women supplant the dream girl, I have also tried to bring the dream girl out of the shadows and into the light of recognition and understanding. A man does not need to put aside his dream girl in order to enjoy a mature, real relationship; he only has to put her in perspective, accepting her as the product of his own inspired imagination. He may have repressed memories of her when his daydreams seemed infantile and he became ashamed of the insecurity that had led to their formation, but she was an important part of his aspirations.

A wise woman will learn as much about her man's dream girl as she can. If she treats a man's dream girl with respect and amusement, not scorn and jealousy, she can, through their shared secret, become even closer to her lover.

My Girl

Up until this very end, I debated whether or not I should share information about my personal dream girl. Now I have decided to.

You knew I had one, because I have been saying that nearly all men do, and if I were an exception, I would not be the one writing this book.

I will get to the true dream girl, the one who came strictly out of my imagination, but first there were the inevitable "crushes" on real girls and the attraction to certain celebrities. I recall feeling I was in love in kindergarten. The first was a tiny little girl with a profusion of curls. She left after the first grade and, instead of being free from the aching obsession, another girl in the class took her clandestine place. Again, don't ask me what the hell I wanted to do with them—I didn't have the slightest idea. It always seemed such a thrill to have *any* contact or communication with them. In the eighth grade, there was the girl I called Coronis in an earlier chapter, but I played Leporello to my friend Jerry's Don Juan. Ironically, he broke off with her around the time I lost a lot of weight and became a source of interest to the girls. I honestly had a shot at her, but I felt as out of my depth as I did when in kindergarten. I think I did right when I threw in the cards.

When it came to celebrities, I tended to focus on beauties who were not yet famous. Nanon Millis was one. She was one of about six dancers on the *Lucky Strike Hit Parade*. An exceptionally pretty blonde, she seemed to stand out from the rest of the line. I learned her name only because *TV Guide* once ran a picture of the dancers and (left to right) named them in the caption. According to the show's format, the top songs would be sung every week. Since some stayed on the list for weeks, it was a challenge for the producers to devise different settings to add variety. The male vocalists, Snookie Lanson and Russell Armes, would often sing to a woman, who had to stand there silently and try not to look embarrassed. When Nanon got picked for this duty, I would cheer and then enthusiastically review her "performance" with my peers on Monday.

Anita Ekberg did make it big, but I knew her when she was an incredibly beautiful and sexy unknown. "Who?" my classmates would exclaim; then I would whip out a magazine and they would say, "Woo!" The local magazine store was run by a man named

Harold. He would always point out to me any new arrivals that featured Anita. Then came *La Dolce Vita* and I told Harold that I could not possibly afford to buy every publication with her picture in it. She wasn't as much fun when everybody knew who she was.

The true dream girl probably came along when I was about thirteen, old enough to know about sex and love, and young enough to avoid them. I wanted to imagine the perfect girl for me. She was based on a chess piece, of all things. I had a plastic set in which there were medieval figures, not the usual abstract standard pieces. The queen was an attractive young woman with long hair and delicate features. Her bearing was erect and confident, her figure womanly without being voluptuous. Her expression was serious, yet soft.

I decided she would do as a model for my dream girl. I imagined her hair to be blond, although it was white. Her black opponent looked just like her and was, I suppose, a brunette.

I had called the chess queen Guinevere, but that did not seem to be a suitable name for a modern young woman, so I made it Gwendolyn. Her last name was, of course, Queen. The chessboard king, dressed in Crusader garb, became her father in the fantasy, a cop named Richard. She didn't have a mother.

The rest of the fantasy was pretty routine and G-rated. We kissed, looked into each other's eyes, walked in the moonlight and waltzed. I never imagined her naked or had any sexual feelings about her, although I am sure I was old enough to have been feeling them toward just about every other female.

I even wrote a "dream girl" song, not specifically about her, but on the dream-girl dilemma. I have no musical talent at all, but I picked out a simple melody on the piano to go with the mawkish lyric. I wasn't going to reproduce the song, since it is so corny, but, from a psychological viewpoint, it shows you what length an adolescent boy can be driven to by loneliness:

> *Oh, somewhere in this big wide world, there's just one girl*
> *   for me.*
> *I know she must be somewhere; where can that somewhere*
> *   be?*
> *I know that somewhere in this world my dream girl must*
> *   exist.*

Oh, how I long to hold her, my lips yearn to be kissed.
But the only place I've seen her is in dreamlands filled with
mist.
Oh, where can my dream girl be?
Oh, where is the one girl for me?

I've known a lot of other girls, with her they can't compare;
Her soft blue eyes, her ruby lips, her silky golden hair.
So many times I've seen her where the stars all brightly
beam,
And I've gently held her close to me, or else so it would
seem.
But alas, then I awaken to find out it's all a dream.
Oh, where can my dream girl be?
Oh, where is the one girl for me?

Obviously, I still remember that hokey lyric line for line, even
though I assure you that I do not sing it in the shower or even in my
head. The song was probably emblematic of the problem with the
dream-girl relationship: it was just too sickeningly sweet and tame.
Gwen was beautiful, loving, and kind, but she never made me
laugh.

So, you may think, that was the end of the dream girl. Well, it
was the end of Gwen, but I acquired another one, the one who still
follows me around. I tried to make Gwen a real girl, but she
couldn't escape the realm of the imaginary.

I then created Glenda as an imaginary female, but she keeps
intruding on the real world.

Glenda is a gremlin. She started, innocently enough, as a
doodle. In my early teens, I had a romance with cards. Poker, even
at the nickel-and-dime level, was a macho pastime and I never felt
more cool than when I was shuffling a deck with dexterity or calling
the hands with impassive objectivity. One day I doodled a devil,
with mustache and goatee, holding an ace of hearts on a flaming
pitchfork, as the smoke formed the name "Red Ace." Someday I
would own a casino called the Red Ace, and that would be its logo.

Then, I drew the devil again, but this time she was a woman, with long blond hair, slanty eyes, and a cupid's bow mouth. She had a horned cap, a cape, and wore a bikini.

I can't draw any better than write songs, but the demon found her way into my notebooks. I called her Glenda because I liked the sound of it. I've never been in a glen, but I always imagine it to be incredibly green, peaceful, and full of leprechauns.

The devilette became a gremlin. Like most people, I felt plagued by disappearing objects and malfunctioning appliances; I now had someone to blame them on. Glenda was still basically a visual thing. To give her added dimension, I would make drawings illustrating the top-ten jukebox hits. Glenda would cavort in her abbreviated garb, sometimes tormenting frustrated suitors, whom I drew as silhouettes.

I took her out of the closet one day when I was the features editor for the New York University newspaper, *Square Journal*. That day, the editor-in-chief said he had an empty half-column to fill and asked me if I had any ideas. It was on the editorial page in a space filled by letters, which were in short supply today, so I said tentatively, "Well, I have this character I've been working on, a female gremlin—"

"Fine, fine!" he said, abruptly.

Thereafter, Glenda and I shared a column. I was the conservative straightman, she was the bold, wisecracking invulnerable critic, who would say the most outlandish and true things about the administration, the student leaders, and any other inflated target. She was my "personal office gremlin, female variety," five-two (not your typical six-inch pixie), always in her red bikini. At first, the column was anonymous, under the byline "Harassed Reporter." When I got a regular column as copy editor in my junior year, I moved Glenda into it.

The students loved her, but I had problems with their mentally modifying her to fit their own dream-girl standards. "I always think of her as a redhead," one student told me.

"How can you say that?" I exploded. "In just about every column, she's distinctly identified as a blonde."

I made the mistake of showing one of my smitten co-workers a doodle I made of her. He gasped in dismay at my lousy artwork and exclaimed, "Oh no! Glenda's beautiful!"

A female colleague wrote in her Christmas column that she wished Santa would bring me "a real gremlin to tell my problems to."

"There's no such thing," I corrected her. "A gremlin is, by definition, an imaginary being. If she's real, she can't be imaginary. A real gremlin is an oxymoron." I stopped short of telling her she was a real moron.

Right to the end, I had to fend off interlopers. For my farewell column, I decided to run a drawing of Glenda. *I* certainly was not going to do it, so I asked our staff artist.

She agreed and produced a creature resembling Tinker Bell, with wings.

"That's not Glenda!" I fumed. "She doesn't have wings. Horns, not wings!"

The artist insisted Glenda *did* have wings. It was *my* gremlin, but I couldn't dissuade her.

I scrapped the drawing and pressed my brother, a fair artist, into service. He came up with a caped, horned silhouette that looked more like a viking than a dream girl, but at least it didn't have wings.

Was I in love with Glenda? Sure. Somewhere along the line, I fell hopelessly in love with her. All my readers knew it, but some of them fell in love, too.

The more I learned about psychiatry, the better I understood Glenda. She was the perfect dream girl because she was as imaginary as one could get. She didn't fawn over me or make declarations of love, she teased me and deflated me. She was sexy, but unapproachable even on a fantasy level. She was strong and courageous, as I would want to be and—hey, she *was* me. When she said, in our column, things I didn't have the guts to say, *I* said them. She was immortal, she was part of me—maybe I could believe that a part of me is immortal.

Occasionally spooky things happen that make me wonder if she's more real than I think. Sometimes I wonder whether I've managed to contact some ghost or stray demon or a rebel guardian angel who prefers bikinis to robes. Sometimes I tell myself that maybe I have some of those untapped spiritual powers the mystics talk about and she helps me realize them.

I used her in my last book, letting her masquerade as a patient in a mock case history. She was far tamer than when she wore her bikini to the newspaper office, but she still had the old charm and sense of humor. (She used her real name.)

And here she is again, maybe where she really belongs most, a dream girl who survives and makes life better, not worse.

My wife knows about Glenda and likes her. (In college, I had a female friend who did not like her, and I knew Glenda didn't like her, either. The woman never had much luck.) My wife, Joy, will say, in tough times, "Ask your gremlin to help." Things always work out.

My wife has also given me many gifts of Jessica Rabbit merchandise. Once she came up with a Jessica dressed in the tight-fitting nurse's uniform she wore in *Tummy Trouble*. "I didn't know this existed!" I exclaimed with delight.

Jessica is only a pseudo-dream girl, but she's fun, as dream girls should be. My wife has put up with my miniature leaden harem of Dungeons and Dragons enchantresses, amazons, succubi, sirens, and captive damsels; my Tinker Bells; my fantasy-female trading cards; my Venuses; my villainesses; and all the toys that have helped fuel my imagination in its quest for the dream girl.

If you let a real woman share your fantasy, the fantasy will never get out of control. Psychiatrists know that delusions lose their hold over a patient once they are shared with the therapist.

Psychoanalyst Robert Lindner, in *The Fifty-Minute Hour*, relates a moving account of how he treated a man who believed himself to be the ruler of a very detailed and intricate fantasy world, which occupied more and more of his time. The therapist, who was going through a mild depression of his own, unconsciously began to get gratification from sharing his patient's fascinating dream world and he pressed the patient for more details about the realm's history and customs. If the patient did not know, the doctor urged him to get the information on his next "visit" there.

Then one day the patient exploded, "Oh, hell, Doc, I haven't believed in any of this crap for months!"

When the flabbergasted therapist asked why the patient had persisted in recounting fantasy adventures, the patient shook his head and said, "I know this sounds crazy, but... I thought you wanted me to."

Don't be afraid of fantasy. The artist, as much as the psychotic, dwells in a fantasy realm; the difference is that the artist knows where the boundaries are.

The dream girl sustains a man until he is ready for real love in the real world, but she can only guide him as far as the frontier between fantasy and reality.

A woman who understands the dream girl can readily replace her on the other side of that boundary line.

About the Author

Anthony Pietropinto, M.D., is a psychiatrist at St. Luke's/Roosevelt Medical Center in New York City, where he supervises residents, and at FEGS Mental Health Center in Brooklyn. He has a private practice in Manhattan, where he resides with his family. He is the co-author of *Beyond the Male Myth*, the best selling nationwide study of male sexuality, *Husbands and Wives*, *Not Tonight, Dear: How to Reawaken Your Sexual Desire*, and *The Clinic*, a novel.